naeyc at 75

1926–2001

REFLECTIONS ON THE PAST • CHALLENGES FOR THE FUTURE

National Association for the Education of Young Children · Washington, D.C.

The painting on the cover, unsigned by the artist, was purchased by then *Young Children* editor Laura Dittman at an art show in the late 1960s. She "immediately knew that it belonged at NAEYC." The painting has hung in the NAEYC headquarters for more than three decades and serves as a constant reminder that the work of staff and volunteer leaders is, in the end, always about the children.

National Association for the Education of Young Children
1509 16th Street, NW
Washington, DC 20036-1426
phone: **202-232-8777 or 800-424-2460**
e-mail: **naeyc@naeyc.org**
online: **www.naeyc.org**

Through its publications program the National Association for the Education of Young Children (NAEYC) provides a forum for discussion of major issues and ideas in the early childhood field, with the hope of provoking thought and promoting professional growth. The views expressed or implied are not necessarily those of the Association. NAEYC thanks the editors and contributors, who donated much time and effort to develop this book for the profession.

ISBN 1-928896-00-6

NAEYC #775

Publications editor: Carol Copple
Copy and production editor: Lacy Thompson
Editorial assistance: Eugenia C. Wilkinson
Design and production: Jack Zibulsky

Contents

Foreword

When planning first began for NAEYC's 75th anniversary, a strong consensus emerged among the Board and staff that the anniversary celebration needed to do more than simply evoke memories (fond or otherwise) for "experienced" members. It needed to capture the essence of the Association's spirit and culture. We wanted the anniversary to affirm our commitment to NAEYC's fundamental mission—to work on behalf of all young children, with primary emphasis on the provision of group programs. And, we wanted the celebration to encourage individual members and others to renew their personal commitment to young children and their families.

This book is designed to meet these anniversary goals. Like all good NAEYC projects, it involved the contributions of many individuals. A number of years ago, as NAEYC's executive director, Marilyn M. Smith urged Affiliate Group leaders to view their organization as an orchestra, where the unique contributions of each member—whether woodwind, percussion, or strings—combine to make more beautiful music than any one musician can produce alone. In this book, our orchestra is comprised of many NAEYC leaders, past and present, who have contributed their thoughts and perspectives to make this volume such a treasure. Of course, good orchestras rely on good conductors, and here we are indeed fortunate that Marilyn agreed to lead the writing group and serve as this volume's editor. Her gracious style, quiet determination, and deep knowledge of organizational development and early childhood education has nurtured so many of us over the years and helped to bring out the best in each of us as we worked to achieve our shared goals. This book represents yet another gift from which the Association will benefit.

As you read this book, I hope you will gain a renewed respect for the NAEYC members and leaders who have preceded us. In addition, I hope this book will help to renew your commitment to continue—and expand—NAEYC's efforts on behalf of young children, families, and the early childhood profession. As this book so clearly illustrates, maintaining our core values while also adapting to changing needs and circumstances has been a hallmark of NAEYC throughout its 75 years.

For this reason the current priorities identified by the NAEYC Governing Board should come as no surprise. They include

- Further nurturing NAEYC at every level and in all activities as a more high-performing, inclusive organization;

- Considering relevant issues and initiating related activities regarding the construct of developmentally appropriate practice and the development of standards and outcomes for the education of young children; and

- Developing an action plan advocating for public policies for comprehensive financing strategies to support a system of high-quality early childhood education.

Certainly, these priorities reflect current critical issues—within the Association, the field of early childhood education, and the broader society. But as these pages underscore, these priorities build upon—and must be guided by—the principles and values that have been at the heart of this Association since its beginning.

As I read this volume, I was struck once again by how glad I am to be a part of NAEYC. We work fervently to improve early childhood programs for children and their teachers. At our best, we are guided by the vision of helping *every* child and family grow and learn to their fullest potential, knowing that this vision requires that we continue to grow and learn as well. On behalf of NAEYC, I challenge you to grow and learn with us as we strive to achieve our mission on behalf of all young children.

— *Kathy R. Thornburg,*
NAEYC president (2000–2002)

Preface

Invited to serve as editor for a book to commemorate NAEYC's 75-year history, Marilyn M. Smith convened a small writing group to explore the prospect. From that first meeting emerged clear agreement about the purpose of such an endeavor—to engage current and future members in thought about the core values and principles that guide NAEYC's work. We share the belief that the role of history is to inform the future. To make wise decisions for the future, we must consider the context of prior decisions as well as new information and knowledge related to an issue. One member of the writing group, Sue Bredekamp, stated it this way:

> As a dynamic profession and organization, we will continue to confront new challenges and revisit old ones. For this reason alone . . . it is critical that NAEYC members understand history. Most issues are not really new, but contexts and knowledge do change. We must heed Lois Meek's words from 1929 when she said we must not "become stereotyped or static." (p. 113)

With this purpose in mind, we sketched out the components for the book and agreed that the first 50 years of NAEYC's history had been so well documented that we should focus on the last 25 years and challenges for the future. Thus, this book is organized in three parts: Understanding Context, Learning from NAEYC's Past, and Looking Forward. This preface briefly describes the organization and intent of each part.

Part 1, Understanding Context, includes a timeline that sets the stage for NAEYC's evolution, listing milestones in early care and education alongside highlights of NAEYC's development. It is placed at the front of the book so that readers can easily refer to it when they are curious about events that were happening in a particular time period. Next are two articles previously published for NAEYC's 50th anniversary. They tell the story of how our Association was born, survived, and developed over its first 50 years. Many ideas that emerge in the remainder of the book will be more clearly understood with these first 50 years as background.

Part 2, Learning from NAEYC's Past, tells the story of NAEYC's recent history, focusing primarily on the years 1976–2001 but sometimes going back a bit further to recount key events that set the stage for what was to come. This section includes three chapters organized around the goals that have driven NAEYC's work from its inception: building a strong organization, improving early childhood professional practice, and building public understanding and support for high quality programs. The authors of these chapters seek to stimulate early childhood educators to think about the future, drawing on what we can learn from the past. Hence, they have organized their respective chapters around core values, beliefs, and themes that have guided NAEYC's work rather than attempting to provide a comprehensive chronological account of the past three decades.

Part 3, Looking Forward, focuses on the future of the Association and its mission. Marilyn Smith's chapter offers guidelines for those who will do the organizing for the future. Principles for effective organizing are gleaned from NAEYC's past, but are applicable for many types of organizations. For the last chapter we reached outside our original writing group and invited Barbara Bowman to present a future agenda for NAEYC and the early childhood field. She considers the present environment and future trends that will have significant impacts on young children, families, and early childhood leaders. In light of lessons learned from NAEYC's history, Bowman offers questions that we as a field and an Association must address in order to substantially improve our mutual work on behalf of all young children.

In the end, our past and our future are embedded in the people who serve as our leaders. Acknowledging all who have contributed to our Association is not feasible. But we have chosen to list the names of all who served in national Governing Board positions throughout NAEYC's 75 years as a reminder of the thousands who also made NAEYC's accomplishments possible through their work in Affiliate Groups, panels, task groups, interest groups, and so on. Preceding this list are photos and short biographical sketches of all former NAEYC Presidents. This material appears as an Appendix.

The wisdom of the leaders on whose shoulders we stand is also reflected in quotes from NAEYC leaders that appear throughout the book. NAEYC leaders past and present were invited to submit thoughts about the Association's beliefs, culture, accomplishments, and challenges. Their words speak for themselves as lessons of importance in the telling of our history and planning for the future.

Throughout the creation of this book we frequently referred to this endeavor as a labor of love—love for not just retelling, but for participating in the history of early childhood professionals organizing to "serve and act on behalf of the needs, rights, and well-being of all young children." The successful continuation of NAEYC's journey to improve care and education for all young children requires the involvement of all who work with and for young children. May each reader take on her or his own labor of love. May we all go forward thinking about how we can engage ourselves and others in meaningful dialogue and planning for organizational and personal actions to benefit children—learning from the past to meet the challenges of the future.

— *Sue Bredekamp, Carol Copple, Jerlean Daniel, Marilyn M. Smith,*
Pat Spahr, and Barbara Willer
Writing Group for 75th Anniversary Book

This book is dedicated to future leaders who accept the torch to further NAEYC's mission to achieve high-quality care and education for all young children. Each person who takes on this goal, now and in the future, is a living tribute to past NANE and NAEYC leaders on whose work they build.

Part 1

Understanding Context

- TIMELINE OF EARLY CARE AND EDUCATION

- NAEYC'S ROOTS—THE FIRST 50 YEARS

NAEYC, as we know it today, is a product of its own organizational history as well as the social milieu in which it thrives. Two chapters establish this context for the reader.

"Timeline for Early Care and Education" (Chapter 1) reminds us that any organization evolves in the context of events in the larger society. We can better understand NAEYC's creation and development over the years by looking at what was happening within the broad arena of education and care of young children. The timeline lists important events in early care and education in the right-hand column, events and activities in NAEYC's development during the corresponding time period in the left-hand column.

When NAEYC's History and Archives Panel identified the creation of this timeline as an important contribution to the celebration of the Association's 75th anniversary, Panel member Edna Ranck took the lead in compiling the first draft. Dorothy Hewes, a specialist in the history of NAEYC and early childhood, and the other Panel members contributed validation, refinements, and additions. Major sources used for this compilation are listed at the end of the timeline.

"NAEYC's Roots—The First 50 Years" (Chapter 2) portrays NAEYC's foundation, in which its purpose, mission, and structure are embedded. Becoming familiar with this foundation helps us recognize and understand NAEYC's great strides forward and significant contributions to the improvement of group programs serving young children and their families. We are fortunate that many important facets of NAEYC's first 50 years were documented for the 50th anniversary celebration. We have selected to reproduce in their entirety two vibrant articles originally published by NAEYC in 1976.

- "NAEYC's First Half Century: 1926–1976" is a product of Dorothy W. Hewes and NAEYC's Organizational History and Archives Committee, which she chaired. The committee, appointed in 1974 to research and document the history of the Association, compiled numerous sources of information: reports, correspondence, and published materials that had been saved by previous leaders of the Association as well as other published materials about events in the history of early childhood education and of the organization. Adding to the richness of this narrative were the reminiscences of the leaders who had shaped the history of the Association and of the field.

Members of the NAEYC Organizational History and Archives Committee (1974–1976) were

Dorothy Hewes, Chairperson • June E. Aimen • Judith Cauman • Bess Ferguson • Cornelia Goldsmith • Glenn Hawkes • James L. Hymes Jr. • Phyllis Richards • Ruby Takanishi • Ralph Witherspoon

• In "From NANE to NAEYC: The Tempestuous Years," Ralph L. Witherspoon covers the critical transition years from 1958 to 1968. His account of the bold and innovative changes that lifted the organization to a new level of functioning is personal and authentic because he "lived" these changes. First, he chaired the committee that recommended organizational changes, and then he served as president during four critical years of the actual transition.

Chapter 1

Timeline of Early Care and Education

**Edna Ranck and NAEYC's
History and Archives Panel**

Timeline of Early Care and Education

	NAEYC	Early Care and Education
1825–26		A child care center opens in a mill in New Harmony, Indiana, founded by Robert Owen.
1830s		Froebelian kindergarten begins in Germany.
1838		*Crêches* are established in France.
1863		The first federally sponsored day nursery for mothers working in Civil War hospitals and factories opens in Philadelphia.
1875		Day nurseries are set up in philanthropic agencies to meet the needs of immigrant families.
1888		The Society for the Study of Child Nature is founded. It will change its name to Child Study Association in 1924.
1891		The Golden Gate Kindergarten Association establishes free kindergartens in the San Francisco Produce Exchange.
1892		The International Kindergarten Union (IKU) is organized in Saratoga Springs, New York.
1895		G. Stanley Hall, one of the first academics to study children through research techniques, invites early childhood teachers to Chicago for a series of lectures on the implications of child development research for the field and thus begins his powerful influence on early childhood education programs.

NAEYC	Early Care and Education	
	The first meeting of the National Congress of Mothers, predecessor to National PTA, convenes in Washington, D.C.	1897
	The National Federation of Day Nurseries is formed. It provides educational activities for children and minimal staff training.	1898
	The first day nursery for Black children opens in New York City.	1903
	The first White House Conference on Children and Youth is held. The theme is "Care of Dependent Children," with focus on mental health and child guidance.	1909
	The U.S. government establishes mothers' pensions to keep mothers at home with their children.	1911
	The U.S. Children's Bureau is established in the federal government. The Bureau publishes seven child-care-related documents between 1919 and 1944.	1912
	The White House Conference on Standards of Child Welfare issues statements that influence child labor laws and maternal and child health programs.	1919
	The 19th Amendment to the U.S. Constitution grants women the right to vote.	1920
	The American Orthopsychiatric Association is established.	1924

Timeline of Early Care and Education

	NAEYC	Early Care and Education
1925–26	Preliminary meetings on establishing a professional organization for nursery school educators begin under the leadership of Patty Smith Hill of Teachers College, Columbia University, in New York City.	Nursery schools link to child development and psychology while day nurseries focus on meeting the needs of poor and immigrant families.
1926–29	The National Committee on Nursery Schools holds national conferences in 1926, 1927, and 1929. The first national conference convenes in Washington, D.C., in February 1926.	
1929	The National Association for Nursery Education (NANE) is formally established as an independent professional organization. The National Committee functions as the executive committee until 1931. Lois Hayden Meek Stolz, the first chair of the National Committee on Nursery Schools, becomes the first NANE president. *Minimum Essentials for Nursery School Education* is the first NANE publication. The idea of NANE merging with the International Kindergarten Union (IKU) is discussed but doesn't happen.	Lois Hayden Meek Stolz edits the 28th Yearbook of the National Society of the Study of Education on the theme, "Preschool and Parental Education."
1930		The White House Conference on Child Health and Protection addresses issues of "day care" and rejects any kind of major federal government role. The conference drafts "The Children's Charter"—the nation's goals for its children and youth.

NAEYC	Early Care and Education	
NANE is incorporated.	Licensing at local and state levels begins for day nurseries but with little consistency or enforcement.	1931
	The International Kindergarten Union (IKU) and the National Council of Primary Education (NCPE) merge to become the Association for Childhood Education (ACE).	
The nine members of the WPA National Advisory Committee's preschool program are all members of NANE.	The Works Progress Administration (WPA) establishes a national preschool program. Nursery schools employ teachers, nurses, and social workers throughout the Great Depression and serve children who are poor.	1933
	George Stoddard, former NANE president, establishes the Society for Research in Child Development (SRCD).	
NANE's leaders urge the Association to organize effectively to extend the WPA preschool program across the country to meet the needs of all preschool-age children. Practical classroom activities and techniques dominate the sixth biennial national conference.	2,000 WPA nursery schools enroll over 72,000 children and employ 6,770 adults.	1935
	The passage of the Social Security Act (August 14) creates the modern welfare program called Aid to Dependent Children, which is designed to provide funds to allow mothers to stay home to care for their children. ADC, later known as Aid to Families with Dependent Children (AFDC), becomes Temporary Assistance to Needy Families (TANF) in 1996.	

Timeline
of Early Care
and Education

	NAEYC	Early Care and Education
1937	NANE selects a conference theme for the first time—"Safeguarding the Early Years of Childhood." This conference is the last held in the segregated South until 1964. NANE took an early stand on equal treatment for all members.	
1938	Nursery schools in public schools are seen as the meeting ground of the community where democracy is practiced.	Elinor Guggenheimer begins a career in child care activism by working to keep local child care centers open in Manhattan.
1939		U.S. Tax Court rules that working mothers cannot deduct child care expenses from gross income because child care is held to be a personal duty.
1940		The White House Conference on Children in Democracy is convened and recommends a program to equalize opportunity in education, employment, and living conditions.
1941	As in 1929, NANE rejects merging with the Association of Childhood Education International (ACEI), formerly the International Kindergarten Union (IKU).	Pearl Harbor, December 7, leads to U.S. entrance into World War II, which rapidly expands the development of early childhood education programs nationwide.

NAEYC	Early Care and Education	
NANE is a member of the National Commission for Young Children, a nongovernment agency serving as a clearinghouse for information about children in defense areas, child care trends, and volunteer training for early childhood programs. NANE suffers low membership and participation as Americans focus on the war effort and the services needed to support it.	Congress appropriates funds to keep selected WPA nurseries open to meet the child care needs of women working in the wartime defense industry. Lanham Act revisions allow public works funds to be used for child care in war-impacted areas. All families, regardless of income level, are eligible. Nonschool-based child care plans are approved by the U.S. Children's Bureau.	1942
At the NANE conference in Boston, participants discuss affiliation structure. {See list of conference sites in Chapter 4.}	Kaiser Shipbuilding, using Lanham Act funds, sets up two child care centers for employees, offering quality care and comprehensive services to families.	1943
	Child care, though federally supported, is viewed as a war need only.	1944
NANE cancels its biennial conference because of the war, issuing instead Volume 1, Issue 1 of the *Bulletin of the National Association for Nursery Education.*		1945
NANE president describes the concerns of every new organization: a lack of members, a lack of funds, and a lack of services to recruit new members due to the lack of funds.	UNICEF is established within the United Nations. Federal support via the Lanham Act is gradually withdrawn after the war is over. Child advocates in California, New York City, and several other large cities fight to keep government involved in supporting child care.	1946

Timeline of Early Care and Education

	NAEYC	Early Care and Education
1948		Nursery schools are seen as positive and day nurseries as negative. Most families with working mothers use a relative, neighbor, or friend for child care. OMEP (the Organisation Mondiale pour l'Education Préscolaire) is founded.
1950		The Mid-century White House Conference on Children and Youth focuses on how to help children develop the mental, emotional, and spiritual qualities essential to individual happiness and responsible citizenship.
1951	During the 1930s and 1940s, NANE members had been in close contact with government personnel involved in nursery education but in the 1950s members are less responsive to legislative information and activities offered by NANE. Legislative advocacy at the federal level remains weak throughout the 1950s.	
1952	During the 1950s and 1960s, membership grows slowly. Funds are provided to establish a limited office capacity, and the use of conferences to raise funds begins in earnest.	The Ding Dong School television program for children is created by Dr. Frances Horwich (Miss Frances), who had been the NANE president in 1947–48. The Southern Association for Children Under Six (SACUS) is established (later renamed Southern Early Childhood Association).

NAEYC	Early Care and Education	
The *NANE Bulletin* is published quarterly and pamphlets are sent on request. Legislative reports are issued regularly, and a conference is convened every two years. The work is done almost entirely through volunteer efforts of the leadership and members. During this period, the NANE headquarters moves with president.	The Children's Bureau publishes a report on working women and the use of child care by employed mothers. President Dwight D. Eisenhower creates the Department of Health, Education, and Welfare (HEW).	1953
"On the Research Side," a regular column on the implications of research for practice, is first published in the winter issue of the Association's bulletin. Many highly regarded researchers serve as the research editor for this regular feature, later renamed "Research in Review."	Internal Revenue Code (IRS) Section 214 (P.L. 591) allows tax deductions for selected child care expenses. Deductions are increased in 1971 and 1975.	1954
The *Bulletin* changes its name to *The Journal of Nursery Education*.		1956
A national headquarters with desk space and a half-time secretary is established at the Elizabeth McCormick Memorial Fund in Chicago. NANE is formally incorporated as a not-for-profit corporation in the State of Illinois.	The Inter-City Day Care Council (NYC) expands to become the National Committee for the Day Care of Children. In 1968 it becomes the Day Care and Child Development Council, and in 1982 the Child Care Action Campaign. Senator Jacob Javits (D-NY) introduces a series of child care bills.	1958
The Edith Lauer Fund awards a $4,000 grant to NANE to support fundraising efforts.	The United Nations proclaims the Declaration of the Rights of the Child, which states "mankind owes the child the best it has to give."	1959

Timeline of Early Care and Education

	NAEYC	Early Care and Education
1960	NANE is allowed six delegates to the 1960 White House Conference and, in addition to sending the president and past president, uses two slots for young professionals and two for college students.	The White House Conference on Children and Youth is convened to promote opportunities for a creative life in freedom and dignity. The American Council of Cooperative Preschools is established. It will change its name to Parent Cooperative Preschools International in 1964. The High/Scope Perry Preschool Project starts.
1961		The International Association for the Child's Right to Play forms in Denmark with 40 nations as affiliates. The American association is established in 1973 in Philadelphia.
1962		Child care assistance is made available to mothers on welfare who are working or in job training through an amendment to Title IV-A of the Social Security Act (AFDC), P.L. 87-543. President John F. Kennedy delivers an address on welfare asking Congress to fund day care for welfare mothers so they can go to work.
1964	NANE becomes the National Association for the Education of Young Children (NAEYC) at its conference in Miami Beach. With the advent of Head Start and growing federal involvement in early care and education, NAEYC becomes more active in policy issues.	The Economic Opportunity Act of 1964 (P.L. 88-452) includes plans for Head Start, a demonstration program offering comprehensive services to preschool children of families with low incomes.

NAEYC	Early Care and Education	
The *Journal* becomes *Young Children*.		1964 (cont'd)
Fundraising efforts, begun with the 1959 seed money from the Edith Lauer Fund, achieve many gifts from "Friends of NANE" and a donation from the Grant Foundation that finally enables NAEYC to appoint its first executive secretary.		
The headquarters office relocates to New York City to be managed by the newly appointed executive secretary who is persuaded to leave retirement to help build a staff and strong headquarters operation. Later in the year, the office moves to Washington, D.C., fulfilling the Association's dream of a permanent presence in the nation's capital.	Head Start begins as a summer program in an anti-poverty initiative. Originally located in the Office of Economic Opportunity, it is subsequently moved to HEW.	1965
Membership grows from 1,000 in 1956 to over 6,000.	The Child Nutrition Act and National School Lunch Act include eligible child care centers in nutrition programs.	1966
The executive secretary is able to retire (again) as NAEYC achieves its goal of appointing an executive director.	The Children's Television Workshop (CTW) creates *Sesame Street,* which is funded by the Ford Foundation, the Carnegie Corporation of New York, and HEW.	
Annual conferences begin.		
NAEYC, concerned about the quality of some of the 1965 summer Head Start training, contracts to research the professional capacity of applicants and to recommend training sites based on curriculum and faculty.		

Timeline of Early Care and Education

	NAEYC	Early Care and Education
1967	The first volume of *The Young Child: Reviews of Research* is published. This and the second volume (1972) are compendiums of research about young children previously published as articles in the Association's journal.	The Educational Resources Information Center (ERIC)/ Elementary & Early Childhood Education Clearinghouse is established. The Federal Panel on Early Childhood initiates the Community Coordinated Child Care (4C) Program and recommends nationwide organizations.
1968		The Child Care Food Program is established in the Department of Agriculture. Federal Interagency Day Care Requirements (FIDCR) are promulgated, but never implemented.
1969	NAEYC purchases its own building at 1834 Connecticut Avenue, N.W., Washington, D.C.	The Office of Child Development (OCD) is created in the U.S. Department of Health, Education, and Welfare (HEW).
1970	NAEYC begins expanding staff and adds an assistant executive director position. The executive staff of NAEYC, and others from a few additional organizations focused solely on young children, meet regularly to advise the director of the Office of Child Development in invited, off-the-record sessions. NAEYC is one of many organizations represented in frequent meetings with the Washington Research Project (precursor to the Children's Defense Fund) to build consensus around components for which to advocate for inclusion in the Comprehensive Child Development Bill (Brademas/Mondale bill).	The White House Conference on Children endorses the Comprehensive Child Development Act. The National Black Child Development Institute is established in Washington, D.C.

NAEYC	Early Care and Education	

NAEYC follows the lead of some of its Affiliates in Chicago and California and establishes the national Week of the Young Child in April. (Over the years, it becomes known as the Month of the Young Child as well.)

When NAEYC holds its annual conference in Minneapolis in November, the Comprehensive Child Development Bill passes the House and is pending in the Senate. Hired picketers protest NAEYC's inclusion of Senator Walter Mondale as a speaker and the Association mounts a telegram campaign in support of the bill.

NAEYC conducts a feasibility study of the consortium approach to implementing the new professional credential (CDA).

President Richard M. Nixon vetoes the Comprehensive Child Development Bill (S. 2007) as it promotes "communal approaches to child rearing over family-centered approaches."

The Internal Revenue Code Section 214 Revision establishes increases in the income ceilings and allowable deductions for child care.

The Child Development Associate (CDA) Consortium is created in HEW to develop the CDA credential, first awarded in 1975.

1971

The executive director resigns for health reasons. The Search Committee completes its search, and the Governing Board names a new director effective January 1973, who stays 26 years.

The appointment of a full-time professional meeting planner heralds a change from volunteers to staff in responsibility for conference planning.

Representatives from NAEYC, ACEI, and NEA's Department of Elementary, Kindergarten, and Nursery Education work weekends to prepare a proposal for OCD funding to establish the CDA Consortium and begin hiring staff.

The National Council of Jewish Women publishes *Windows on Day Care*.

The Office of Child Development establishes a School-Age Day Care Task Force with representatives from HEW and Labor.

1972

Timeline
of Early Care
and Education

	NAEYC	Early Care and Education
1973	Membership Action Grants (MAG grants) are established.	Marian Wright Edelman founds the Children's Defense Fund in Washington, D.C.
		The National Head Start directors form the forerunner of the National Head Start Association (NHSA).
		The Division for Early Childhood (DEC) of the Council for Exceptional Children is formed to focus on young children with special needs.
1974	NAEYC sponsors a small conference on the preparation of teachers for early childhood education programs and is challenged by presenters and conferees to develop a new model of teacher education.	The Title XX amendment to the Social Services Act (P.L. 93-647) allows funds to be used for child care. In the Omnibus Budget Reconciliation Act of 1981, this amendment becomes Social Services Block Grant (SSBG).
		The Child Abuse Prevention and Treatment Act (P.L. 93-247) is enacted.
1975		Stride Rite opens the first modern, on-site employer-supported child care center. By 1978, 105 companies have sponsored child care centers.
		Congress enacts the Education for All Handicapped Children Act (P.L. 94-142), later known as the Individuals with Disabilities Education Act (IDEA).
		The Head Start Performance Standards are promulgated.

NAEYC	Early Care and Education	
NAEYC celebrates its 50th anniversary. Observances include the publication of *NAEYC's First Half Century, 1926–1976* and, at the Anaheim conference, the ceremonial burning of the headquarters mortgage, a speech by first president, Lois Hayden Meek Stolz, and participation of all living Association presidents. NAEYC has 28,000 members.	The Dependent Care Tax Credit (20%) defines child care as an employment expense and benefits all families. In 1981 the credit increases to 30% and a sliding scale is created. The National Association of Early Childhood Specialists in State Departments of Education is formed.	1976
An article titled "Public Policy Participation as a Moral Responsibility" is published in the September issue of *Young Children*.	The National Association of Early Childhood Teacher Educators (NAECTE) is established. The Bush Center in Child Development and Social Policy is established at Yale University. The National Center for Clinical Infant Programs is founded. It later changes its name to ZERO TO THREE. The *Child Care Information Exchange*, a journal for center directors, is created.	1977
The NAEYC archives are placed at Indiana State University, Terre Haute. NAEYC begins involvement with the National Council for Accreditation of Teacher Educators (NCATE).	The Child Care Employee Project is founded in Oakland, California, and moves to Washington, D.C., in 1984. The organization's name is later changed to the Center for the Child Care Workforce. Early childhood faculty in community colleges form a network that will later become American Associate Degree Early Childhood Educators (ACCESS).	1978

Timeline
of Early Care
and Education

	NAEYC	Early Care and Education
1979		*Children at the Center: Final Results of the National Day Care Study* is published. This federally funded study connects higher quality care to small group size and trained caregivers.
1981	The Governing Board votes to explore the feasibility of a center endorsement project to address concerns about the quality of early childhood programs. This work results in NAEYC's accreditation system. The Board approves *Early Childhood Teacher Education Guidelines for Four- and Five-Year Programs* (December). Contributions from the family and friends of Rose H. Alschuler, founding member and first secretary/treasurer of the Association, fund the development work.	Social Services Block Grant replaces the Title XX funding stream and, over time, decreases. The first annual *Children's Defense Budget* is published by CDF. The Family Resource Coalition forms and later changes its name to the Family Resource Coalition of America.
1982	NAEYC publishes Volume 3 of *The Young Child: Review of Research,* for the first time consisting of chapters written expressly for the book (previous volumes were compilations of articles from *Young Children*). The authors are leading researchers committed to disseminating child development information to practitioners responsible for services to children and their families.	The National Association for Family Day Care is established. The National Coalition for Campus Child Care formally incorporates as a membership organization.

NAEYC	Early Care and Education	
	The Child Care Action Campaign is established in New York City	1983
	The Ecumenical Child Care Network is established.	
NAEYC adopts	The High/Scope Foundation publishes *Changed Lives: The Effects of the Perry Preschool Project*, a report showing positive impact of child care.	1984
Position Statement on Nomenclature, Salaries, Benefits, and the Status of the Early Childhood Profession;		
Position Statement on Family Day Care Regulation.	The Human Services Reauthorization Act (P.L. 98-558) creates the Dependent Care Development Grant to fund child care resource and referral agencies, school-age programs, and special needs child care.	
NAEYC publishes "Results of the NAEYC Survey of Child Care Salaries and Working Conditions" in *Young Children* (November).		
The Accreditation system is field tested in Santa Clara County, California; Dallas, Texas; Broward County, Florida; and Minneapolis-St. Paul, Minnesota. *Accreditation Criteria and Procedures* is approved and published by end of year.		
The Governing Board approves *Guidelines for Early Childhood Education Programs in Associate Degree Granting Institutions*. The Alschuler Fund supports this work.		
With grant support from Carnegie Corporation of New York, NAEYC begins development work for Child Care Information Services.		

Timeline
of Early Care
and Education

	NAEYC	Early Care and Education

1985 NAEYC officially begins its national voluntary accreditation project through the National Academy of Early Childhood Programs.

NAEYC publishes "Early Childhood Education's Past as Prologue: Roots of Contemporary Concerns" in *Young Children* (July).

NAEYC establishes the Council for Early Childhood Professional Recognition to administer the national CDA credential program. The council becomes a separate organization in 1989.

1986 NAEYC publishes "Birthday Thoughts" in *Young Children* (January).

The Annual Conference celebrates NAEYC's 60 years.

NAEYC publishes "NAEYC Then and Now: 1926–1986" in *Young Children* (March). The article includes these membership growth figures:

1926, a committee of 25 members; 1936, 250 members; 1946, 600 members; 1956, 900 members; 1966, 9,000 members; 1976, 31,000 members; and 1986, 50,000+ members

and this on Headquarters growth:

1926–1957, all operations are performed by Board members and committees; 1958–1963, donated space in Chicago with a paid secre-

Temporary Child Care for Handicapped Children and Crisis Nurseries Act (P.L. 99-401) passes.

The Human Services Reauthorization Act Amendment, Title VI (P.L. 99-425), creates scholarships for training for the Child Development Associate (CDA) Credential.

tary; 1965, rented space in Washington, D.C., and a paid executive director; 1969, building at 1834 Connecticut Avenue NW is purchased (50% occupancy by NAEYC); 1976, mortgage is paid off (100% occupancy by NAEYC).

NAEYC supports the Act for Better Child Care (ABC), along with many early childhood education colleague organizations.

The first issue of NAEYC-sponsored *Early Childhood Research Quarterly (ECRQ)* is published.

NAEYC adopts

Position Statement on the Liability Insurance Crisis;

Position Statement on Developmentally Appropriate Practice in Early Childhood Programs Serving Children from Birth through Age 8;

Position Statement on Developmentally Appropriate Practice in Programs for 4- and 5-Year-olds; and

Guidelines for Developing Legislation Creating or Expanding Programs for Young Children: A Position Statement of NAEYC.

NAEYC publishes "NAEYC Publications: Then and Now" in *Young Children* (November).

Timeline
of Early Care
and Education

1987

NAEYC's headquarters expands with the purchase of the adjoining town house at 1832 Connecticut Avenue, NW, Washington, D.C.

NAEYC publishes

Developmentally Appropriate Practice in Early Childhood Programs Serving Children from Birth Through Age 8—Expanded Edition;

"NAEYC at 60: Visions for the Year 2000" in *Young Children* (March).

NAEYC adopts

Position Statement on Quality, Compensation, and Affordability in Early Childhood Programs;

Position Statement on Licensing and Other Forms of Regulation of Early Childhood Programs in Centers and Family Day Care; and,

Position Statement on Standardized Testing of Young Children 3 Through 8 Years of Age.

NAEYC's book compilations of research articles take a new approach, focusing on one theme per book, and adopt a new series name, Research Monographs. The first volume is titled *Quality in Child Care: What Does Research Tell Us?*

NAEYC becomes one of 90 organizations that form the national Alliance for Better Child Care (ABC).

The National Association of Child Care Resource and Referral Agencies (NACCRRA) is incorporated. The national office, originally in Rochester, Minnesota, moves to Washington, D.C., in the fall of 1992.

The U.S. Children's Bureau celebrates its 75th anniversary.

NAEYC	Early Care and Education	
NAEYC adopts Position Statement on Developmentally Appropriate Practice in the Primary Grades, Serving 5- Through 8-Year-Olds. NAEYC sponsors the Colloquium on Early Childhood Teacher Education during which the Position Statement on Early Childhood Teacher Education Guidelines for 4- and 5-Year Programs is reviewed. An executive summary of the colloquium is published in *Young Children* (November). NAEYC adopts an anti-discrimination policy. Members approve revised change in Bylaws.	The Family Support Act of 1988 offers the first open-ended entitlement for eligible child care for parents in mandatory work and training programs and a year of transitional child care to parents leaving welfare for the workforce. The ABC bill is introduced (S.1885/H.R. 3660). Over 100 child care bills are introduced in the 101st Congress. U.S. Department of Education creates Even Start.	1988
NAEYC adopts Code of Ethical Conduct. NAEYC establishes a Department of Public Affairs. NAEYC has 62,000 members, having gained 60,000 members in the 25 years since 1964.	The National Child Care Staffing Study shows how low wages and staff turnover affect the quality of child care. Follow-up reports in 1993 and 1998 indicate little change. The National Center for Children in Poverty (NCCP) is established in Columbia University's School of Public Health. President George H. Bush's Education Summit, led by then-governor Bill Clinton, adopts six goals, the first of which is that all children will start school "ready to learn." The Center for the Future of Children is founded at Stanford University and funded by the David and Lucile Packard Foundation.	1989

Timeline of Early Care and Education

	NAEYC	**Early Care and Education**

1989 (cont'd)

The United Nations adopts the Convention on the Rights of the Child. The convention recognizes that children have the right to "a name and a nationality, to health care services, education, [and] protection against discrimination, abuse, neglect and injury, and economic exploitation...."

The Families and Work Institute is founded.

1990

NAEYC adopts

Guidelines for Appropriate Curriculum Content and Assessment in Programs Serving Children Ages 3 Through 8: A Position Statement of the NAEYC and the National Association of Early Childhood Specialists in State Departments of Education;

Position Statement on Media Violence in Children's Lives;

Position Statement on School Readiness; and

Position Statement on Guidelines for Compensation of Early Childhood Professionals.

NAEYC holds the opening event of its 1990 Annual Conference on the steps of the U.S. Capitol with speakers including Senators Edward Kennedy, Massachusetts; Paul Wellstone, Minnesota; Christopher Dodd, Connecticut; and John Chafee, Rhode Island; Representative Dale Kildee, Michigan; and Councilman H.R. Crawford, District of Columbia. November 15 is declared "NAEYC Day" in Washington, D.C.

The National Child Care Survey shows a growing need for quality infant and toddler care.

President George H. Bush signs into law the Omnibus Budget Reconciliation Act/Child Care and Development Block Grant (P.L. 101-508), the first U.S. law that specifically addresses child care funding support. Title IV of the Social Security Act now includes JOBS/Transitional Child Care and At-Risk Child Care.

NAEYC	Early Care and Education	
The National Institute for Early Childhood Professional Development is established to improve the quality and training provided for individuals who care for and educate young children. NAEYC publishes *The Demand and Supply of Child Care in 1990*.	The National Commission on Children, chaired by Senator John D. Rockefeller, IV, West Virginia, issues its recommendations in *Beyond Rhetoric: A New American Agenda for Children and Families*.	1991
NAEYC purchases the building at 1509 16th Street, N.W., Washington, D.C., and prepares to move operations there in January 1993. First Annual National Institute for Early Childhood Professional Development is held in Los Angeles.	Nonprofit initiative known as Child Care Aware launches a national toll-free number to help parents find child care in their local area. The Association of Childhood Education International (ACEI) celebrates its centennial, having begun as the International Kindergarten Union (IKU) in 1892 in Saratoga Springs, New York. The American Business Collaboration for Quality Dependent Care (ABC) is established.	1992
NAEYC adopts Position Statement on Violence in the Lives of Children; and Position Statement: A Conceptual Framework for Early Childhood Professional Development. NAEYC works with America Tomorrow Leadership Information Service (ATLIS) to provide member access to an electronic communication system.	Secretary Donna Shalala creates the Health and Human Services Advisory Committee on Head Start Quality and Expansion. The Communications Consortium Media Center is established and helps develop and coordinate media outreach on child care issues.	1993

Timeline
of Early Care
and Education

	NAEYC	Early Care and Education
1994		The National Association for Family Child Care (NAFCC) and the National School-Age Care Alliance (NSACA) both work on accreditation programs.
		The Carnegie Corporation of New York publishes *Starting Points: Meeting the Needs of Our Youngest Children* focusing on birth to three years of age.
		AmeriCorps CARE & Action for Children (ACT) is initiated within the Corporation for National Service.
		The Head Start Reauthorization Act includes a set-aside for services for families with children below the age of three years.
1995	With support from the Robert R. McCormick Tribune Foundation, NAEYC hosts an invitational think-tank meeting focused on a thoughtful and critical review of NAEYC's accreditation system over the past decade and lessons learned for the future. NAEYC adopts Position Statement on Quality, Compensation and Affordability (Revised); and Position Statement on Responding to Linguistic and Cultural Diversity: Recommendations for Effective Early Childhood Education.	The study report *Cost, Quality and Child Outcomes in Child Care Centers* shows that 70% of child care centers are mediocre and only one in seven centers offers quality care. Secretary Donna Shalala establishes the Child Care Bureau in the Department of Health and Human Services. The National Head Start Fellowships Program is established under the reauthorization of the Head Start Act.

NAEYC	**Early Care and Education**	

NAEYC is among the national organizations that support the Stand for Children mass demonstration organized by the Children's Defense Fund and held at the Lincoln Memorial in June. More than 300,000 people come to Washington, D.C., for the one-day event. NAEYC contributes 1834 Connecticut Avenue headquarters space for Stand for Children offices.

NAEYC celebrates its 70th anniversary.

NAEYC adopts

Position Statement on Technology and Young Children Ages Three to Eight; and

Position Statement on the Prevention of Child Abuse in Early Childhood Programs and the Responsibilities of Early Childhood Professionals to Prevent Child Abuse.

Call for applicants to serve on NAEYC panels is initiated.

Annual Report: *Approaching the New Millennium: Lessons from NAEYC's First 70 Years.*

A conference on brain development in young children shows the value of quality interactions between adults and children and generates media interest.

The National Institute of Child Health and Human Development (NICHD) publishes an initial report on the effect of child care on children.

The Personal Responsibility and Work Opportunity Act passes, with a requirement to spend at least 4% of the funds to "provide comprehensive consumer education to parents, increase parental choice, and improve the quality and availability of child care."

The Alliance of Work/Life Professionals (AWLP) is established.

1996

29

Timeline of Early Care and Education

	NAEYC	**Early Care and Education**
1997	NAEYC publishes *Developmentally Appropriate Practice in Early Childhood Programs,* Rev. ed. (includes the "NAEYC Position Statement on Developmentally Appropriate Practice in Early Childhood Programs Serving Children from Birth through Age 8," revision adopted in 1996); and adopts Position Statement on Licensing and Public Regulation of Early Childhood Programs (revised).	President William J. Clinton and Hillary Rodham Clinton host a White House Conference on Child Care in October, and announce a child care initiative for $21.7 billion over five years. Rob and Michelle Reiner start the *I Am Your Child* public awareness campaign. NACCRRA establishes Learning Options, an online early education opportunity spin-off. The Individuals with Disabilities Education Act (IDEA) is reauthorized, strengthening early childhood services.
1998	NAEYC adopts Position Statement on Learning to Read and Write: Developmentally Appropriate Practices for Young Children, jointly with the International Reading Association. NAEYC's executive staff (executive director and chief operations officer) announce plans to leave their positions at end of 1998. Search committee conducts a search and the Governing Board appoints the new executive director to begin in January 1999. NAEYC revises its Code of Ethical Conduct.	The National Research Council of the National Academy of Sciences releases the landmark report *Preventing Reading Difficulties in Young Children.*

NAEYC	**Early Care and Education**	

New executive director assumes duties and appoints a deputy executive director.

NAEYC adopts Position Statement on Developing and Implementing Effective Public Policies to Promote Early Childhood and School-Age Care Program Accreditation.

History and Archives Panel is reactivated in preparation for NAEYC's 75th anniversary in 2001.

NAEYC launches Accreditation Reinvention Project with appointment of a national commission to develop recommendations for the next era of NAEYC's accreditation system.

| | The *Child Care Information Exchange*/ Exchange Press sponsors First World Forum on Early Care and Education, in Honolulu, Oahu, Hawaii. Subsequent forums convene in Singapore (2000) and Greece (2001). | 1999 |

Membership reaches 103,000.

NAEYC begins implementation of a new organizational structure.

| | Committees of the National Academy of Science publish *Eager to Learn: Educating Our Preschoolers* and *From Neurons to Neighborhoods: The Science of Early Childhood Development*. | 2000 |

NAEYC celebrates its 75th Anniversary (1926–2001) through interactive Website opportunities and articles in *Young Children* throughout the year. Anniversary activities culminate with member celebration at the Annual Conference in Anaheim, California, with several past presidents participating in the Presidential Seminar and selected students giving presentations on lessons from the past for our future.

NAEYC recognizes the first NAEYC Interest Forums.

First meeting of the Affiliate Council is held.

| | Bipartisan Congressional Caucus on Child Care is formed.

The Act to Leave No Child Behind is introduced in the U.S. Congress by Senator Christopher Dodd (S. 940) and Representative George Miller (H.R. 1990). | 2001 |

Sources for the 2001 NAEYC Timeline

Boyd, S.T. 1981. An historical perspective of the NAEYC through interviews with past presidents. Unpublished dissertation. Terre Haute, IN: Indiana State University.

Child Care Action Campaign. 1999. *Child Care Action Campaign: The first 15 years.* New York: Author.

Cohen, A.J. 1996. A brief history of federal financing for child care in the United States. Theme issue, Financing Child Care. *The Future of Children* 6 (2): 26–40.

Elkind, D. 1987. The child: Yesterday, today, and tomorrow. *Young Children* 42 (4): 6–11.

Greenberg, P. 1987. Lucy Sprague Mitchell: A major missing link between early childhood education in the 1980's and progressive education in the 1890's–1930's. *Young Children* 42 (5): 70–84. (A review of Antler, J. 1987. *Lucy Sprague Mitchell: The making of a modern woman.* New Haven, CT: Yale University Press.)

Halpern, R. 1987. Research in Review. Major social and demographic trends affecting young families: Implications for early childhood care and education. *Young Children* 42 (6): 34–40.

Hewes, D.W. [1976] 1996. *NAEYC's first half century 1926–1976.* 70th Anniversary reprint. Washington, DC: NAEYC.

Hewes, D.W. 1998. *"It's the camaraderie!"—A History of Parent Participation Preschools.* Davis, CA: Center for Cooperatives, University of California.

Hymes, J.L., Jr. 1991. *Early childhood education—Twenty years in review: A look at 1971–1990.* Washington, DC: NAEYC.

Lascarides, V.C., & B.F. Hinitz. 2000. *History of early childhood education.* New York: Falmer Press.

Ranck, E.R. 1997. *NACCRRA at ten: A commemorative history of the National Association of Child Care Resource and Referral Agencies.* Washington, DC: NACCRRA.

Ranck, E.R. 1998. Highlights and lowlights of the past two decades: *Child Care Information Exchange* matures along with the profession. *Child Care Information Exchange* 120: 12–16.

Snyder, A. 1972. *Dauntless women in childhood education 1856–1931.* Washington, DC: Association for Childhood Education International.

Takanishi, R. 1979. *An American child development pioneer: Lois Hayden Meek Stolz.* (An oral history).

Witherspoon, R.L. 1976. From NANE to NAEYC: The tempestuous years. *Young Children* 31 (5): 333–38.

Chapter 2

NAEYC's Roots

The First 50 Years

- Dorothy W. Hewes and the NAEYC Organizational History and Archives Committttee

- Ralph Witherspoon

The following selection is reprinted in its entirety from: Hewes, D.W., & the NAEYC Organizational History and Archives Committee. 1976. NAEYC's First Half Century: 1926–1976. *Young Children* 31 (6): 461–47.

NAEYC's First Half Century 1926–1976

The National Committee on Nursery Schools

Dorothy W. Hewes and the NAEYC Organizational History and Archives Committee

Although nursery schools began to proliferate during the 1920s, very young children attended public and private schools from the early days of the American colonies. In 1826, just one hundred years before the first conference of the Committee on Nursery Schools, Robert Owen's industrial child care facility in New Harmony, Indiana, enrolled more than one hundred children. Brook Farm included communal child care as part of its utopian program in the 1840s. Day care for working mothers became institutionalized during the Civil War, and Froebelian kindergartens were popular from the 1880s onward. Various philosophies of "infant schools" competed with one another, either as philanthropies or as proprietary programs.

By 1920, when about one-half million four- and five-year-olds were enrolled in kindergartens, the English nursery schools provided a unique model for appropriate early childhood experiences. Mary Dabney Davis described the popularity of this "new unit at the foot of the educational ladder" as resulting from recent knowledge about potential learning abilities of young children and from the development of techniques of conditioning behavior, combined with population shifts toward cities (Davis 1932). Nursery schools were established for educational experimentation, for demonstration of methodology, or for purposes of research, but not for the relief of working mothers or neglected children. Professional researchers and educators began to organize nursery schools, and those programs which actually began to operate in the 1920s were deluged with requests for information. There were perhaps 3 nursery schools at the beginning of the decade and at least 262 when it closed. Obviously. some sort of structured professional organization was inevitable.

Following several years of discussion, the first preliminary meeting of nursery school advocates was held in New York City in May 1925. Patty Smith Hill, who had carefully selected the 25 members of this advisory committee, was chosen as chairman. Victoria Dike, who had issued the invitations, was asked to be secretary. There was no treasurer. The main concern was whether a new association should be formed, or whether the nursery school people should join an already established organization. A subcommittee composed of Arnold Gesell, Lois Meek (Stolz), Abigail Eliot, and Louise Stanley was named to investigate alternatives (Hewes 1976).

At a subsequent meeting, it was decided to hold a public conference in Washington, D.C., in February 1926.

According to Mary Dabney Davis, that initial conference 50 years ago was characteristic in many respects of those that followed. As a member of the original committee, she later wrote:

It included discussions of the functions of nursery schools, their part in the total educational program, their service for parent education, and their programs for health and family welfare. Descriptions of practice were given. These included reports about the Bureau of Educational Experiments, a Montessori Training School, the Under-Age Kindergartens of Washington, the Child Welfare Research Clinic of Teachers College, the Ruggles Street Nursery (School) and Training Center, the Chicago University Cooperative Nursery School, and the Chicago Public School Nursery School . . . . Dr. [Arnold] Gesell of the Yale Psycho-Clinic and Dr. Bird Baldwin of the Child Welfare Research Station at the University of Iowa described research in progress in the field of child development. (Davis 1964, pp. 106-107)

The second conference, held at the Majestic Hotel in New York City on April 22 and 23, 1927, had 295 registered representatives from 24 states, the District of Columbia, Hawaii, and England. Although 50 were nursery school teachers and directors and 61 were students, the range of professional positions included home economists, social workers. psychiatrists, psychologists, college presidents and instructors, and others. Listed separately were five directors and teachers of day nurseries and play groups, an early indication that they were not yet accepted as part of the nursery school movement. At that conference, in addition to reports of research and descriptions of programs, the membership again considered alternatives for its continuation. Patty Smith Hill said:

The business problems you are asked to consider and help us to decide are as follows:

1. Shall we organize, electing officers, and continue as a separate organization?

2. Shall we disband as a separate organization, appointing a committee to appeal to all present organizations interested in nursery school education, to make a place in all their programs for the consideration of nursery school problems?[1]

A long list of potential organizations pointed up the increased interest in the nursery school concept, for in those days of prosperity, when the average citizen assumed that every year would find the economy getting better, there was a tacit acceptance of spending money on small children. Money from the Laura Spelman Rockefeller Memorial Fund, administered by Lawrence Frank and Beardsley Ruml, was available for research in child growth and development. Freudian emphasis upon the importance of early childhood and behaviorist theory which stressed early habit training were also winning recognition.

With the momentum of public interest, the 1929 conference in Chicago was exciting and successful. After a brief introduction on "The Philosophy Underlying Early Childhood Education," social psychologist Goodwin Watson explained a new conference procedure and threw the meeting open to discussion. For two afternoons, participants met in small groups to exchange ideas on topics which are still viable. Among them were these:

- How can nursery school children be trained to adjust to the world as it may be rather than to the world as it is?
- What is meant by "integrating" the physical, mental, and social experiences of the child? Does any experience fail to do this?

- What, if anything, does the nursery school contribute to the child that he does not get eventually without nursery school?
- How can one define the province of parents and specialists in the education of young children? Does the parent have any unique rights?[2]

Some of the general issues which emerged as a result of these discussions were formulated as problems appropriate for further research, such as:

- Does adult interference with children's quarrels increase or inhibit self-control?
- Is a nursery school justified in developing and using techniques which are not likely to be used in the home?
- Is the time really ripe for the encouragement of nursery units in public education, or should an attempt be made to maintain them only in experimental situations?
- Should there be a differentiation in levels of training for teachers who fill different types of positions?
- How much practical experience with children should be required in training courses?[3]

In the business session concluding the 1929 conference, a final determination was made. The loosely organized National Committee on Nursery Schools was inadequate. People wanted to belong to a formal organization. As members of a variety of professions—nursery school people, pediatricians, home economists, social workers, nurses—they wanted an integrated association. Protests came from administrators of teacher training

1929

Conference participants asked, "How can nursery school children be trained to adjust to the world as it may be rather than to the world as it is?"

programs, who saw disruption of their integrated sequence of nursery school, kindergarten, and primary grades. They predicted that it would make acceptance of nursery schools into public schools more difficult. Officers of other associations were present, convinced that the new group should join their organizations. When the decision to form the National Association for Nursery Education was determined by a vote of 80 to 5, it was a particular blow to Alice Temple. As president of the International Kindergarten Union (IKU), and for thirty years a leader of the kindergarten movement and a close friend of Patty Smith Hill, she was reorganizing the IKU into the Association for Childhood Education (ACE) to include the nursery schools as an integral unit.

It is unclear why the nursery school pioneers would not merge with the kindergartners, although some reports indicate that the IKU was viewed as a conventional group of female teachers, while the new nursery school association included prominent men in its membership and was multidisciplinary. The NANE president of 1931-33, George Stoddard, recently expressed the opinion that the new Association was a bond that pulled the new child study centers together.

> It gave us all a sense, not only of working in Iowa, or in New York, or in New Haven, or Chicago, or Stanford, or Minneapolis, but a sense of being together in a real educational movement. Back there . . . it was a case of men's liberation. . . [Women] practically monopolized the field . . . all the way up through elementary education . . . . But we men, and many women, too, like Lois Meek

> [Stolz], Beth Wellman, Florence Goodenough, others that I could name, joined forces on behalf of this great movement to secure a better educational environment and a better educational experience. (Senn 1975, p. 20)

Whatever the reasons for the decision of the original Committee on Nursery Schools to form an independent organization, it resulted in many dual memberships in NANE and ACE, with official cooperation and competition waxing and waning to the present time. Until the 1950s, some local and regional groups actually paid a portion of the membership dues to ACEI rather than to NANE, and older members still use the ACEI term "branches" rather than the NAEYC "affiliates."

With the 1929 decision to form the National Association for Nursery Education, it was determined to continue the National Committee for Nursery Education as its Executive Committee until 1931. Lois Meek (Stolz), who had been involved with preliminary planning for almost a decade, was elected chairman. Rose Alschuler, who can now chuckle over the realization that Patty Smith Hill had invited her to be on the original committee because she was an influential lay leader of the public school nursery school movement, was elected secretary-treasurer. Since there were no funds, she donated $500 to the cause! The meeting adjourned with plans to meet again in two years to vote on a constitution and by-laws. The gestation period was over, with NANE born into the chaos of bank failures beginning the Great Depression.

From its earliest years, the Association has held certain basic philosophic orientations. Emphasis has been upon the young child in the family and community. Although NAEYC is a national association, there has been a realization that programs of benefit to children must have strong local services geared to community needs. Affiliation with other professional groups has been important. A combination of research reports and practical information has been evidenced in publications and conference schedules, with professional men and women from a diversified range of occupations contributing to the developing expertise of the early childhood education profession. As NANE concluded its initial structural planning between the 1929 conference and that of 1931, it established the foundation for NAEYC as it is in 1976.

The Challenge of the Thirties

With the Philadelphia conference of November 1931, NANE moved from the commercial atmosphere of hotels to the academic one of Temple University. Conference arrangements indicate a well-organized group. Exhibits of nursery school materials were open all day. Automobiles were scheduled to take observers to a variety of nursery schools which were listed as philanthropic, educational, or cooperative. Reduced railroad fares enabled members to purchase return tickets at half price. Active membership was restricted to those trained for work in the field of nursery education or professionally engaged in it, with

associate membership available for parents and others. Dues were set at $2 per year for active members, $1 for associates, with the conscious effort to make them low enough for anyone to afford. Patty Smith Hill received the first honorary membership in recognition of her efforts in behalf of the new Association. Apparently this was a successful, though not particularly eventful, conference.[4]

The 1933 Toronto conference was destined to be a landmark event for NANE. It is interesting to note little recognition of the depression which was devastating the country. Even the keynote talk by Lillian Gilbreth, engineer and efficiency expert now best known as the mother in *Cheaper by the Dozen* but then introduced as having 11 children, seemed to avoid real issues when she spoke on "The Challenge of the New Deal to Nursery Education."

The routine conference schedule was disrupted by a special Executive Committee meeting at two o'clock on the first afternoon. NANE President-elect Mary Dabney Davis, Senior Specialist in Nursery-Kindergarten-Primary Education for the U.S. Office of Education, announced that a national preschool system had been authorized just three days earlier on October 23. This program, initiated under the Federal Emergency Relief Administration but better known as the Works Progress Administration (WPA) nursery schools, was supposed to develop the physical and mental well-being of preschool children in needy unemployed families or neglected or underprivileged homes. Administration was to be through state educational offices and local school districts.

A committee was named that afternoon to draw up a statement and by eight o'clock that evening it was presented to the membership. Characteristic of NANE, not only was Mary Dabney Davis given immediate pledges of cooperation but concerns were expressed that only with the greatest of care could such an extensive new program be started without harm to children. It was also characteristic that discussions continued through most of the night. By morning, a mimeographed report was ready for distribution, recommending that age limits of children be from two years to public school legal admission, that a permanent advisory and supervisory committee be established, and that NANE ally itself with health and educational programs and with professional organizations sponsoring such programs. In addition, the report stated:

> We recommend that the permanent Committee enlist the services of institutions in a position to furnish trained workers in the field of preschool education and professional care and to be responsible for training programs, thus forming a network of centers that would offer for the untrained worker: first, guidance through supervision; second, opportunity for understanding children's needs through free attendance in training classes; third, opportunity for acquiring right attitudes toward children, through conferences and sympathetic contacts with experienced and trained persons in the field who hold professionally accepted standards and ideals for young children.

> We recommend that a program of education and counseling for parents be included as an essential aspect of the program of each preschool unit.

> We recommend that the officers of the Association together with the permanent Committee be authorized to take any action they deem necessary for coordinating with the National Association for Childhood Education and the National Council of Parent Education.[5]

[Behind the official story of these nursery schools is the account given by Lois Meek Stolz. Some months earlier, a young man from the staff of Harry Hopkins, then administrator of the Federal Emergency Relief Administration, had called at her office in the Child Development Institute of Teachers College. As he waited for her, he watched children at play and began to ask why there shouldn't be nursery schools for poor children, too. "Suppose we had them," he asked. "Who could you employ? Nutritionists, maintenance workers, all kinds of people besides teachers!" By the time they had finished lunch, there were great visions of nursery schools across the nation—and largely through the work of NANE members, that dream came true .[6]]

Full of enthusiasm, nursery school leaders went home from Toronto ready to implement the recommendations. Although only Abigail Eliot and Lois Meek (Stolz) were delegated NANE representatives to the National Advisory Committee which was established to determine policies and procedures, all nine members belonged to NANE. Mary Dabney Davis, who was program administrator of the federal nursery schools through their first year, was also NANE president.

By the time of the St. Louis conference two years later (1935), a network of free and inexpensive training programs had been established. Materials were being published to provide guidance for the education of both children and their parents. Individuals worked with schools in their own communities, telling each other stories of parental dedication as equipment was improvised to supplement that provided by the government. Parents made valiant efforts to keep children in classes—including the father in northern Minnesota who put a large wash tub on a sled, lined it with a warm comforter, and pulled his two children through the snow in bitterly cold weather. In its report for the first year, the NANE-initiated National Committee wrote, "Though there have been many difficulties and only a beginning has been made, the emergency nursery schools have been epoch-making in the history of early childhood education" (White, n.d.).

Almost two thousand WPA nursery schools were in operation by 1935 with every state except Delaware having some of the 72,404 enrolled children. Employment was provided for 6,770 adults; half were teachers, with the others including janitors, clerks, and a variety of other employees (White, n.d.).

Impact of the federal programs was recognized by Mary Dabney Davis in her presidential report:

> There were innovations in the administration of the 1935 conference. For the first time the conference was held at the invitation of a superintendent of schools. For the first time special courses were offered, one at the request of local public elementary school teachers, principals, and supervisors of instruction, and another for emergency nursery school teachers, beginning teachers, and college students. And for the first time a large number of organizations interested in education, public health, family welfare, and civic betterment sent official representatives to participate in the discussion. All of these "first times" indicate new responsibilities and opportunities for members of the National Association for Nursery Education.[7]

Mary Dabney Davis was aware of the temporary nature of federal funding, for in her review of the emergency preschools she asked how NANE could be organized to most effectively help extend the nationwide program for the next five or ten years to more adequately care for the nation's 9.5 million children between the ages of two and five.

The St. Louis conference also broke the precedent of having scientific research papers and discussion groups as primary program elements. Emphasis was upon classroom techniques, with such topics as fingerpainting, nature study, creative painting, and music. It also revealed that previously untrained teachers, through inservice courses, were often able to teach well and tended to be more willing to move away from institutional patterns to their own innovations.

Another indicator of change in 1935 was the introduction of the new Society for Research in Child Development (SRCD) as an organization which permitted professionals from different fields to devote their energies to the child, without feeling they were stepping outside their own professions. Was this not the purpose of the original Committee on Nursery Schools? Although SRCD was introduced by George Stoddard, NANE's immediate past president, it marked the departure of many research-oriented child study members from Association leadership.

By the seventh biennial conference in Nashville (1937), half of those registered were representing organizations concerned with young children but were not members of NANE. Rather than the physicians, psychologists, and professors who attended NANE conferences ten years earlier, these were social workers, public health employees, and teachers. For the first time, the conference had a theme—*Safeguarding the Early Years of Childhood*—and Lawrence K. Frank gave a general session address on "The Fundamental Needs of the Child." Program emphasis had definitely shifted from correlation of research findings to coordination with other community programs, from an association dominated by university-trained members to one incorporating a wide variety of backgrounds. In the period of social awareness which characterized the New Deal, with its experimentation in funding art and music and community endeavors, the nursery school people became more egalitarian, and conference programs began to reflect wider issues.

That 1937 conference was the only one held in the segregated South until 1964. Although only a minority of the membership was non-white, the situation imposed there was felt to be intolerable: Individuals report having held meetings on the first floor of buildings because elevators were not allowed to carry racially mixed groups. Groups took separate taxis for the same reason. However, one integrated committee simply walked into the hotel dining room, asked the manager for a "quiet table in the corner" so they could transact their business, and got it. From that year on, conference planning committees quietly but firmly insisted that all of their members were to be treated equally or their business would be removed to another hotel or another city.

The emphasis of the Association by the late thirties is reflected by President Ruth Andrus:

Nursery schools in public schools are the meeting ground of all individuals and agencies in a community interested in safeguarding young children . . . but questions arise which involve basic conflicts in our present culture. . .Community committees made up of lay and professional people, including representatives of local government units, should be developed for each nursery school or nursery education center. This . . . . involves practice in fundamental concepts of democracy, and is particularly difficult to achieve in our society where specialists strive for power and individuals have very little opportunity to participate in a group process. (Andrus 1938, p. 9)

The Frantic Forties

As the depression era merged into prosperous preparations for a second World War, NANE went into a period of relative inactivity. Across the country, teachers dropped from WPA nursery schools were hired by public schools or became homemakers. Conferences were still held every second year—New York City in 1939 and Detroit in 1941. The question of a possible merger with ACEI recurred and was again rejected. Then, with a rapidity which stirred the nation, America became totally involved in fighting the war. In her presidential letter of July 1942, Amy Hostler wrote:

> Without doubt the majority of us are serving our schools, our immediate communities and possibly state or national agencies in new ways. Many of these new activities are related to planning and action which is necessary to safeguard the general well-being of young children in the future as well as in the present emergency. . . . Many of you will remember the final stirring meeting of the October conference when announcement was made of the establishment of the National Commission for Young Children. . . .As a nongovernmental agency sponsored by well-known educational organizations, the Commission has been serving as a clearinghouse for individuals and for agencies on information concerning child care in defense areas, trends in the needs of day care, training of volunteers for work in the field of child care and development. Mrs. Rose Alschuler, Chairman, divides her time between field and office work. . . . As part of your war effort will you write to Mrs. Alschuler what you are doing in your locality to further nursery education.[8]

While dwindling remnants of the WPA nursery schools were closing in 1942, plans were being made to fund child care through federal legislation now remembered as the Lanham Act. Once again, NANE leaders rallied to the cause of children. Not only was it important to provide professional staffing for centers, but volunteers were also needed. Dorothy Baruch, named chairman of the registration committee, sent a letter to all known training centers asking for recruits:

> You know of the difficulties and dangers to which children under school age have been subjected in defense areas. We now have the added dangers of disasters brought on by war situations. Nursery education is being strengthened at every possible point. We must aid in this in order to guarantee the physical and mental health of these children and thereby safeguard our future citizens.[9]

Oddly enough, during this period the Association almost faded away. Theodora Reeve, one of the stalwarts who kept it going then (she was president in 1956–58), remembers, "During the war years, there was real danger that NANE could not, perhaps should not, survive. Membership crept down below 100, as I recall. But as Jimmy Hymes used to say, 'NANE won't die and you can't kill it.'"[10]

Because of travel curtailment, there was no 1945 conference. Instead, a mimeographed *Bulletin of the National Association for Nursery Education* was sent to members, with Volume 1, Number 1 issued in April. The work of the Association was being carried on by committees, and the *NANE Bulletin* served as a communication medium. James Hymes's 1946 presidential report in the *NANE Bulletin* saw community interest in children high and potential major gains coming.

> . . . our Association is handicapped desperately by lack of funds, by lack of a permanent headquarters, by lack of any paid staff. One answer is more members. The key to this answer is more service that will attract members. Yet funds are needed if real service—to members and to children—is to be given. This is a vicious circle—a frustrating cycle in the light of the need for national leadership in nursery education—which the Governing Board faced as it attempted to plan ahead. (1946, p. 1)

With each announcement of a conference, membership would rise in the area hosting the meeting. For the 1947 San Francisco conference, membership rose to 762, and for many years hovered around a thousand. Then, in the words of the 1947-48 president, Frances Horwich, "Slowly we emerged and moved forward."[11] It was a long and arduous climb, however. By 1962, outgoing President Glenn Hawkes wrote in his message to the membership:

> For over thirty years we have attempted to operate on a shackling budget while our goals have been soaring. As I approach the end of my term of office I would be remiss were I not to SHOUT this to your attention. "Somethin's gotta give."

Organizational duplication must be eliminated. Reorganization must take place. An executive secretary must become a reality. More publications must find their way to your desk. The quality of the Journal must be maintained. We must be represented more often when national issues are discussed and determined. This cannot occur without additional financial resources. It is as simple as this. . . . And not to deceive you, some of what you must do will affect your pocketbook. (1962, p. 154)

The great shake-up was at hand, with NANE about to become NAEYC.

From Frustration to Fulfillment

It was a common joke in the forties and fifties that one requirement for the Association's president was storage space under the bed—and perhaps room in the closet too—since "headquarters" for NANE was the president's home. Although it is now commonly accepted that an association becomes efficiently functional only if it can afford full-time paid personnel, the first awareness of such possibility for NANE was apparently at the Governing Board meeting in 1945. The situation was again pointed out by Millie Almy, as 1952 incoming president:

> How is it possible for such an organization to accomplish so much? A *Bulletin* four times a year, numerous helpful pamphlets, cooperative relationships with many organizations concerned with young children, a biennial conference, up-to-the-minute legislative reports, committees

formed as new demands and new problems in nursery education arise—how can all this be done with no paid staff other than a part-time clerical worker? How indeed, can a limited income be spread so far, to produce so many bulletins and pamphlets and to distribute so much information? . . . NANE owes its success to long hours of hard work generously given by members who care so deeply about young children that they are just as ready to fill out membership cards, post bills, edit copy, heckle their friends for news items, dicker with printers as they are to write articles, make speeches, or meet the press. (1952, p. 3)

Six years later, President Theodora Reeve sent an exuberant letter to Affiliate Groups to announce that "a dream of many years and many NANE Boards has at last come true! NANE has a headquarters office, at the Elizabeth McCormick Memorial Fund in Chicago. Can you imagine the increased efficiency with which the organization business can be accomplished through the establishment of such an office?"[12] It was only desk space, with Greta Bresler as half-time secretary, but the $40 monthly rent included a typewriter. The Publication Distribution Center remained at the University of Rhode Island, with Russell Smart and Helen Carpenter responsible. Journals were mailed from California. Business was coordinated, and there was finally an address for NANE.

In addition to the paid secretary, June Aimen was asked to serve as "organizational consultant." She spent one day a week at the office to answer mail and take care of Association business in

return for parking fees and the price of a baby-sitter. Later, she was elected to the NANE Board to facilitate services. She recalls that "before the establishment of the headquarters office, mail was usually addressed to the president—and oftentimes that name was obtained from an old journal—so Frances Horwich was still receiving mail—mostly complaints about why they hadn't received their Journal—for more than ten years after she was out of office!"[13] Soon the Chicago workers were handling conference mailings, processing memberships, and doing a myriad of other tasks. The publications office was moved to Ames, Iowa, and Bess Ferguson set up a system to increase sales by inventorying and mailing publications requests that were processed in Chicago. Attorney Philip Aimen contributed his services to straighten out legal complications and to incorporate NANE as a "not-for-profit corporation" in Illinois—a status held to this time.

As the Association continued to grow, the need for outside funding intensified. Members made contributions, but the amounts raised were meager. An appeal at the 1951 conference in New York City brought in only $279.35—but the Program Planning Committee had viewed $188 on hand a month earlier as a cause for rejoicing. There was a ripple of excitement at Minneapolis two years later, when a mysterious stranger was reported to have given a check for $25,000. Unfortunately, it was a misunderstanding about the $25 donation from a regular contributor, Judith Cauman,

sponsors emerged during the fifties, booklets specifically written for church programs and parent cooperatives were added to a greatly expanded series of curriculum aids.

By 1957, William E. Martin of Purdue reflected the standardization of nursery education when he asserted at the Cincinnati conference that "the stories, the songs, the food, even the free play constitute a culture which is remarkably uniform from one nursery school to another, from one part of the country to another." This was in large part attributable to NANE publications and their wide distribution.

In addition to leaflets and booklets, NANE published an increasingly professional periodical. Beginning with the mimeographed *NANE Bulletin* which was sent out as a wartime expedient in 1945, the publication was put together wherever a willing editor happened to live. When first issued by the Committee on Public Relations, with Marjorie Craig of the Metropolitan Life Insurance Company of New York as chairman, emphasis was upon Association business and items about members. By the second year, legislative reports were given prominent attention. In October of 1946 there was an article about "Parent Education and Television" with Amy Hostler's prediction:

> It is stated there are over 5,000 receiving television sets in the New York metropolitan area alone. When the difficulty of distance is overcome there will be many more sets in operation. It is a

new medium and promises much to educators of the future. Those of us who are strongly convinced that the child's first teachers can play a vital part in helping to promote greater understanding of children and their needs should be aware of television development, and recognize its potentialities in this major job of public education." (1946, pp. 6-7)

For several years, the *NANE Bulletin* was a simple compilation of Association news, stapled together and mailed to the members about four times a year. Then, in 1956, with increased membership and the assistance of outside funding, its name was changed to *The Journal of Nursery Education*. The professional appearance gave no inkling of its origins in the garage of Editor Docia Zavitkovsky. Each issue included legislative information, recent official business, a chatty "On the Personal Side" section, research reports, and book reviews. Many well-known authorities in child development and early childhood education were introduced to the public through its pages, and others already well-known in related professions were introduced to nursery school workers. In a farewell column, after editing the *NANE Bulletin* and *The Journal of Nursery Education* for ten years, Docia Zavitkovsky and her assistant, Mary Alice Mallum, wrote:

> Planning and putting the Journal together, making contacts and occasional frantic calls to friends for articles which in those days were hard to come by; cutting and pasting the complete layout; typing and pasting corrections on the off-set printing copy; getting copy to the printer; and

then maintaining address files; putting Journals into envelopes; typing and licking address labels; licking and applying thousands of stamps; sorting, stacking and wrapping Journals by states; transporting Journals to the post office—all these became routine tasks.

One of the biggest problems was answering mail, especially letters such as these, "My Journal hasn't arrived. Where is it? Send it." (No name given.) or "I haven't received my Journal. Perhaps it is because I have moved several times. Will you please send it?" (No address given.) (Zavitkovsky & Mallum 1961, p. 3)

Gradually, the volunteer staff who had taken care of publication duties "after work" received the help of paid specialists, with Bess Ferguson taking over in 1958 to become managing editor. By early winter 1962, when Cornelia Goldsmith became editor, there were two assistants. A survey mailed to approximately 1,300 members by Alex Saryan and the Mental Health Materials Center, at the request of the 1963 NANE Board, brought overwhelming agreement that the reading and comprehension level of the Journal was "just about right" but recommended an increase to six issues a year and the need to increase circulation to nonmembers. These changes were soon implemented, together with an updated format. When the reorganized Association made its debut as NAEYC at Miami Beach in 1964, the very first copies of *Young Children* were there for inspection. The change in title was seen as a more realistic frame of reference for the organization's objectives, and in her new role as executive

secretary, pro tem, Cornelia Goldsmith challenged the membership to move forward.

Change in name and in organization is indeed timely, symbolizing the new role we hope to play. In recognizing the potentialities in young children, we have perhaps failed to recognize our own. Let us learn from the children that the zest for living and learning refuels itself, and be on our way.

The national voice of NAEYC is no longer a whisper. Joined with others it may become a lion's roar. As we value ourselves, we will be valued. As the young child is valued by us, he will be valued by others. (1965, p. 212)

Since 1964, *Young Children* and NAEYC have grown through a synergistic relationship, each promoting growth of the other. NAEYC's publication program now is implemented by professional editorial staff with the voluntary assistance of the Editorial Advisory Board.

MEMBERSHIP STRUCTURE

Other facets of the Association have also been part of the developmental process. Of these, the system of Affiliate Groups is of paramount importance. The affiliation process actually has been long and painful. During the early years, everybody knew everybody else and had some input into Association business. With growth and diversity, the need for more structure became apparent. After several years of debate, this became official business at Boston in 1943, when delegates decided to maintain a "close working relationship" with regional, state, and local organizations but to postpone plans for formal affiliation.

By the 1950s, the situation was becoming critical. Theodora Reeve, president from 1953 to 1958, considers the development of affiliates to be one of her most important accomplishments. Added incentive was given in 1956, when memberships directly with NANE were $5.00 but those through local, state, or regional affiliates were only $3.50. Katherine Read (Baker) chaired the organizing committee and by 1958 reported 30 Affiliate Groups, with 3 more in process.

Only with a permanent office staff could the development of affiliates proceed smoothly. There was a decline to 28 groups in 1962, but in the tumultuous struggle of reorganization the desire for affiliation grew stronger. Procedures changed with a new constitution, adding inducements of *Young Children* and voting rights for each group member. Five more affiliates were ready to be chartered when the Association officially became NAEYC. By 1966, there were 48, and over half of these had changed their own acronyms to substitute "AEYC" for the previous "ANE." Affiliation continues to bring members into NAEYC (there are now 190 Affiliate Groups), but for the main body of membership it is hard to realize that until recently only a few officers of thriving local and regional groups were regular dues-paying members of the national organization.

Throughout the changes of emphasis, however, the Association has demonstrated a concern for all aspects of the education, development, and well-being of young children, which has combined an open-minded interest in new ideas with dedication to those which have proven their worth.

PUBLIC POLICY

As a correlate of the increased size and prosperity of NAEYC, there has been incremental clout in public policy at the federal level. In the beginning, when national affairs were simpler and expectations lower, members "knew somebody" or worked with other members to affect conditions. Certainly, the WPA nursery schools reflected NANE concerns in their formative stage, and even wartime Lanham Act preschool programs were influenced by professional nursery school philosophy. By the 1950s, when the Association was going through its own struggle for survival, it could not assume strong legislative positions. Attempts by Theresa Mahler and others to arouse membership involvement seem to have been futile. A major legislative affairs workshop at the 1951 New York conference had three sessions with outstanding leaders but virtually nobody attended. Eight years later, an appeal in *The Journal for Nursery Education* for Affiliate Groups to send names of legislative chairmen brought no response at all! Although individual members were dedicated to public policy concerns, the Association was ineffective.

As the Association grew larger, it gained recognition. The reaction to Eveline Omwake's presidential letter in the January 1969 issue of *Young Children* was gratifying—and somewhat frightening. Criticizing federal programs, she said, in part:

> An honest look at the last few years, when it seemed as if we were at last beginning to move ahead in early childhood education, is a disheartening exercise. Although there have been a few obvious advances in services for children and their families, considering the grand investment of money and effort since 1965 the actual changes are unimpressive. . . . The makeshift operations of early days are now the model recommended by OEO under the pressure of financial cutbacks. . . . We have to face the reality that the once promising Head Start project has already begun to go downhill. Still another grim aspect . . . is the present deplorable condition of day care . . . [and] the lack of any solid foundation for a good national program. . . . The federal agencies had a great opportunity to vitally affect children's lives and influence early childhood education in positive ways. They muffed it when they began to exploit the children's program to bolster the economy. (1969, pp. 130-131)

This candid statement, which followed resolutions passed at the NAEYC conference the previous November, was sent to legislators and policymakers. Surprisingly strong agreement was evidenced, and responses indicated that NAEYC was considered an association to be reckoned with.

In the past decade, with permanent Washington headquarters for the Association and with articulate and effective executive directors—Milton Akers from 1966 to 1972 and Marilyn Smith since that time—the Association has moved into a level of public policy activity undreamed of by the original National Committee on Nursery Schools.

Analysis of public policy efforts, interrelationships with other organizations, responsiveness to minority causes and representation, the work of committees (in particular the work of the Task Force appointed in 1969), and the relationship of NAEYC's growth to federally funded programs must be dealt with in future reports.

As we look backward over the past half century, to view the development of the Association against the dominant attitudes of psychologists and other behavioral scientists, it is interesting to recall that the National Committee on Nursery Schools was made up of professionals who were leaders in a "whole child" approach to education. A behaviorist orientation to child development, with stress on habit-training, dominated the field from the early 1930s until the 1950s. With a shift to developmental emphasis, accompanied by renewed interest in Piaget and the genetic theorists, there has been a resurgence of interest in nursery schools. Throughout these fluctuations, however, the Association has demonstrated a concern for all aspects of the education, development, and well-being of young children which has combined an open-minded interest in new ideas with dedication to those which have proven their worth.

References

Almy, M. "Greetings from the New President." *NANE Bulletin* 7, nos. 3-4 (1952): 3–4.

Andrus, R. "The Nursery School . . . A Child Welfare Center." New York City Chapter, ANE, 1939. Reprint from *Progressive Education,* October 1938.

Davis, M.D. "How NANE Began." *Young Children* 20, no. 2 (November 1964): 106–109.

Davis, M.D. *Nursery Schools.* Washington, D.C.: U.S. Office of Education. Bulletin no. 9. 1932.

Goldsmith, C. "The Impact of a Growing NAEYC on Young Children." Address to NAEYC Conference, October 31, 1964, Miami Beach, Fla. *Young Children* 20, no. 4 (March 1965): 209–212.

Hawkes, G.R. "From the President." The Journal of Nursery Education 17, no. 4 (September 1962): 154.

Hewes, D.W. "'Patty Smith Hill—Pioneer for Young Children." *Young Children* 31, no. 4 (May 1976): 297–306.

Hostler, A. "Parent Education and Television." *Bulletin of the National Association for Nursery Education* 2, no. 1 (October 1946): 6–7.

Hymes, J.L. "The President's Plans for the Future." *Bulletin of the National Association for Nursery Education* 1, no. 4 (May 1946): 1–2.

Omwake, E.B. "From the President." *Young Children* 24, no. 3 (January 1969): 130–131.

Senn, M.J.E. "Insights on the Child Development Movement in the United States." *Monographs of the Society for Research in Child Development* 40, nos. 3–4 (1975).

White, E.N. *Report of National Advisory Committee on Emergency Nursery Schools, 1934–35.* Published by the Committee. Undated.

Witherspoon, R. "From NANE to NAEYC: The Tempestuous Years." *Young Children* 31, no. 5 (July 1976): 333–338.

Zavitkovsky, D., and Mallum, M.A. "From the Editors." *The Journal of Nursery Education* 17, no. 1 (November 1961): 3–4.

Endnotes

[1] Patty Smith Hill, "Report of the Second Conference of Nursery School Workers," 1927: 7.

[2] "Report of the Third Conference of Nursery School Workers." 1929: 7-10.

[3] Ibid.

[4] "Proceedings of the Fourth Conference of the National Association for Nursery Education." 1931.

[5] "Proceedings of the Fifth Conference of the National Association for Nursery Education," 1933: 99–100.

[6] Lois Meek Stolz, August 1975: personal interview.

[7] "Proceedings of the Sixth Conference of the National Association for Nursery Education," 1936: 6.

[8] Amy Hostler to NANE Board. July 1942. Mimeographed.

[9] Dorothy Baruch. Undated mimeograph.

[10] Theodora Reeve to Dorothy Hewes. August 28, 1975.

[11] Frances Horwich to Dorothy Hewes. July 30, 1975.

[12] Theodora Reeve to Responsible Officers of NANE Affiliated Groups. March 18, 1958. Mimeographed.

[13] June Aimen to Dorothy Hewes. February 4, 1976.

The following selection is reprinted in its entirety from: Witherspoon, R. 1976. From NANE to NAEYC: The Tempestuous Years. *Young Children* 31 (5): 333–38.

From NANE to NAEYC

The Tempestuous Years

It is fitting in this bicentennial year that we review the origins of NAEYC, for no one will deny that NAEYC plays a significant role in 1976 in the life and education of our nation's young children and their families.

Ralph L. Witherspoon

The ten-year episode in the history of NANE-NAEYC described here deals only with the critical transition period when NANE was reorganized as NAEYC. There is intended no implication that the events prior to and since this period were not equally important. Likewise, many persons whose contributions were significant cannot be included. They represent a close-knit, always dedicated, group of people who never lost hope in the cause they believed in, namely, that young children are more important than recognized by the larger society of which they are a part. Children deserve more attention and better care, services, and educational opportunities. While this is still true in 1976, remarkable progress is being made, and NAEYC and allied organizations play an important role in this progress. The continuous struggle to define the Association's philosophy, purpose, and modes of influence are not reported here. Instead, this article reports a chronicle of events and the many key persons involved in keeping NANE alive and in getting NAEYC established.

It would be difficult for the majority of today's NAEYC members to grasp the magnitude of the difficulties faced by the Officers and Board of NANE and/or NAEYC during the ten transition years from 1958 to 1968. Most members today see NAEYC as a big, active organization, invincible as "Washington, D.C." itself. Yet, slightly more than a decade ago, the major resources of the Association were made possible by faith that in the future there would be greater efforts on behalf of young children. A relatively few "believers" made personal and financial sacrifices which kept the Association alive. They continue to do so today but with the support of thousands of members rather than a few hundred.

Cornelia Goldsmith, NAEYC Executive Secretary 1964–1966.

I have reviewed past issues of the *Journal of Nursery Education,* the initial issues of *Young Children,* and minutes of Governing Board meetings during this period of NANE-NAEYC history. It became necessary to guard against the often biased effects of nostalgia, for I was in the "thick of things" throughout the entire period either as a Governing Board member, as the last president of NANE, the first president of NAEYC, or on the Board as past president.

Establishment of a National Headquarters

During 1958, a national headquarters was established in Chicago, while the Journal of the Association continued to be mailed from California and other publications distributed from Rhode Island. This achievement was made possible by several gifts and the generous support and help of the Elizabeth McCormick Memorial Fund and the Fund's Executive Director Don Brieland. NANE was fortunate to have shared the efficient services of the Fund's secretary, Greta Bresler, and the devoted guidance of June Aimen, NANE organizational consultant representing the Officers and Board, along with a responsible Headquarters Committee. This arrangement continued with all or some responsibilities until the complete move to Washington, D.C., in 1964.

Shortly after the establishment of the Chicago office in February of 1958, the distribution and production of materials and the Journal were faithfully carried out by Bess Ferguson from her home in Ames, Iowa, until the establishment of an executive, editorial, and publications office in New York in 1965. The New York office was managed by Cornelia (Nell) Goldsmith. The membership processing functions remained in the Chicago office. Later that year the executive office was moved to Washington, D.C., with the editorial and publications office remaining in New York.

On September 15, 1964, Cornelia Goldsmith became the first and only Executive Secretary of NANE and, with the reorganization, became NAEYC's first Executive Secretary in October of that year. All this was made possible by an untiring effort to secure adequate funds and to increase membership. Seed money had been provided by the Edith Lauer Fund during 1959 and 1960 with the restricted purpose of encouraging other contributions to employ an executive secretary. The Development Committee, chaired by Blanche Persky, succeeded in obtaining Grant Foundation funds in 1963.

Of critical importance during these tempestuous years was the continuous flow of funds from "Friends of NANE." Major gifts were made by many individuals and by Affiliate Groups nationwide as they sought to become a part of and to have a voice in a strong national organization dedicated to bettering the lives of young children everywhere. While existing previously, "Friends of NANE" was spawned spontaneously as a formal effort at the 1962 Philadelphia Conference and continued well after the establishment of NAEYC. There were also gifts from other interested persons.

In retrospect, it was these combined efforts that made it possible for NAEYC to be what it is today. While it is impossible because of space limitations to mention by name all who should be recognized in this development, it was, in my opinion, the insistence on the part of the Board

members and the Officers during the presidencies of Edna Mohr (1959-60) and Glenn Hawkes (1961-62) that enabled NANE to survive, and NAEYC to become a reality. As a Board member, it appeared to me that by every realistic criterion, NANE should have died a natural death or merged with existing viable organizations. There were, indeed, strong efforts to achieve both of these ends. Nevertheless, optimism and purpose prevailed, although proposed budgets and projected membership goals never fully materialized during these transitional years. Membership during the years 1958-63 averaged around 1200 and dues were $5 a year.

Eveline Omwake, NAEYC President 1967–1970.

In 1960 I was named chairman of an MANE-NANE Committee to study organizational problems and to make recommendations for reorganization as well as needed actions. Ethel Kunkle, Judith Crane, and Viola Theman represented MANE (Midwest Association for Nursery Education); representing NANE were Edith Dowley and Eveline Omwake. This committee later became the Long Range Committee which did the investigations and studies that resulted in the recommendations for and eventual reorganization as NAEYC. The MANE Committee members resided in Florida, California, and Connecticut, yet NANE was never able to provide more than token funds for expenses during the four years of this

NAEYC Past Presidents at the 1962 Philadelphia Conference: Lois Hayden Meek Stolz (1929-31) Ruth Updegraff (1937-39) Frances Horwich (1947-51) Millie Almy (1952-53) Harriet Nash (1954-55) Theodora Reeve (1956-58) Edna Mohr (1959-60) Glenn R. Hawkes (1961-62) Ralph Witherspoon (1963-66)

committee's existence. Fortunately, Board member Phyllis Richards was a graduate student at the university where I served. Without her help, the long hours needed to carry out the "leg work" duties of the committee likely never would have been accomplished. The committee piggy-backed on national or regional meetings we mutually attended, or depended on the mail for most committee deliberations and implementation. One such meeting took place in the conference hotel's furnace room during the St. Louis Conference! Somehow, the work got done and reorganization became a reality four years later in 1964.

At one Board meeting, President Glenn Hawkes urged the members to think positively ·

and plan as though there was a large membership and adequate finances, even though both seemed impossible goals at the time and, indeed, were not fully realized until several years later. Looking back, one can appreciate the wisdom of this approach. Securing funds from the Grant Foundation in 1963 was a breakthrough for much activity, but a condition of the grant was that no funds were to be available until an executive secretary was actually appointed and an office established.

This Herculean task as executive secretary, for indeed that is what it was, was undertaken by Nell Goldsmith after much persuasion from friends. Moving parts of the headquarters' functions from Rhode Island, Iowa, and Chicago to New York, and later all the functions to Washington, D.C., was not done without trauma, especially when adequate membership and operational funds were still to be achieved. While funds were available to temporarily pay an executive secretary and minimal staff, to redesign and produce an expanded Journal, and to buy furniture and equipment for a headquarters, membership dues and sales continued to lag behind projected needs, a fact which promised to cause difficulties.

One can best catch the spirit of Nell's determination to make NANE a success by noting the following incident. Shortly after the move to the Alban Towers Hotel in Washington, D.C., and at the first Executive Board meeting when NANE finally had a "home" and new furniture and with everyone feeling exhilarated, the Association's auditor told the group bluntly that the new furniture would be "out in the streets" in six months because there was no possible way to save the Association. Nell quickly countered with "Sir, the furniture will be here six months from now and so will we." And we were, but not without great personal sacrifice on the part of the new executive secretary. Present and future members of NAEYC should be grateful that Nell, because of her devotion to seeing that the needs of young children were rightfully met, gave up her beautiful New York apartment for far-from-adequate living conditions in Washington, D.C., postponed work on preparation of her important book (Goldsmith 1972), and with great financial as well as personal sacrifice

literally saved the Association from dissolution at a time when it was on the verge of the greatness that it since has achieved. Of course, there were and still are problems, but Cornelia Goldsmith's sterling efforts got the Association "over the hump" and "saved the day" for NANE-NAEYC.

NAEYC Becomes a Reality

The 1964 Miami Beach Conference was an historic event. Despite damage to the conference hotel by a recent hurricane and cloudy weather, electrifying excitement filled the air as most of the longtime supporters of NANE witnessed the official birth of NAEYC. The anticipation of the fulfillment of impossible dreams of many years for a better life for young children made it all worthwhile. The employment of an executive secretary, active participation of Affiliate Groups in the affairs of the Association, an expanded program for more children including those of early school age, a truly national headquarters with full-time paid personnel, help with travel expenses for Officers, Board, and Committee members, a newly designed and improved Journal with a new name were for the first time either a reality or in sight. Obviously this had not happened and the Association would not prosper without the participation of many people—today more than

Milton Akers, NAEYC Executive Director 1966–1972.

NAEYC Governing Board, 1964. Seated from left to right: Blanche Persky, Lola Emerson, Glenn Hawkes, Phyllis Richards, Ralph Witherspoon, Edith Dowley, June Aimen, Greta Bresler, Cornelia Goldsmith. Standing left to right: Mary Minnie, Mary Ellen Durrett, Evengeline Ward, Adele Goldstein, Flo Kerckhoff, Sylvia Lapin, Bess Ferguson, Norma Law.

finished but the Association is strong and viable and highly respected in the educational world.

New Horizons

The flood of available funds for early childhood education during the middle and late 1960s made possible NAEYC participation and leadership in many ventures. The ever optimistic outlook of Milton Akers, the new Executive Secretary (renamed Executive Director in 1966), and the skillful leadership of President Eveline Omwake, brought involvement at all levels of membership in national opportunities. Membership grew by leaps and bounds. New headquarters space was needed. In 1969, "our very own" headquarters at 1834 Connecticut Avenue, N.W., Washington, D.C., became a reality when NAEYC began procedures to purchase the picturesque and beautiful building now well known to members and friends. Thus began a new era in the fulfillment of dreams for a better world for young children. NAEYC was at last solidly on its way to becoming the significant force that it is in the world of 1976.

27,000! Truly, the earlier decisions of the Officers and Board to set these goals for the Association rather than give up or merge with existing groups were the right ones.

The timing was perfect. The education of young children, the new hope of the future, was in the throes of a national revolution. No one in their wildest dreams a few years prior to this event could have seen the proliferation of financially supported programs for young children that have since become a reality. In 1976 NAEYC's task is far from

While researching the reference materials needed to write this chapter of the NANE-NAEYC story, many names of persons not previously mentioned here appeared over and over again. In the effort to recognize some of those who labored hard during the transition period and who are well known to NAEYC members today, the following seem to stand out. My apologies to the many others who rightfully should be included if space permitted. The order of presentation has no relationship to the importance of their contributions. All served with distinction. They are: Millie Almy, Rose H. Alschuler, Katherine Read Baker, Minnie P. Berson, Alma Bingham, Bernice Borgman, Evangeline Burgess, Judith Cauman, Carrie Cheek, Ruth J. Dales, Shirley M. Dean, Laura L. Dittmann, Mary Ellen Durrett, Lola B. Emerson, Gabrielle Faddis, Barbara Fischer, Bernice H. Fleiss, Ira Gibbons, Sadie Ginsberg, Minerva Golden, Adele Goldstein, Marjorie (Craig) Gray-Lewis, Helena Guernsey, Willard W. Hartup, James Hymes, Ruth A. Jefferson, Alice Keliher, Florence (Gould) Kerckhoff, Dorothy J. Lane, Mary B. Lane, Sylvia Lapin, Norma A. Law, Elizabeth Ann Liddle, Thelma McClure, Polly McVickar, Ethel Macintyre, Marjorie Maynard, Mary V. Minnie, Shirley G. Moore, Harriet C. Nash, Josephine Newberry, June Patterson, Mildred A. Reed, Theo Reeve, Katherine M. Reeves, Judy Schoelkopff, Frank Self, Aladine Shomaker, Russell C. Smart, Marilyn M. Smith, Bernard Spodek, Jeannette (Galambos) Stone, Elizabeth Vernon, Evangeline H. Ward, Esther Weir, Docia Zavitkovsky, and Julia Zimmerman.

Reference

Goldsmith, C. 1972. *Better Day Care for the Young Child.* Washington, DC: NAEYC.

Learning from NAEYC's Past

The nucleus of NAEYC's work is represented in the three goals that have guided the Association through its lifetime: (1) building a strong organization; (2) improving early childhood professional practice; and (3) fostering public understanding and support for high-quality programs. Each of the three chapters in this section focuses on one of these goals. The intent of these chapters is to highlight lessons we can learn from our past to incorporate into our deliberations as we go forward.

The author of each chapter analyzes NAEYC's actions, products, and processes within one given goal area, identifying values and principles that she believes have been key in what occurred. This way of rendering NAEYC's history is intended to stimulate thought and debate about the efficacy of these guiding principles for future decisions and actions. In light of this purpose, these chapters do not attempt to present an exhaustive recounting of events during the past 25 years. Rather, each chapter is organized around key principles and values and uses selected examples from our history to illustrate these themes. In some cases the same initiative appears in two or three of the chapters, reminding us that one program effort, such as accreditation, can be viewed from the perspective of each of our goals.

The authors of these three chapters have intimate experience in the events they describe, which makes their stories and messages both authentic and engaging. They are not the first to speak for the principles and values about which they write. Rather they were participants, with many others, in the development of guidelines and processes. In many cases they and their contemporaries rediscovered what had guided previous leaders of our Association and found the same principles and processes to be effective once again.

"Building and Maintaining a High-Performing, Inclusive Organization" (Chapter 3) by Jerlean Daniel is organized around five fundamental values that have enabled NAEYC to build and maintain the strong foundation without which it could not accomplish its mission. These values are inclusiveness, effective structure and processes, fiscal stability, consensus building, and "staying on message." Her insight about these fundamentals is based in her knowledge and experience of organizational leadership, including firsthand experience as NAEYC president (1994–1996), two four-year terms of service on the Board, and leadership in numerous Association initiatives and studies. She also has a keen capacity for observing, listening, and analyzing. Daniel ends her account of each of these five organizational values with challenges to carry our thinking further. Jerlean Daniel is on the faculty of the Learning Research and Development Center at the University of Pittsburgh.

"Improving Professional Practice: A Letter to Patty Smith Hill" (Chapter 4) by Sue Bredekamp introduces four principles that have permeated NAEYC's work on standard setting since its inception. By writing in the form of a letter to NAEYC's founder, Patty Smith Hill, Bredekamp conveys a strong sense of the continuity in the Association's conception of and commitment to improving professional practices and standards. Sue Bredekamp's staff leadership role in NAEYC's work on setting standards from 1981 through 1998 enables her to tell this important story in personal terms. Reading this account, other leaders will find great relevance in the external and internal struggles inherent in making change. She discusses the four themes in using standards to improve practice with respect to two kinds of standards—those for professional preparation and development and those for practice. At present, Sue Bredekamp is director of research for the Council for Professional Recognition.

In "Advocating for Young Children and the Early Childhood Profession: A Letter to Jimmy Hymes" (Chapter 5), Barbara Willer

also uses the letter form as a vehicle for looking at the past. She addresses her letter to former NAEYC president James L. Hymes Jr., who is revered for his leadership in both child development and advocacy. As she writes her letter to Jimmy, Willer conveys the integration and influence of child development knowledge in NAEYC's policy and advocacy work. Following a summary of key policy issues affecting young children over the last quarter century, she describes how NAEYC's policy involvement and influence parallel the growth in membership and staff. The extension of professional improvement initiatives into policy work comes alive in many examples. Willer concludes by articulating three major characteristics that have stood the test of time in moving NAEYC's policy and advocacy work toward greater effectiveness. The view from which Willer writes is as staff leader of the Association's policy work from 1985 until 1999 and as deputy executive director of NAEYC from 1999 to the present.

Chapter 3

Building and Maintaining a High-Performing, Inclusive Organization

Jerlean Daniel

Throughout the 75-year history of NAEYC there have been five consistent values that have undergirded the organization and contributed significantly to its standing as a high-performing, inclusive organization. First and foremost, NAEYC is an organization that values inclusiveness, recognizing that a broad-based cadre of participants is needed to fulfill its mission. Second, the Association reviews the effectiveness of its organizational structure and processes as they relate to fulfilling that mission. Third, the organization focuses on maintaining fiscal viability. Fourth, NAEYC is committed to consensus building as a pivotal strength. Finally, for 75 years, NAEYC has persistently stayed on message, putting children first. These five factors make up an integrated whole, and each gives voice and integrity to the other four. Just as our strengths are integrated, so too are our challenges. The future effectiveness of NAEYC will require continued commitment from a membership in dogged pursuit of its mission.

> . . .the purpose of this Association is to serve and act on behalf of the needs, rights, and well-being of all young children, with primary focus on the provision of educational and developmental services and resources. (NAEYC Amended Bylaws, Article I, 1991)

Inclusiveness

NAEYC's definition of inclusiveness is not limited to race and ethnicity. While race, ethnicity, and culture are critical components of inclusiveness, NAEYC's scope is much broader. Inclusiveness begins at the level of ideas.

NAEYC's mission sounds simple enough, but a close analysis reveals the complex interplay among several factors beginning with the needs of children and those of their families and communities. New insights gained through research and the field's practical challenges also contribute to the complexity of the task. The "right" solutions for children require ongoing input from a variety of people with differing perspectives. In 1972 President Evangeline Ward reaffirmed NAEYC's commitment to

inclusiveness of ideas and the dignity of each individual's participation in the change process.

> Educational means rather than sanction or formal endorsement procedures are utilized to effect growth and change among the membership and the many publics we serve through providing information by which they can engage in dialogue leading to independent decisionmaking. (Ward 1972, 3)

There is a basic trust implicit in this statement that informed decisionmaking will bode well for the organization and its mission. Thus, coercion or exclusionary tactics are unnecessary.

Ed Klugman, a former Governing Board member from New England, describes in a personal communication how the organization's responsiveness to new challenges has served to revitalize NAEYC.

> We moved from NANE to NAEYC;
> We moved from education and information about policy to information, education, and position statements supporting points of view;
> We moved from a "resolution process" to a "membership expression of opinion" process, to a dialogue with the Governing Board;
> We moved from caucuses to interest forums;
> We moved from individual Affiliates to our new structure of State Affiliates, local Affiliate Chapters, and regional Affiliate Alliances.

Each of these changes revitalized the effectiveness of NAEYC's communications within the Association as well as with the broader society.

Inclusion that welcomes people at all levels builds the capacity of our membership and our other publics—parents, policymakers, and so on—who constitute our community of learners. An example of capacity building is the Association Development Process (ADP) begun in the early 1990s. ADP included a community participation inventory, an opportunity to assess our outreach to the various constituencies affected by and effecting our work. Local Affiliates are the means by which most people enter the organization. Increased capacity at the local level strengthens Affiliates. Because the local and national components of NAEYC are interrelated and mutually dependent, ADP strengthened the organization at all levels. Quality improvements to early care and education programs are enhanced when policy changes and resource shifts have the support of a broad-based constituency. ADP, originally piloted in several states, has now been folded into NAEYC's new structure.

NAEYC's commitment to an open membership policy has been supported by attempts to keep basic membership dues as inexpensive as possible and to make it convenient for anyone to join. Concurrently, a commitment to inclusive membership requires the provision of services that are relevant and meaningful for the multiple audiences that share our goals. One prescribed set of services will not serve the needs of everyone. NAEYC membership spans program auspices, funding sources, job titles, educational attainments, races, and ethnicities. NAEYC is a place where all people who want to improve the lives of children and families can find a home.

NAEYC's openness is also reflected in the affordable prices of the resources the Association produces and distributes, including books, posters, brochures, and videos. For many years book prices, for example, have remained in the range between $5 and $10. Keeping a book like *Developmentally Appropriate Practices in Early Childhood Programs* so inexpensive has made it possible to put over one million copies in the hands of early childhood people, including practitioners in the field where practice can be improved.

Choices made in creating and evolving NAEYC's accreditation system also reflect the theme of inclusiveness. The goal of NAEYC's accreditation is to improve center-based early childhood practice wherever it is being offered. Thus, accreditation is a voluntary system with an umbrella large enough to cover early childhood programs of various types and operating under various philosophies. Program accreditation is not an award for members only.

Accreditation is one of the field's best professional development tools because it allows individuals and teams of practitioners to reflect on their own practice as measured against a professional standard. The professional standard is a combination of research, regulations, and accepted professional consensus about practice. Participants rank themselves and make improvements in their everyday practice. The voluntary program accreditation process again affirms our commitment to lasting change through education for informed decisionmaking. Validators visit when programs deem themselves ready. If there is still work to be done, programs can keep working on their quality enhancements in preparation for another validation visit.

THE CHALLENGES OF INCLUSIVENESS

NAEYC's inclusiveness encompasses both ideas and people. The decisionmaking that moves the Association closer to fulfilling the mission of high-quality early care and education programs for all children is strengthened when the intellectual and experiential capital of each participant is considered. The early childhood field—and NAEYC in particular—must accept the challenge of the 1997 revision of the developmentally appropriate practice (DAP) guidelines. We must work through what it really means to consider cultural context in relation to research and practice, to negotiate cultural

differences as DAP guidelines challenge us to do. My concern is "If we cannot blend what we think we know [from research and practice] with a child's real-life situation and what is meaningful to parents, then we will lose our stature in the field" (Daniel as cited in NAEYC 1998, 7). Effective, high-performing organizations stay in touch with the gaps in the knowledge base and put together structures and processes that will advance the thinking in the field to close the gaps.

While NAEYC's commitment to inclusiveness is a strength, fulfilling the commitment remains NAEYC's greatest challenge. Inclusiveness requires ongoing vigilance. It is not a task to achieve and then be put behind us. Inclusiveness only exists to the degree that the organization and its members tend to it regularly. Without inclusiveness NAEYC cannot achieve its goals for all children.

To the degree that we successfully achieve diverse participation within NAEYC, we will strengthen our leadership endeavors in the broader arena of child and family work. Diversity will help NAEYC to be more relevant, articulate, and insightful as members shape "what ought to be" for children and families. While we still have work to do, it is a fact that throughout our history we have listened to each other and created policies, processes, and structures

NAEYC has dared to be the place where all who care about and work with children are welcome, but this continues to be a tremendous challenge.

— Carrie Cheek

within the organization that make inclusiveness a fundamental part of NAEYC.

Structure and processes

Organizations in their prime closely examine their structures and processes as they relate to achieving their missions. The changes of the 1960s—from NANE to NAEYC, the establishment of a national headquarters with staff, and the eventual move to Washington, D.C.—set our organization on a path filled with opportunities for increased efficiency and effectiveness. (Highlights of this progression in establishing an effective coordinating unit are presented in the special section on the headquarters at the end of this chapter.)

Another critical change took place in 1964 with the refinement of the Affiliate structure. Phyllis L. Richards, who served as vice president in charge of Affiliate Groups during those years, says it best.

> The Affiliate Groups were vital then; they are vital now. A major strength of NAEYC has been and continues to be its grassroots structure and mentality. The smallest voice can be heard.

Inclusiveness informs the operations of the Affiliate structure. It also gives NAEYC many roots in local communities and thus a strong national base from which to work. (The evolution of a workable structure to connect NAEYC with local and state groups is described in a section on Affiliate Groups at the end of this chapter.)

Each decade since the 1960s has included deliberations about our organizational structure and processes. By August 1971 NAEYC was studying its fifth draft of a proposed reorganization plan (Ward 1971). Comments from the membership were solicited throughout the process. The fifth draft included a proposal for Governing Board elections based primarily on geographic representation. Secondary considerations were diversity among the types of programs represented, racial and cultural diversity, and competencies (for example, fiscal) needed on the Board at any given time (NAEYC 1971a, 352-B).

This representative form of Governing Board was rejected because the Board felt that the organization's commitment to inclusiveness would be undermined by a framework based on a single form of representation, such as geography.

> No matter what the organizational structure of NAEYC is, very little will really change unless all members, from local groups to national Board members, are committed to ensuring appropriate representation for the diversity of our membership. (NAEYC 1971b, 96-A & 96-B).

The Board wanted all of the membership to participate in representing all young children.

I believe that NAEYC was a genuine pioneer in the cultural diversity, multiculturalism, antibias movement in the field of education in general, and especially in early childhood. Not only did we offer leadership on this nationally, but internationally as well. That surely speaks to core values and beliefs.

— Lilian Katz

As part of these deliberations, the Bylaws and mission statement were revised to include the words *to serve and act on behalf of the needs, rights and well-being of all young children*. The charge to the Nominations Committee was also rewritten to define diversity as including program type, race, culture, competence, position, and geography (NAEYC 1971b, 96-C). This same definition continues to govern the nomination process today.

The practical impetus for each of NAEYC's structural reviews was threefold: increased organizational size, need for effective communication, and need to facilitate membership participation in the decisionmaking processes of the organization. Each of these issues is fundamental to the healthy maintenance of NAEYC's overriding value of broad and substantive participation. A policy for attractive, affordable, open membership; a committed core of volunteers; and a professional staff promoting a clear, worthwhile mission caused NAEYC's ranks to swell over time. Each growth spurt in membership put pressure on communications channels within the organization. If NAEYC was to use the full potential of its membership, the flow of

> We moved from 500 members to over 10,000 members while I served on the Governing Board and today number more than 100,000.
>
> — Ed Klugman

NANE/NAEYC membership growth: 1926–2000

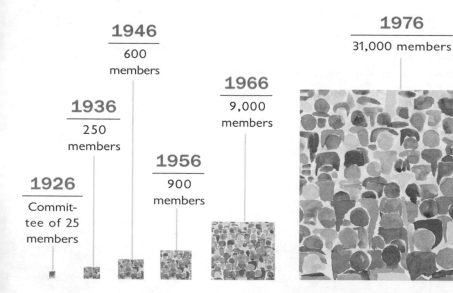

1926
Committee of 25 members

1936
250 members

1946
600 members

1956
900 members

1966
9,000 members

1976
31,000 members

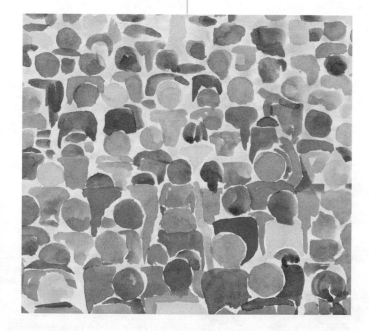

1986
50,000 members

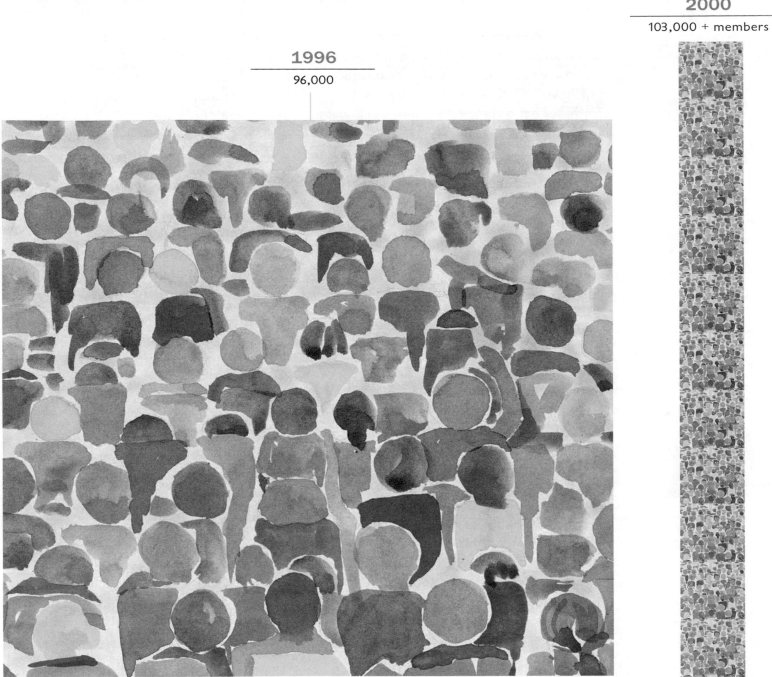

1996

96,000

2000

103,000 + members

71

ideas had to be unencumbered. As a membership organization, NAEYC must remain responsive to its members. If each member is to "own" NAEYC, each person has to clearly see her or his opportunities to impact decisionmaking.

In the 1980s members were surveyed regarding structural changes they would propose and the reasons for the suggestions. For the most part, members did not want to make any major changes at that time. But it was important that the questions were asked and the responses were given due consideration.

Additionally, in the 1980s NAEYC gave considerable attention to how it was positioned to advocate effectively for higher-quality early childhood programs. It was during this period that NAEYC established a clearer definition of and tone for its public policy voice. A series of position statements, including those regarding developmentally appropriate practice, licensing, and quality, compensation, and affordability, used the mission statement as the basis for policy related to the issues of the times. These documents fortified NAEYC's work on the national and the local grassroots levels. As Phyllis L. Richards said recently,

> Even though attention to the basic issues of childhood may change over time, the power of the many voices being represented enables NAEYC to speak confidently, clearly, loudly, knowledgeably, effectively for children and families.

The national organization was increasingly able to offer materials and advocacy strategies to local Affiliates. It was, however, a two-way street. Several state and local Affiliates were quite effective in their local regions. *The Affiliate* newsletter, begun in 1974, became a vehicle for sharing information among the growing number of Affiliates and the national headquarters.

Following two decades of Affiliate Day at the national Annual Conference, a separate Leadership Conference was begun in 1983. This conference was yet another example of the development of a structure to improve communication among the components of NAEYC. It continues to be an opportunity for Affiliate leaders to gather firsthand information and to participate in deliberations on a variety of issues from public policy to organizational governance. Affiliate leaders attending the first Leadership Conference in Washington, D.C., gave critical input to Governing Board deliberations concerning whether or not to establish a system of accreditation for early childhood programs (NAEYC 1997b, 10).

Late in the 1990s, after more phenomenal growth in the membership base—by then more than 100, 000—yet another structural assessment took place. Looking into the new century, staff and Governing Board members grew concerned that it was time to put into place a more clearly participatory governance structure that would formalize inclusion and have clear communication channels. High-performing organizations do not wait until systems break down to make critical adjustments to enhance effectiveness. As in previous structure studies, membership input was repeatedly sought through a variety of forums and other channels.

NAEYC's new structure is designed to build state capacity, not only to better address state policy issues but also to better support networks of local Affiliate Chapters. It establishes a formal representational structure, the Affiliate Advisory Council, to advise the Board and staff on Affiliate issues. The new structure also creates Interest Forums to encourage groups of members who share a common interest related to the NAEYC mission to network, exchange ideas, and learn together.

While focusing on its own growing niche and the structures and processes to support sustained influence on early childhood quality, NAEYC has also provided a seedbed for fledgling groups. Because our membership is so diverse, NAEYC is a fertile meeting place for people with related interests and concerns.

A critical function of organizations in their prime is proactive support of new initiatives that give their work new insights and energy (Adizes 1988). Numerous other organizations have been important participants in particular aspects of early care and education work.

NAEYC has supported groups whose founders began meeting at NAEYC conferences. Some of those groups eventually incorporated with their own staff, boards, and conferences. The National Association of Child Care Resource and Referral Agencies (NACCRRA), the Center for the Child Care Workforce (CCW), and the Ecumenical Child Care Network (ECCN) are examples of groups that began as interest groups or caucuses.

Other organizations hold some of their meetings and/or conferences during NAEYC conferences. Examples of such organizations are the National Association of Early Childhood Specialists in State Departments of Education (NAECS/SDE), American Associate Degree Early Childhood Educators (ACCESS), and the National Association of Early Childhood Teacher Educators (NAECTE).

NAEYC has different types of relationships with other types of organizations. There are projects on which NAEYC and

All who wish to better the lives of young children are INCLUDED in the umbrella of caring that characterizes NAEYC. I pray that this caring, personal aspect of NAEYC will never be drowned in the need for organizational streamlining or computerized efficiency as the organization grows. Keep the caring flowing!

— Alice Honig

other organizations work together based on mutual interest and the strength brought to the project because of the partnership. Several examples of such partnerships are discussed elsewhere in this volume: for NAEYC, American Psychological Association, and the Ad Council, see chapter 5; for NAEYC and NCATE, see chapter 4; for NAEYC, NBCDI, and CDF, see chapter 5.

THE CHALLENGES OF MAINTAINING EFFECTIVE STRUCTURES AND PROCESSES

The challenges of inclusive and effective structures and processes are both external and internal. The partnerships described above are a form of external inclusiveness. The challenge is to recognize that NAEYC does not have to, and in fact cannot, rectify every issue in the early care and education field alone. The temptation is great to try to do so because improving quality is multifaceted, touching on regulations, compensation, training, accessibility, and other issues. Our effort can feel incomplete if some aspect is left untouched. Targeted partnerships and supportive collaborations extend our responsiveness without overburdening our organizational capacity.

Internally, there is clearly a need to periodically reexamine what we are doing,

and why and how we are doing it. The impulse to recreate structures and processes can, however, become cumbersome and ritualistic, robbing the organization of its agility in terms of timely responsiveness or proactive efforts around specific issues. The main challenge of structural alteration is to not change for the sake of changing, but rather to make changes advisedly, anticipating trends and stressors on the organization. One constant stressor on any organization is the need for fiscal stability.

Fiscal stability

Starting in the early 1970s the executive staff and the executive committee of the Governing Board began working collaboratively and tirelessly to establish fiscal policies and structures that would put NAEYC on solid financial footing. The cornerstone of the work in this area was the decision to build fiscal stability from the inside out with the organization building steady sources of income from its own products and services. It also meant a spending pattern that included safe investment of "rainy day" savings and close monitoring of even the most well thought-out expenditure. Cost projections for proposed projects included Board deliberations on the centrality of the activity to the mission and the availability of staff and volunteer expertise, as well as the availability of financial resources.

NAEYC made the decision to try to avoid the soft money grants that regularly were available from government sources, even if they served NAEYC's mission. Soft money runs out or shifts focus. It did not seem wise to bank NAEYC's future on such shifts, controlled from outside the organization. NAEYC sought to fill a need in the field for improved quality through professional development and advocacy. With that goal in mind, NAEYC needed the flexibility to march to its own drummer. In addition, it did not make sense for NAEYC to compete with its own membership for soft money grants. Many of our members were participants in other organizations, including universities that filled the need for research or service-oriented bodies with specific areas of expertise and structures more ably suited to use the grant money to advance the knowledge base of the field.

Overall, NAEYC has worked to fulfill its mission by growing within budget. The mortgage on the original headquarters building on Connecticut Avenue was paid off in 10 years. Expansion to an adjoining building on Connecticut Avenue and the new headquarters on 16th Street were financed with rainy-day expansion funds rather than with a mortgage. Our NAEYC prospered.

An example of NAEYC growing within budget was the establishment of the National Institute for Early Childhood Professional Development in 1991. The Carnegie Foundation responded favorably to an NAEYC proposal to start the Institute. The three-year start-up grant included a plan for an annual conference, the proceeds from which NAEYC could use to stabilize the program. NAEYC was able to gradually take full responsibility for funding what has evolved into its Professional Development Division. The annual conference, known as the National Institute for Early Childhood Professional Development, continues and provides a service to the field by offering an advanced level of programming for early childhood educators who prepare and support early childhood professionals and for leaders interested in their own professional development.

THE CHALLENGES OF MAINTAINING FISCAL STABILITY

There is a real tension in the balancing act between essential and desired services and how to pay for them without compromising the fiscal integrity of the organization. There

NAEYC is not 'single-minded' in goals setting, but is selective in moving in new directions through an analysis of what the needs are and what the organization is capable of doing well at a given point in time.

— Jan McCarthy

are services that are part of the membership package, such as discounts on conference fees and a subscription to *Young Children*, all of which are meant to support, at an affordable cost, a cadre of loyal members. There are also services that are essential for and desired by the early childhood field and that directly serve our mission, such as NAEYC accreditation. Some NAEYC services and activities generate income and some do not. Income-generating activities do not have greater priority at NAEYC, and therein lies the tension. The challenge is to find diversified funding sources in an under-financed field.

National membership dues do not cover the cost of the basic membership package, including *Young Children*. While most local Affiliate dues were increased, national dues remained constant for 13 years until the 2001 increase. A $25 discount for joining through the Affiliate structure helped counterbalance the boost in cost. The commitment to inclusion has led NAEYC to continue to absorb the full cost of processing memberships and producing and delivering the journal to all members. Two questions that must be continually revisited are (1) at what level of fee can NAEYC sustain the inclusiveness to which it is committed and (2) how can the Affiliate structure, with a much smaller base, support Affiliate expenses and

keep membership affordable for the greatest number of practitioners in local areas? In some instances, the demographics and mix of professionals in local memberships are not very diverse. We have not studied the degree to which dues or other factors are the primary contributors to a given group's homogeneity.

The importance of NAEYC's accreditation as a vehicle for states to enhance early childhood program quality has put quite a bit of stress on NAEYC's structure and processes. An important fiscal consideration is that validators currently serve as volunteers. Keeping up with the workload has become challenging, and the demand is projected to continue growing. The Board has created a national commission to reinvent accreditation in ways that are fiscally viable and programmatically sound. This is a positive challenge because accreditation is essential to the field and central to NAEYC's mission, but essential services come with costs.

All of NAEYC's strengths and challenges as an inclusive, high-performing organization are evident in NAEYC's accreditation system. Could it be that accreditation, arguably NAEYC's most significant gift to the field, cannot be fully realized unless the Association lets go and allows it to become a freestanding entity? Organizations in their prime create vibrant new offspring organizations (Adizes 1988). Perhaps other monies would be available to the National Academy of Early Childhood Programs if it were not attached to NAEYC. The tension here is that accreditation is the product of our pivotal process, consensus building. As such, a significant portion of the membership of NAEYC views accreditation as a precious personal gift that each of them helped to create. Every voice was heard. It is *NAEYC Accreditation*, not just accreditation (Ethiel 1997). It is our flagship "on message" contribution to early childhood education. It *is* enhancing program quality for a diverse mix of children. Here we are, where we want to be, but the challenges can seem overwhelming.

Consensus building

Consensus building is vital because NAEYC values inclusiveness and recognizes the importance of structure and processes. Consensus building is fundamental to the evolution of NAEYC as a high-performing, inclusive organization. It is NAEYC at its best.

Critically important to NAEYC's credibility as an inclusive organization is having taken the time, again and again, to build consensus around the difficult issues in the field. In one situation after another, NAEYC has brought to the table as many of the disparate, knowledgeable perspectives as possible to examine proactively issues that could threaten young children's development and well-being. Through consensus building, NAEYC has focused on many important issues, such as those pertaining to quality (accreditation), practice (DAP), staff working conditions (compensation), children's lives and development (violence), regulations (licensing), and policies (for example, standardized testing). (See Bredekamp and Willer on position statements in this volume). Building consensus is hard work, and it can be emotionally draining to work through a process of such openness. But, it is clearly worth the effort in the long run. Taking the time to build consensus has repeatedly allowed NAEYC to advance the knowledge base of the early childhood field, far beyond where we would have been had we steadfastly held to a single narrow perspective. Consensus building is a time-tested strategy that we must carry into the future.

Originally the terminology developmentally appropriate practice appeared in NAEYC's accreditation materials. It seemed that everyone had a different definition for the term. NAEYC's subsequent original position

NAEYC is distinctive in that it includes people at many different educational and professional levels who share a common commitment to the well-being of young children. There are very few professional organizations that can make that claim. What is perhaps even more remarkable is that we can trust and communicate with one another as colleagues across wide differences in training and professional rank.

— David Elkind

statement on developmentally appropriate practice (NAEYC 1987) evolved after a couple of year's worth of consensus building that blended research and professional practice knowledge. Drafts of the statement were repeatedly circulated among the membership for input. Ten years later, when the document was revised, it went through the consensus building process within a blue ribbon panel of early childhood experts with disparate knowledge and points of view about 10 years' worth of advances in research and practice. The revised position statement again makes it clear that high-quality early childhood programs should first consider the developmental needs of the child (NAEYC 1997a).

THE CHALLENGES OF CONSENSUS BUILDING

In the 1980s and 1990s, there were a few times when the Governing Board moved too quickly to a vote on complex issues. Too quickly meant that time was not used to reach consensus. The telltale sign was always a split vote—9 to 7, or 7 to 6 with abstentions. When that happened, the Board was destined to revisit the issue until consensus was built. Without consensus, the Board could not move forward. One perspective "winning" over another did not create the kind of climate that allowed the Board to do its best proactive work as stewards of the organization. The message was jumbled because the group's best thinking had not had time to incubate.

Consensus building takes time. A rush to resolve a complex issue without first building consensus among diverse views can lead to decisions that do not advance the knowledge or functioning of the field. People need time to gather information, reflect, discuss, reassess, revise, and so on in order to reach a higher level of thinking and collaboration.

Staying on message

In spite of the complexities of the early childhood field, NAEYC has managed to adhere to its mission by staying on message. The essence of the message is that in NAEYC children come first. The message is brought to life by NAEYC's pursuit of quality in early care and education programs and services. Ellen Galinsky notes that when all the various deliberations about complex policies were over,

> …we always reconfirmed that the commitment to quality was immutable.

In the mid-1980s the Governing Board decided that there needed to be a task force to advise the Board on compensation issues.

A thoughtful dialogue ensued as the Board discussed the range of issues impacting compensation. Clearly, compensation and quality are intertwined; retention of trained teacher/caregivers is very difficult when compensation is inadequate. Young children need continuity and consistency in the adults they interact with to build relationships. Turnover, caused primarily by lack of fair compensation, undermines quality. The NAEYC task force became known as the Quality, Compensation, and Affordability Task Force. Thoughtful deliberation allowed the group to make recommendations that reflected the complexities of the issue while at the same time keeping children first.

THE CHALLENGE OF STAYING ON MESSAGE

Staying on message when the message is too narrowly focused can result in tunnel vision, an oversimplification of issues that can stultify organizations. High-performing, inclusive organizations avoid this pitfall by contextualizing the issues as NAEYC does through thoughtful study. In some way NAEYC's approach seems counterintuitive. It might appear more logical to block out competing ideas as a way of staying on message. The challenge is to resist that kind of effort to control the message—control that excludes new or dissenting ideas. We

need to take into the future what Shirley Dean describes as NAEYC's culture and spirit.

> Its (NAEYC's) openness to ideas, yet its insistence upon thoughtful study which involves a large, diverse group in the process and in the final decision.

Conclusion

The five consistently valued, integrated themes discussed in this chapter have given NAEYC immense credibility as a high-performing, inclusive organization. NAEYC has found its niche. It is the inclusive home for all who work on behalf of young children. NAEYC consistently develops structures and processes that formalize its commitment to inclusiveness. It further stabilizes its work on behalf of children and families by operating from an internally sound financial base. NAEYC invites open dialogue as it seeks to expand the knowledge base of the field of early childhood, trusting and acting on the belief that the new insights gained through consensus building will inspire reflective practices and policymaking among both the committed and the yet to be convinced. From its dynamic position as an inclusive, high-performing organization, NAEYC has delivered a message that has consistently and thoughtfully put children first.

What I find so compelling about NAEYC that constantly drives me to keep giving is that NAEYC does make a difference in the lives of children, their families, and the early childhood professionals who care for and educate them.

— Pat Phipps

References

Adizes, I. 1988. *Corporate life cycles: How and why corporations grow and die and what to do about it.* Inglewood Cliffs, NJ: Prentice Hall.

Ethiel, N., ed. 1997. *Reflections on NAEYC accreditation: Lessons learned and goals for the future.* Washington, DC: NAEYC.

NAEYC. 1971a. NAEYC reorganization. *Young Children* 26 (6): 352-A–352-I.

NAEYC. 1971b. A letter from the NAEYC Governing Board to the membership. *Young Children* 27 (2): 96-A–96-C.

NAEYC. 1987. NAEYC position statement on developmentally appropriate practice in early childhood programs serving children from birth through age 8. In *Developmentally appropriate practice in early childhood programs serving children from birth through age 8.* Exp. ed., ed. S. Bredekamp, 1–16. Washington, DC: Author.

NAEYC. 1991. NAEYC Bylaws revisions. *Young Children* 46 (2): 61–69.

NAEYC. 1997a. NAEYC position statement: Developmentally appropriate practice in early childhood programs serving children from birth through age 8. In *Developmentally appropriate practice in early childhood programs.* Rev. ed., eds. S. Bredekamp & C. Copple, 3–30. Washington, DC: Author.

NAEYC. 1997b. Summit themes and next steps. *The Affiliate* 24: 10.

NAEYC. 1998. NAEYC: Past, present and future. *The Affiliate* 26: 7.

Ward, E. 1971. From the President. *Young Children* 26 (6): 323–25.

Ward, E. 1972. From the President. *Young Children* 28 (1): 2–4.

Witherspoon, R. 1976. From NANE to NAEYC: The tempestuous years. *Young Children* 31 (5): 333–38.

Headquarters—The essential coordinating connection

NANE/NAEYC has headquartered in numerous settings, moving as the organization and staff grew. For the first 32 years the home and office of the serving president functioned as the Association headquarters, with some services originating from the homes of other volunteers. With each change of guard, records had to be packed and moved to a new site; members had to be informed of a new address for dues payments, publication orders, conference registration, or communication with the Board—often a different address for each function. It is no wonder that the leaders and members were delighted when a headquarters address was established in Chicago in 1958. Another landmark occurred in 1969 when the Association stopped renting and became an owner.

The images on the following pages chronicle highlights of NANE/NAEYC's headquarters over the years. The structures themselves depict the escalating growth of paid staff to coordinate the work of the leaders and provide services to the members and the field. Most amazing is the tenacity of the leaders during the first four decades. While struggling with the problems of multiple and frequently changing addresses and an all-volunteer force, they never lost sight of the organization's mission. They produced articles, conferences, and position statements to promote better practice and learning environments for young children.

TELEGRAM

NANE HEADQUARTERS ESTABLISHED FEBRUARY 1.
ADDRESS: 155 EAST OHIO STREET, CHICAGO 11, Ill.
TELEPHONE: SUPERIOR 7-9430. ORGANIZATIONAL
CONSULTANT, JUNE E. AIMEN.

HEADQUARTERS MADE POSSIBLE BY CONTRIBUTIONS TO
TOOLS AND MECHANICS FUND. APPRECIATION EXPRESSED
TO ELIZABETH McCORMICK FUND FOR MAKING
RENTAL OF PERMANENT HEADQUARTERS SPACE POSSIBLE.

YOUR HEADQUARTERS COMMITTEE: CHAIRMAN, GLENN
HAWKES, MEMBERS, EDNA MOHR, MILLIE ALMY, THEO
REEVE, JUDITH SCHOELLKOPF.

1958—Establishment of the first NANE (National Association for Nursery Education) Headquarters in Chicago

The establishment of the first NANE headquarters in Chicago represented such a milestone that the telegram shown was sent to *every* member. The Elizabeth McCormick Memorial Fund provided a desk and typewriter in return for $40 monthly rent. Finally, the Association had one central address and its first paid staff member. Serving as "organizational consultant," June Aimen worked part-time in return for parking and money to pay someone to stay with her own children for a few hours daily. She kept information flowing and coordinated among the volunteer leaders and members.

The stability afforded by the first office enabled NANE leaders to give attention and energy to their dream of hiring a full-time director. With funds from the Grant Foundation and member donations, Cornelia (Nell) Goldsmith of New York City was hired as executive secretary in 1964. By the spring of 1965, she had moved the headquarters to a rented apartment in the Washington, D.C., Alban Towers Hotel. The bedroom served as her apartment and the living/dining room was the headquarters.

At the first Executive Committee meeting at Alban Towers, the auditor predicted that the furniture would be "out in the streets" in six months because there was no possible way to save the Association. Nell Goldsmith countered, "Sir, the furniture will be here six months from now and so will we" (Witherspoon 1976, 336).

1965—NAEYC moves to Washington, D.C., taking up quarters in the Alban Towers Hotel at 3700 Massachusetts Avenue, N.W.

In September of 1966 NAEYC relocated to rental property designed for office space and welcomed the new Executive Director, Milton (Milt) Akers. Prior to this, Cornelia (Nell) Goldsmith had been persuaded to leave retirement and writing to help the Association transition from NANE to NAEYC, consolidate the organization's functions to one site, and represent the Association's voice on behalf of children at a crucial time—all until a permanent executive could be found. Milt Aker's arrival allowed Nell to return to her retirement and writing, having helped NAEYC make enormous gains and having saved "the Association from dissolution at a time when it was on the verge of the greatness that it since has achieved" (Witherspoon 1976, 336).

1966—Headquarters moved to 1629 21st Street, Washington, D.C.

In January of 1969, Executive Director Milton (Milt) Akers located the available property at 1834 Connecticut Avenue and by May had concluded all of the essential arrangements and negotiations—including convincing the Board that the organization's limited funds should be used for a down payment—and moved headquarters to its very own space.

When NAEYC moved into 1834 Connecticut Avenue, there was ample space to rent out apartments in addition to housing all headquarters functions. This situation quickly changed as Milt's vision, talents, and energy stimulated new publications and programs, new advocacy and media initiatives, and increased membership involvement. When Milt left NAEYC in 1972, all building space was fully devoted to organization staff and activity.

1969—NAEYC purchases Headquarters building at 1834 Connecticut Avenue, N.W., Washington, D.C.

Part 2

1987—NAEYC expands headquarters on Connecticut Avenue

Sixteen years after the purchase of the 1834 Connecticut Avenue property, NAEYC membership had tripled from 15,000 members in 1969 to 47,000 members in 1985, and staff had grown from 14 people to 27 people. The headquarters building simply could not hold another desk and two departments were moved to off-site rented space.

In 1976 NAEYC celebrated the Association's 50th anniversary by paying off the mortgage. This action had released funds to be saved for future space expansion, so when the adjoining townhouse at 1832 Connecticut Avenue became available in 1987, NAEYC was in a position to purchase and renovate it so that all departments could be rejoined in one site in the spring of 1988.

Continuing membership growth, to 83,000 by 1992, and the related increase in staff to approximately 50 required the addition of more headquarters space. Thus, in the summer of 1992, NAEYC was again preparing to move some departments to off-site rented space.

On the first day of the July Governing Board meeting in Washington, D.C., staff learned of the pending auction of the eight-floor building at 1509 16th Street, N.W. Lana Hostetler, president, J.D. Andrews, chief operations officer, and Marilyn Smith, executive director, made a "running" visit to all eight floors during the lunch break. At the closing session of the meeting, they described their visit and the Board approved serious investigation of making a bid on the property. A rash of activity and conference calls with the Board ensued as J.D. Andrews won the auction bid for NAEYC. Operating within the context of the economic recession, he negotiated a purchase price far below the building's value. Renovation began in October, and NAEYC staff started the year of 1993 in the new headquarters.

As membership and staff needs continue to expand, in 2001 NAEYC is using the original headquarters buildings on Connecticut Avenue as well as the large building on 16th Street. Linked by computer and telephone, staff are able to communicate without being in the same building.

1992—NAEYC purchases building on 16th Street, N.W., Washington, D.C.

Affiliate Groups—The essential local and state connection

There are 'turning points' in the lives of institutions as well as individuals. The meeting of the Chicago Association for Nursery Schools Board, with Milt Akers in attendance, in the mid-1960s was indeed such a turning point. By the show of hands—by the stroke of a bell—we went from being essentially a local organization to being a part of a strong organization (NAEYC) with a great national commitment to young children. We became Chicago AEYC. It was a splendid moment. It was a true turning point!

— Charlotte Collier

NAEYC's Affiliate Group structure made it possible for NAEYC to grow into an inclusive and national umbrella for the early childhood field. When Association leaders finally figured out a workable system for incorporating existing local, state, and regional groups with similar purposes, membership growth soared.

A successful plan for NAEYC's Affiliate structure was not easy to develop. From 1950 to 1964, the Board launched one approach after the other, learning from the failures until they came up with the design that worked best for all. The plan called for every member of an affiliated group to become a member of the national organization. Those members also in Affiliate Groups receive the benefit of a lower dues rate for national services than those who join only the national group.

This new Affiliate structure was one of several major changes that were put into effect in 1964. The organization changed its name from NANE to NAEYC, the name of the journal changed to *Young Children* with six (rather than four) issues per year, an executive secretary was hired, and plans were put in place to establish office headquarters in the nation's capital. A crystal clear vision of the Association's mission guided its devoted, voluntary leaders to these wise decisions—

the vision of building a strong national voice for children.

Significant growth in membership and an increase in the number of Affiliate Groups followed these bold changes. In 1964 when the new affiliation process went into effect, membership stood at 1,500. One year later NAEYC had 7,000 members and five years later, 17,500.

The number of affiliated groups started with

• 68 Chartered Affiliate Groups by 1966;

and grew to

• 100 Affiliate Groups by 1970,

• 235 Affiliate Groups by 1980,

• 440 Affiliate Groups by 1990, and

• 450 Affiliate Groups by 2000.

In 2000 NAEYC entered a new era with its Affiliate Groups, with the adoption of a restructuring initiative. Following several years of intense study and dialogue, the restructuring establishes clearer definitions of the roles and responsibilities of the national, state, local, and regional groups within the NAEYC Affiliate structure; enhances Affiliate capacity by intensifying technical assistance services; creates an advisory Affiliate Council; and reserves two positions on the Governing Board as Affiliate Liaison seats.

NAEYC Chartered Affiliate Groups—May 1966

ALABAMA

Jefferson County Nursery and Kindergarten Teachers Association

ARIZONA

Arizona Association for the Education of Young Children

Tucson Association for the Education of Young Children

CALIFORNIA

California Association for the Education of Young Children

Central California Association for Nursery Education

East Bay Association for the Education of Young Children

Northern California Association for the Education of Young Children

Peninsula Branch, Northern California Association for the Education of Young Children

Sacramento Valley Association for the Education of Young Children

San Diego Association for Nursery Education

San Francisco Association for the Education of Young Children

Southern California Association for Nursery Education

Tri-Counties Association for the Education of Young Children

CONNECTICUT

Connecticut Association for the Education of Young Children

Hartford Association for the Education of Young Children

Mid-Fairfield Pre-School Association

New Haven Association for the Education of Young Children

South Fairfield Association for the Education of Young Children

DISTRICT OF COLUMBIA

National Capital Area Association for the Education of Young Children

FLORIDA

Department of Early Childhood Education

ILLINOIS

Chicago Association for the Education of Young Children

INDIANA

Indiana Association for the Education of Young Children

IOWA

Iowa Association for the Education of Young Children

KANSAS

Kansas Pre-School Association

Topeka Pre-School Association

MAINE

Southern Maine Association for the Education of Young Children

MARYLAND

Baltimore Association for Pre-School Education

MASSACHUSETTS

Boston Association for the Education of Young Children

Southern Massachusetts Association for the Education of Young Children

Western Massachusetts Association for the Education of Young Children

Worcester Area Association for the Education of Young Children

MICHIGAN

Pre-School Association of Metropolitan Detroit

MINNESOTA

Minnesota Pre-School Association

MISSOURI

Association for the Education of Young Children of Missouri

Greater Kansas City Nursery Education Council

St. Louis Association for the Education of Young Children

NEW HAMPSHIRE

New Hampshire Association for the Education of Young Children

NEW JERSEY

New Jersey Association for Nursery Education

Morris-Union Chapter, New Jersey Association for Nursery Education

NEW YORK

New York State Association for the Education of Young Children

Capital District Chapter, New York State Association for the Education of Young Children

Early Childhood Education Council of Nassau-Suffolk Counties, Inc.

Early Childhood Education Council of New York City

Early Childhood Education Council of Western New York

Ithaca Chapter, New York State Association for the Education of Young Children

Mid-Hudson Association for the Education of Young Children

Rochester Chapter, New York State Association for the Education of Young Children

Rockland County Chapter, New York State Association for the Education of Young Children

Syracuse Chapter, New York State Association for the Education of Young Children

Westchester Association for Nursery Education

OHIO

Akron Area Association for the Education of Young Children

Cincinnati Association for the Education of Young Children

Springfield Pre-School Association

OREGON

Oregon Association for the Education of Young Children

PENNSYLVANIA

Delaware Valley Association for Nursery-Kindergarten Education

RHODE ISLAND

Rhode Island Association for the Education of Young Children

TENNESSEE

Tennessee Association on Children Under Six

TEXAS

Austin Pre-School Association

Houston Area Association for Nursery Education

Texas Association for the Education of Young Children

UTAH

Utah Association for the Education of Young Children

VIRGINIA

Tidewater Pre-School Association

WASHINGTON

Puget Sound Association for the Education of Young Children

Tacoma Association for the Education of Young Children

WISCONSIN

Madison Association for the Education of Young Children

Milwaukee Association for the Education of Young Children

REGIONAL GROUPS

Midwestern Association for the Education of Young Children

New England Association for the Education of Young Children

Chapter 4

Improving Professional Practice

A Letter to Patty Smith Hill

Sue Bredekamp

Patty Smith Hill is recognized as the founder of NAEYC. In 1926 she formed the National Committee on Nursery Schools, the group that became the National Association for Nursery Education (NANE), and later the National Association for the Education of Young Children (NAEYC). Patty Hill was motivated by the "proliferation of all types of nursery schools despite the lack of standards or curriculum plans, and the threat of some unqualified person taking leadership" (Hewes 1976, 297). Although never president of the organization, Patty Hill was its first member and her work dominated the nursery school movement during its early years. Most important, throughout its 75-year history, the Association has continued to reflect her influence and philosophy of education (Hewes 1976).

Concern over the growing number of nursery schools, the absence of standards for their operation, and the risk of unqualified teachers led NANE to publish its first book, *Minimum Essentials for Nursery School Education* (NANE 1929). The book's foreword written by Lois Hayden Meek Stolz, first NANE president, captures the goals of the early nursery school movement:

> The formation of the National Committee on Nursery Schools was a direct outgrowth of the desire of the specialists in nursery school education to keep a critical attitude toward the movement, to protect it from propagation at the hand of untrained enthusiasts and to encourage an experimental, open-minded attitude towards the development of new programs, techniques and organization . . . the need to insure certain minimum standards in nursery schools and at the same time to protect the movement from becoming stereotyped and static were at once the concern and the dilemma of the Committee.

These goals sound remarkably fresh and current as the Association enters the 21st century. The purpose of this letter is to report on the progress NAEYC has made in its 75-year history toward the goals Patty Hill and her colleagues cared so much about— improving professional practice and professional preparation and development.

Dear Patty Smith Hill,

As the organizer of the National Committee on Nursery Schools, you undoubtedly would like to know what the organization has accomplished in its 75 years of existence. You may be surprised to learn that the organization you founded is now the world's largest membership association of early childhood educators. This letter focuses on what you would find most interesting—NAEYC's progress on issues of early childhood professional practices and standards. Your initial concerns about the need to improve the qualifications of early childhood teachers and the need to improve the standards of practice in programs for young children have largely driven the work of the Association during the last 25 to 30 years. Significant progress has been made, but much more needs to be done. In fact, the concerns you expressed 75 years ago remain uppermost as this work continues. NAEYC must constantly strive to set standards for the field while also remaining open and flexible as we gain new knowledge and the social and political contexts change.

The work of establishing standards and criteria for quality has evolved into two interrelated strands: setting standards for practice in early childhood programs and setting standards for professional preparation and development of teachers. Before reporting on NAEYC's accomplishments in each of these areas, it is important to review the principles and values that underlie this work, each of which had its origin in your work and that of the founders' group.

Major values of NAEYC's work on professional standards

The standard-setting work of the Association, which began with its very first publication, has recognized the importance of stating informed positions on potentially controversial issues. Beginning in the late 1970s, NAEYC has used the strategy of developing and promulgating official position statements to influence practice, policy, and public opinion. In using this strategy, the Association's approach has consistently reflected four key values.

The first value is the need to base positions or standards on research knowledge and the wisdom of expert practitioners. The nursery school movement grew out of the child study movement, so the emphasis on research and child study is foundational to all the work of the Association and the field.

Because NAEYC's position statements are well grounded in research, they provide a solid basis for decisionmaking and political debate.

The second value that drives the standard-setting work of NAEYC is the involvement of large numbers of people in the development process, to bring diverse perspectives to the table with the goal of building consensus around the final product. Again, this is a value that you understood well, Patty. You believed in inviting potential opponents to the table, such as Montessorians, as well as nonprofessionals, such as Rose Alschuler, who were becoming actively involved as leaders in public school programs at the time (Hewes 1976). Your motive was to "educate" these people to your way of thinking. Today, we bring diverse perspectives together to negotiate differences, so that each party can learn and change as a result of the exchange of diverse perspectives. Really listening to and respecting diverse perspectives make the process of establishing position statements lengthy, and at times even painful, but inevitably result in stronger, more defensible, more useful statements.

A third value that has persisted is, in Jimmy Hymes's terms, *the child development point of view* (Hymes 1955). You and your colleagues in the child study movement launched the concept that programs should be derived from the study of children's development and learning. From this work came the emphasis on the role of play in children's development, child-centered programming, responsiveness to individual differences in children, and other key principles of good early childhood practice.

We still refer to the "whole child" as a shorthand way of describing this perspective. It reflects the fact that all dimensions of children's development—physical, social, emotional, and cognitive—must be considered in effective programming. The whole child view leads to provision of comprehensive services, such as those in Head Start that incorporate health, nutrition, mental health, social services, and parent involvement along with education. Finally, the whole child perspective requires the diverse array of professionals who work with and for children and who belong to NAEYC: teachers/caregivers, early childhood special educators, medical personnel, social workers, family support experts, and many others.

It is clear that as knowledge of child development and learning has expanded, our views of what constitutes good practice have expanded as well. Nevertheless, the child development value that permeated the early nursery school movement continues to influence NAEYC's work to this day.

A final value that dominates all of NAEYC's work, but especially the setting of standards, is commitment to our mission of acting on behalf of the needs and rights of young children. This value is primary in all decisions. At times, focusing on this mission can put NAEYC's standard-setting work at odds with some members' desires. For example, programs operated or directed by NAEYC members may be turned down for accreditation. College faculty who are active in the Association may find that their teacher preparation programs do not meet NAEYC's standards. Members of the Association may find that they themselves do not meet the professional qualifications identified as important by NAEYC. These situations create tensions and risks for the Association. When standards are set, some compromises must be made; standards cannot be set so high that they are unachievable. Nevertheless, when the toughest decisions have been made about whose interests are paramount, the Association has always put children's best interests first, as its mission requires.

*   *   *

Before describing some of NAEYC's specific achievements in improving profes-sional practice, I'd like to share a minor note of history that I think you, Patty, would particularly have appreciated. As I mentioned earlier, you cultivated a relationship with Rose Alschuler even though she was not "qualified" in the field. Rose became the first secretary of NANE, and during its earliest days, when lack of funds threatened its continued existence, it was Rose herself who anonymously contributed $500—an enormous amount of money in those days—to keep it going (Stolz 1977). Then later when Rose died, she left a bequest of $10,000 to NAEYC toward the goal of improving professional preparation. That money was used to hire a consultant to develop teacher education guidelines. I was that consultant in 1981, and I continued to work for NAEYC, ultimately as director of accreditation and professional development, until 1998. So, I would like to personally thank you for welcoming Rose Alschuler when others might not have. This one example—and there are many others like it—demonstrates the value to the field and the organization of keeping an open-minded attitude toward different perspectives and qualifications.

Since my experience with standard-setting work began with the teacher education guidelines, I'll begin by describing the strand of work on improving professional preparation and development.

Standards for professional preparation and development

During its first 40 years of existence, the Association continuously worked toward the goal of improving professional practice primarily through two channels: national conferences and publications—particularly the publication that began as a mimeographed newsletter and grew to the full-color, peer-reviewed *Young Children* we know today. (Highlights of NAEYC publications and conferences, key means of improving professional practice, appear on pages 116–124.)

Then in 1965 with the launching of Head Start and the resulting need for training large numbers of early childhood staff, NAEYC was thrust into taking a more active leadership role in providing guidance on professional preparation. Many NAEYC leaders worked tirelessly in that famous summer of 1965 and in subsequent years as early childhood education expanded rapidly from a nursery school movement for mostly middle-class children to a major strategy in the war on poverty.

THE CHILD DEVELOPMENT ASSOCIATE CREDENTIAL

During the 1970s, the most significant effort toward improving professional standards was the development of the Child Development Associate (CDA) National Credentialing Program. The program was funded by the federal government through the Head Start Bureau but was conceptualized from the outset as a new credential for the entire early childhood field. CDA credentialing was based on the assumption that a vehicle was needed for assessing and recognizing the knowledge and competence for working with young children that many individuals had acquired through various nontraditional means.

NAEYC leaders were integrally involved in developing the Credential. For instance, a key leader was Dr. Jenni Klein, chief of the Education Branch of Head Start, who led the entire CDA development effort as project officer during its early years. Significant investment was made in the development of the competency standards for the CDA Credential, including input from diverse constituencies of the field. That investment paid off in the degree to which the competencies were accepted as a framework of basic training for early childhood professionals. (See Bouverat & Galen 1994; Bredekamp 2000). It soon became clear that individuals are rarely "natural" teachers; they acquire competence through training. Based on this knowledge, the federal government funded several CDA training models, many of which continue to this day.

The CDA program strongly influenced the field during its early years although it struggled

NAEYC is faithful to the core value of serving children and striving to improve the quality of their experiences by educating (and inspiring) their child-care-providers.

— Nancy Fraser

financially. Finally, in the mid 1980s, NAEYC agreed to take over management of the program toward the goal of seeking a permanent home for it. To do so, NAEYC established a completely separate nonprofit organization, the Council for Professional Recognition, which has administered CDA since 1985. Under the Council's leadership, the CDA program has become more closely linked to college credit. And in collaboration with NAEYC's work on professional development, the CDA Credential has been clearly defined as the entry-level qualification to work in the field of early care and education.

Joining NCATE

While work on CDA occupied a great deal of energy from many in the field, others were concerned that more attention needed to be paid to the more traditional avenues of higher education for early childhood teachers. Under the leadership of President Jan McCarthy in the late 1970s, NAEYC joined the National Council for Accreditation of Teacher Education (NCATE). By so doing, the Association achieved a voice among the many groups that govern teacher education programs at the baccalaureate level and beyond. NCATE accreditation procedures require that individual teacher education programs within colleges of education conform to the standards of their professional organizations. For example, mathematics teacher education programs must meet the standards of the National Council of Teachers of Mathematics. In joining NCATE, NAEYC gained the authority to directly affect colleges of teacher education that prepare early childhood educators. However, NAEYC had no standards for teacher education at that time. Therefore, the Alschuler bequest was used to develop the teacher education guidelines for four- and five-year programs. Guidelines were also developed for masters and doctoral programs.

In developing the guidelines, NAEYC used a consensus-building process that served as the basic model for later efforts. The process included commissioning papers from experts that summarized what was known about effective teacher preparation; reviewing existing teacher education curricula and state standards; holding open hearings at NAEYC conferences; preparing a draft of standards that was sent to 250 experts for review and rating; revising drafts; gaining final review and approval from the appointed commissioners and then the Governing Board. Such a process is lengthy but serves several purposes. It not only establishes standards that are defensible due to expert input and review, but also informs those who will be using the standards. Having participated in development, individuals are more likely to understand and use the guidelines and less likely to resist them. In fact, the developers, some of whom may be the most ardent critics during the process, often become the strongest advocates for the standards.

Since development of the guidelines, NAEYC has used them to review teacher preparation programs that participate in NCATE accreditation (NAEYC 1996a). Through that process, weaknesses in early childhood teacher preparation programs become evident. The primary problem was and still is the great diversity of programs. There is no consistent definition of college preparation in early childhood education due in large part to the widely varying sets of state certification standards (the standards set by each state for licensing teachers to practice). To address this issue, NAEYC worked with the Association of Teacher Educators to develop a position statement on early childhood teacher certification that called for specialized certification covering the period birth through age 8 in every state (adopted 1991, see NAEYC 1991). In the intervening years, significant progress has been made toward the goal of increasing the number of states that offer early childhood certification. However, the diversity of what is required in those programs has only increased (McCarthy, Cruz, & Ratcliff 1999).

DEVELOPING GUIDELINES FOR ASSOCIATE-DEGREE PROGRAMS

In 1985 NAEYC developed guidelines for associate-degree-granting institutions, an important contribution to the field because so many child care teachers get their professional preparation in two-year institutions. Unfortunately, these guidelines have never had the same impact as those for four-year colleges because there is no NCATE to lend them authority or see that they are enforced in programs. Given this void, faculty from associate-degree programs proposed that NAEYC develop an accreditation system. Without incentives, however, colleges do not willingly seek multiple accreditations. Therefore, NAEYC, working collaboratively with ACCESS (American Associate Degree Early Childhood Educators), has investigated and field-tested the possibility of an approval system for associate-degree programs. Even this has proven challenging because of the diversity of programs. Some are clearly transfer programs, and most of students' professional work takes place at the four-year institutions they enter. Others are terminal degree programs, after which graduates immediately become responsible for groups of children. Other programs serve both functions. Any approval system must have adaptations to cover both kinds of programs and means to make clear what is being approved.

THE NATIONAL INSTITUTE FOR EARLY CHILDHOOD PROFESSIONAL DEVELOPMENT

By 1990 NAEYC had invested a great deal in work on setting standards for professional preparation yet there was still no clear system of early childhood professional preparation and development. In addition, during the 1980s tremendous effort had been spent trying to improve the quality of programs for young children (described later in this chapter). It became clear that unless similar effort was made on professional preparation, the goals for children would never be achieved.

Toward this end, NAEYC sought a start-up grant from Carnegie Corporation of New York to launch the National Institute for Early Childhood Professional Development. The Institute served three key functions during the 1990s that helped shape the landscape of professional preparation today: convening leaders, building consensus, and developing collaborations.

First, the Institute convened a national conference for the leaders of the field. These individuals needed a forum for com-

ing together to discuss their differences and commonalities, and to attempt to resolve them. For example, associate-degree and baccalaureate-degree faculty were called upon to discuss face-to-face the key issue of articulation—the transfer of credits between their programs. This direct discussion had never occurred before.

The Institute advanced collaboration in other ways as well. For example, at the first annual meeting, the Center for Career Development in Early Care and Education at Wheelock College launched its work with state teams on professional development initiatives, which has had significant positive effects in the intervening years. Celebrating its 10th anniversary in 2001, The Institute conference has become the meeting place for the leadership of the early childhood field.

The Institute has continued its work through significant collaborations with many different groups. All of NAEYC's teacher education standards were revised to reflect more current knowledge and also to reflect NCATE's move to performance-based standards and measurements. NAEYC worked tirelessly with the Division for Early Childhood (DEC) of the Council for Exceptional Children to develop standards for early childhood special educators and to

NAEYC believes in the ability of trained, caring adults to make a difference in the lives of young children. It encourages us to become the best nurturers, teachers, and caregivers we can be through constant learning, self-reflection, and growth in our skills and commitment to young children. This belief is the core that fuels the fire for excellence and service.

— Alice Honig

gain endorsement of its standards for early childhood educators in general. This professional preparation work extended to collaborative efforts with organizations not already mentioned, including the National Association for Family Child Care (NAFCC), the National School-Age Care Alliance (NSACA), and the National Association of Early Childhood Teacher Educators (NAECTE).

Perhaps the Institute's most important work has been conceptual. As mentioned earlier, the field has lacked a coherent system of professional preparation and development, at least in part because the field is so diverse, spanning different age groups and settings. To help achieve coherence, NAEYC staff and leaders worked to develop the position statement "A Conceptual Framework for Early Childhood Professional Development" (adopted 1993, see Willer 1994). This work was actually very difficult. In linking specific professional levels to academic qualifications, NAEYC was directly challenging the qualifications of its members and leaders. Many family child care providers were affronted because they could not find themselves on the lattice even though their work was considered excellent by their peers and the families they served.

Others criticized NAEYC for calling for such qualifications when low compensation was still such a serious problem. It probably is safe to say that the work managed to offend everyone in the field in some way. Nevertheless, we proceeded. Again, taking our time, holding meetings with diverse constituent groups, convening hearings at conferences, circulating drafts for review, and writing conceptual articles in the journal to build understanding (Bredekamp 1992; Bredekamp & Willer 1992). Finally, the framework was agreed to by the Governing Board and the language of the "career lattice" is now commonly adopted throughout the field.

An important characteristic of all standard-setting efforts is that they never end. Just about the time a set of standards is developed, new knowledge becomes available and misunderstandings arise that necessitate revisions. So the review and revision process is ongoing. Each set of professional preparation standards has been reviewed and revised at least once and this process will continue ad infinitum.

Integrally connected to NAEYC's work on professional preparation standards is its work on standards for programs for young children, to which I turn now.

Standards for practice

Perhaps you would be most pleased, Patty, to know that just as you personally dominated the early nursery school movement in this country in your day, your educational philosophy continues to be reflected in NAEYC's work today (Hewes 1976). We now have a name for it—developmentally appropriate practice—and though our conceptualization of practice is more complex, reflecting new knowledge and experience, the fundamentals are the same (Bredekamp & Copple 1997). Many of your beliefs remain core values emphasized in our work. These include the observational study of children, curriculum that focuses on active learning and builds on and expands children's interests, play as key in children's development and learning, and a multidisciplinary approach that includes families and is responsive to cultural and socioeconomic variations.

In the last 25 years of its history, NAEYC has become the established standard-setter for the early childhood field. Because the first publication of NANE in 1929 was *Minimum Essentials for Nursery School Education*, we know that a primary concern at the outset was to set standards for practice in a field that was just beginning to grow and that included many untrained people. That same situation, on a much larger scale, motivated NAEYC to launch development of a national accreditation system for early childhood programs in 1981.

NAEYC ACCREDITATION

NAEYC's accreditation is now the largest effort in the United States to directly influence the quality of early childhood programs. In the beginning, however, none of us knew exactly what we had gotten into. The idea came from discussions among Governing Board members and the executive staff, J.D. Andrews and Marilyn Smith, about future directions for the Association. By 1980, NAEYC had grown significantly in membership and financial security. It had almost doubled membership in the 1970s. Some Board members wanted NAEYC to endorse schools of education, but the executive staff drew the members' attention to the quality of early childhood programs. Most NAEYC members worked directly with children and already the majority of U.S. children were spending some time in centers. The Board decided to use $500,000 of NAEYC's savings to explore the feasibility and development of a "center endorsement project." Having just completed my

I continuously discover that we owe so much to the beginning founders of NAEYC for setting the tenets of Early Childhood Education in the form of principles and beliefs that are still solid and firm. By building on these tenets, NAEYC leads us toward the goal of high-quality early childhood education.

— Shizuko Akasaki

consulting work on the teacher education guidelines project, I was hired to consult on this new project.

No other NAEYC effort to influence quality through standards was more thoroughly developed, nor involved so many people as that for the creation of the National Academy of Early Childhood Programs. (The history is completely described in Bredekamp & Glowacki 1996). A prestigious steering committee guided the effort: Chair Barbara Bowman, Bettye Caldwell, Docia Zavitkovsky, Jan McCarthy, Earline Kendall, and Sally Kilmer. Committee members and staff held meetings with Affiliate Groups throughout the country over several years. One of my own responsibilities was to conduct a comprehensive review of research on the effects of various program indicators on outcomes for children and to examine existing instruments and state standards. Several drafts of proposed criteria for accreditation were circulated for review. A final draft appeared for review in *Young Children*, which then circulated to 40,000 people. Many thousands of people, with varying perspectives, participated in the development process over four years, and a field test of the system was conducted in four states: Texas, Minnesota, California, and Florida.

While the criteria were being developed, committee members and staff also investigated and reviewed various models of accreditation and designed one that we felt best met the needs of our unique field. At the time, the only widely known model of quality control was state licensing, a mandatory system of government regulation setting minimum standards and punishing infractions. Its purpose was to provide a baseline of consumer protection for children and families. Accreditation, on the other hand, is voluntary, sets high quality standards, and gives recognition to those who achieve them.

As with most accrediting bodies, NAEYC placed considerable emphasis on the self-study portion of the system. The idea was that programs would engage all participants—administrators, teachers, assistants, parents, even children—in the process of examining the quality provided and making improvements to more closely meet the accreditation criteria. Self-study and improvement is based on the concept that changes initiated from within would be more lasting and meaningful. When program personnel decide they are in substantial compliance with the criteria, they invite NAEYC validators in to verify that compliance, and then a decision is made on the results.

I care passionately about what happens to young children and their families in this country and believe that NAEYC is one of the best vehicles to translate that caring and commitment into action. NAEYC enables research knowledge to reach NAEYC members who work directly with children and families day in and day out.

— Ellen Galinsky

Accreditation is by definition an exclusive system; it sets high standards and recognizes those who achieve them, excluding those who don't. However, NAEYC's goal from the outset was to accredit not a small minority of the most excellent programs in the country but a far wider base. In fact, the goal was to engage as many programs as possible in a process to bring about real and lasting improvement for children. The founders of accreditation dreamed that one day parents in this country would be able to choose from among many accredited programs the one that would best fit their needs and values for their children. Certainly, this goal has not been achieved, but accreditation has had several serendipitous effects. For the broader field, accreditation has definitely raised public awareness about quality and provided a benchmark against which state standards or programs can be measured. For the organization, accreditation greatly expanded the constituency of members and participants. All types of early childhood programs, for-profit and nonprofit, under every possible sponsorship or auspice, have achieved accreditation. This fact alone has demonstrated the Association's inclusiveness and helped it build a membership of more than 100,000.

More than 10,000 early childhood programs and thousands of validators are involved in accreditation. As accreditation has grown, it has naturally encountered growing pains. Among the challenges has been the difficulty of applying a single set of standards to the diverse kinds of programs that exist and to programs that function in various social and cultural contexts. Over the years, the standards have been revised and validators have been trained and retrained toward the goal of improving quality control while also maintaining flexibility and open-ness—the same goals that the National Committee on Nursery Schools sought to achieve. But now, as then, this is a difficult challenge and will continue to be because knowledge and contexts will always be changing. Keeping a huge system of indi-viduals—each with her or his own values and biases—working toward the same goals while also interpreting quality within an acceptable range is a significant challenge. NAEYC is now engaged in a project to reinvent accreditation to ensure that the system is able to respond to greatly in-creased demand as well as the changing contexts of the field (Goffin 2001).

Accreditation has played a major role in the entire field of early childhood education. Patty, I'm sure that you, Lois Meek, and your other colleagues in the 1920s could never have imagined how your initial effort at

Early in my career I became dismayed as I encountered so many disparate views about curriculum and practice in early care and education. Then I watched NAEYC take leadership to quantify and define those elusive elements of quality and involve early childhood educators in agreeing on practices that enhance the lives of children. Thank you, NAEYC for the Developmentally Appropriate Practice position statements and the accreditation system that guide so many of us who are trying to find ways to help families and children.

— Pearl L. Waxman

standard-setting would grow and change to become the benchmark standard for the field of early childhood center-based programs.

Each of NAEYC's standard-setting efforts has addressed one problem only to uncover or even create new problems (Bredekamp 1999). Work on accreditation was no exception. It contributed to another strand of NAEYC's work, defining standards or guidelines for developmentally appropriate practice, that has had an even larger impact than accreditation.

DEFINING DEVELOPMENTALLY APPROPRIATE PRACTICE

Two trends led NAEYC to its work on developmentally appropriate practice (DAP), for which it has become very well known. One trend was toward programs for 4-year-olds in public schools and the other was a need identified by accreditation. Accreditation standards used the phrase "developmentally appropriate" in several places, specifying that programs must provide "developmentally appropriate materials" or that teachers have "developmentally appropriate expectations of children." As soon as NAEYC validators started conducting validation visits in 1985, we found that these terms required more detail because these phrases and other parts of the standards were being interpreted so many different

My dream is that every child would have a developmentally appropriate preschool experience, regardless of income, because I think it is good for children. To me, that ought to be the right of every American child.

— Helen Taylor, St. Petersburg Times (10/88).

ways. While developing the accreditation criteria, the steering committee had identified the need to define *developmentally appropriate* but the task had seemed daunting at the time (and this later proved true). We also assumed that people in the field knew what we meant by the phrase. Developmentally appropriate practice was a shorthand term used so widely within the field, it seems impossible to identify its true origins. I personally became familiar with the term during an internship I served in the Education Branch of the Head Start Bureau in 1980. At that time, the Carter administration launched a Basic Educational Skills initiative in Head Start. Education Chief Jenni Klein consistently conveyed the message that basic educational skills were a fine goal as long as teaching practices were developmentally appropriate.

In 1985 the NAEYC Governing Board convened a Commission on Appropriate Education of 4- and 5-Year-Olds because of members' concerns about the increasing emphasis on academics in kindergartens and the trend of public schools beginning to serve 4-year-olds. The commission consisted of 29 members from very diverse backgrounds and was chaired by Bernard Spodek who prepared the final report. The report, which consisted of a listing of learning and development goals for 4- and 5-year-olds, was presented to the Board. However, minority reports were also received, each of which expressed concern that the listing of learning goals describing what children should learn did not address the key issue of *how* they learn and develop. But the minority reports came from two different perspectives. K. Eileen Allen voiced the concern that special education knowledge, especially the proven benefits of behavior reinforcement, was not acknowledged in the Commission's work. Jimmy Hymes and Jenni Klein each submitted letters expressing their concerns that the report did not present a whole child perspective and did not sufficiently address child development and the processes by which children acquire the competencies listed. Due to the lack of unanimity among the commission members, the Board did not approve the report and directed the staff to work on the task of defining appropriate education of 4- and 5-year-olds.

The three reports of the 1985 commission seem oddly reminiscent of the three reports that the Committee of 19 of the International Kindergarten Union issued in the early 1900s (Snyder 1972)—don't they, Patty? Given the charge of deciding on kindergarten curriculum, you and the other members could not come to consensus. Susan Blow advocated a more structured, uniform kindergarten curriculum; you, Patty, wanted a play-oriented, more child-centered ap-

proach; and Lucy Wheelock attempted to write a compromise but failed. The IKU and NANE went on to become separate organizations. This early division of the nursery school movement from kindergarten/ elementary schooling persists to this day and is only now being significantly addressed as more public schools enter the arena of preschool education.

Returning to the story of developing NAEYC's statement on developmentally appropriate practice, I began working on the project with Marilyn Smith, and we quickly identified the need to take a developmental approach. We realized that rather than singling out 4- and 5-year-olds, we should be addressing the issue across the full age-span that corresponds to NAEYC's mission— birth through 8. In fact, the very concept of developmental appropriateness makes most sense when thinking about what is appropriate for different age groups. For example, what is safe and healthy for a toddler is not the same as what is safe for a 7-year-old.

NAEYC contracted with Bess-Gene Holt to prepare an initial draft of principles of developmentally appropriate practice. In that draft, Bess-Gene gave us the early, now well-known, definition of developmentally appropriate practice as having two dimensions: age-appropriateness and individual

For more than 40 years, NAEYC's conferences and publications have afforded me an important forum for professional growth and collaboration. At the 2000 conference a young early childhood educator asked what we did before we had the developmentally appropriate practice guidelines. My description of how each person had to piece together concepts and philosophies gleaned from other professionals underscored the great value in the integrated definitions of development and guidelines for practice in developmentally appropriate practice.

— Rosalind Charlesworth

appropriateness. We also worked with experts from the National Center for Clinical Infant Programs (now ZERO TO THREE) to define developmentally appropriate practices for infants and toddlers. Others who contributed were Teresa Rosegrant and Jan Brown McCracken. I edited the first version of *Developmentally Appropriate Practice* published in 1986, covering the age range of birth through kindergarten (Bredekamp 1986). But immediately, we began work on a section on primary grades, which Polly Greenberg helped write. In 1987 NAEYC published *Developmentally Appropriate Practice in Early Childhood Programs Serving Children Birth through Age 8* (Bredekamp 1987; NAEYC 1987).

Despite the fact that NAEYC's mission incorporates the primary grades, the Association has never been especially influential with public schools, nor have primary teachers been well represented in the membership except in a few Affiliate groups. This fact no doubt goes back to the group's history as a preschool organization, even separate from kindergarten in its early days. The 1987 version of the statement on developmentally appropriate practice was NAEYC's first direct venture into standard-setting for primary grades. To this day, we regularly encounter school administrators and public school teachers who know little of NAEYC but who are familiar with the "green book."

The 1987 *Developmentally Appropriate Practice* struck a chord in the early childhood field and beyond. This edition became the best-selling book in NAEYC's history with more than 700,000 copies sold. Widely used in early childhood courses, it has been seen as having presented a codification of the research-based and practical wisdom of generations of early childhood educators.

My personal opinion as to why the position statement and book on developmentally appropriate practice had such influence was the Governing Board's decision to include examples of both appropriate and inappropriate practices for each age group. This was quite a risk because we had never stated any position in negative terms before (with the exception of "staff refrain from corporal punishment" in accreditation criteria). As a college instructor I had often taught concepts by giving negative exemplars as well as positive and I fully believe that that is an important element of the conceptualization process.

Early on, however, I proposed to the Board that we present appropriate and inappropriate practices as a continuum from more appropriate to less appropriate. Several Board members felt that such a strategy was wishy-washy and that NAEYC shouldn't communicate that it was ever acceptable to be a little

104

naeyc at *75*

less appropriate. The decision to articulate an either/or view of developmentally appropriate practice in the 1987 edition was all-important. By doing so, we ensured that the document would be noticed because it was significantly different from other early childhood textbooks. But we also created another set of issues and opened the door for misinterpretations that would need to be addressed in the future.

CURRICULUM AND ASSESSMENT

Along with the increased academic pressures on young children in the late 1980s came a movement toward increased reliance on the use of standardized tests to make important decisions about children such as placement and readiness for school. Head Start had initiated a set of measures that relied heavily on paper-and-pencil testing and took a great deal of time in administration. NAEYC members requested that the organization take a stand on these issues and the result was a position paper on standardized testing, developed by a group of assessment experts including Asa Hilliard, Sam Meisels, Lorrie Shepard, and others (adopted 1987, see NAEYC 1988). For two reasons this position paper was not widely circulated for review and comment to members prior to approval. One was the need for a timely response to the issues confronting the field

and the other was the (erroneous) assumption that most members did not have the background in testing necessary to provide an informed review. In retrospect, not following usual procedures was a mistake. Not because the statement is not sound; it is. But failing to obtain consensus meant that the Association missed a vital opportunity to engage members in an educative process about the content, to make the statement more user friendly for practitioners, and to enable it to really influence practice. Almost 15 years later, we still have incredible misunderstanding in our field about the important issues of testing and assessment, which might have been reduced if a healthy dialogue had been conducted then.

Shortly after *Developmentally Appropriate Practice in Early Childhood Programs Serving Children Birth through Age 8* was published, it was criticized for its overreliance on knowledge of child development as the basis for practice (Spodek 1991). Spodek and others were justifiably concerned that the influential document did not address the issue of curriculum content for young children. Again, NAEYC seemed to be revisiting past debates about what the content of curriculum should be. Developmentally appropriate practice is not about curriculum, what to teach and when, except in the broadest sense in which *Developmentally Appropriate Practice*

I was elected secretary of the Association in 1965 when we had just changed from NANE to NAEYC and the field of early childhood education was starting to expand dramatically. I saw the potential in NAEYC to raise standards and improve the intellectual base of the field among leaders and practitioners. It was this hope that kept me involved in governance for over 20 years.

— Bernard Spodek

supplies some principles for curriculum planning. Rather, *Developmentally Appropriate Practice* is about how to teach. So even with the wide distribution of the book, the problem that prompted the creation of the 1985 Commission on Appropriate Education of 4- and 5-Year-Olds still remained: What should the content of early childhood education programs be?

To address this problem, NAEYC began a collaboration with the National Association of Early Childhood Specialists in State Departments of Education (NAECS/SDE). The goal for the collaboration was to describe developmentally appropriate curriculum goals across the age span. We reviewed documents and research, and held meetings throughout the country but were far from agreeing on a set of learning goals. We feared setting goals that were too narrow by age, or limiting individual variation. We also struggled with conveying the subtleties of developmental progression across time. One strategy we used was giving groups of educators examples of curriculum to evaluate. We simply asked, what do you like about and what don't you like about the sample curriculum, and why? Their answers to the why question were surprisingly consistent. We realized that our own members implicitly applied a set of guidelines for evaluating curriculum. Having been unable to reach

I think we have lost much that made the 1940s and 1950s so rich in development—listening to children, learning how to observe children and enter into the child's world unobtrusively.

— Mary B. Lane

agreement on what children should be learning, we settled for developing a set of guidelines for making decisions when choosing or developing curriculum. Because our position statement on testing had more to say about what not to do than what to do, and because curriculum and assessment must be tightly linked, NAEYC and NAECS/SDE also developed assessment guidelines to accompany the curriculum guidelines (adopted 1990, see NAEYC & NAECS/SDE 1992).

Recognizing that NAEYC and the field still had not achieved the original goal of articulating developmentally appropriate learning goals, I began working with Teresa Rosegrant on a two-volume set of publications titled *Reaching Potentials* (Bredekamp & Rosegrant 1992, 1995). For the first volume, *Reaching Potentials: Appropriate Curriculum and Assessment for Young Children,* I invited experts in each of the subject matter areas (literacy, math, science, social studies, physical education, the arts, health) to answer the question of what children, birth through 8, should be learning. Just as we were working on these books, a parallel trend was occurring in which each of the various professional organizations, beginning with the National Council of Teachers of Mathematics, and each began setting curriculum standards for their specializations. School reform soon became standard-based reform with initiatives coming from not only specialty organizations but also from government-funded national and state standard-setting projects. Due to these trends, we delayed publication of the second *Reaching Potentials* volume so that authors could respond to the standards in their respective areas. In many cases the national standards did not directly address preschool or earlier years so authors adapted or critiqued what was provided.

The curriculum question seems to have been at the root of your division with Susan Blow and her colleagues almost a hundred years ago, Patty, and was also the dispute among the members of 1985 Commission on Appropriate Education. The question persists to this day. NAEYC's efforts at addressing the curriculum question in the early 1990s, which resulted in the curriculum and assessment guidelines, were not only insufficient but also reactive. Rather than assuming leadership on defining what the content of the early childhood curriculum should be, NAEYC reacted to what others said or rejected the notion of specifying anything at all.

This reluctance to specify learning goals was also evident in the organization's initial response to the National Education Goals Panel Goal 1, "By the year 2000, all children will start school ready to learn." As a field, our initial response focused on our perspective that children are born ready to learn and that schools should be ready for children, not children ready for school. Thus we rejected the concept of school readiness for many years, failing to take the lead on coming to an acceptable definition. The Goals Panel (advised by key NAEYC leaders) did use a comprehensive definition with five dimensions of readiness, but it took a decade for early childhood educators to realize that Goal 1 was not detrimental to their work and mission. In fact, focus on readiness for school appears to mobilize broad support for early childhood education as no other rallying cry has done.

REVISING THE POSITION ON DEVELOPMENTALLY APPROPRIATE PRACTICE

The process of standard setting is never ending. In fact, it is an iterative process in which questions continually repeat themselves and solutions must be revisited and revised, creating new questions. The 1987 edition of *Developmentally Appropriate Practice* enjoyed a remarkable honeymoon period during which it was widely embraced by the field, almost evangelically so. Within a few years, however, developmentally appropriate practice—the book and the concept—came under considerable scrutiny. The criticism and questioning, although challenging for

We must have the ability to use research well and wisely but not be immobilized by a lack of it. In these cases, rather than waiting for the science to emerge, we must let good judgment by seasoned practitioners prevail.

— Sharon Lynn Kagan

NAEYC, created a tremendous opportunity for thoughtful debate and deliberation within the early childhood field.

Criticisms of the 1987 edition of *Developmentally Appropriate Practice* are thoroughly described elsewhere (Bredekamp 1997; Bredekamp & Copple 1997). To briefly summarize they include: (1) the either/or oversimplification of practice; (2) overemphasis on child development and underemphasis on curriculum content; (3) the passivity of the teacher's role, the failure to recognize the value of teacher direction; (4) lack of awareness of the significant role of culture in development and learning (White, middle-class bias); (5) lack of application for children with disabilities and special needs; (6) overemphasis on the individual child and underemphasis on relationships and social construction of knowledge; (7) naivete about the significant role of families. Other weaknesses could be cited, but these are the primary ones around which considerable debate occurred. Critiques of *Developmentally Appropriate Practice* from all these perspectives regularly appeared in the literature and point/counterpoint sessions became a common feature at conferences.

At one such session at NAEYC's 1991 Annual Conference in Denver, Rebecca New and Bruce Mallory challenged *Developmentally Appropriate Practice* on the issues of responsiveness to cultural diversity and special needs. Lilian Katz and I were in the position of "defending" *Developmentally Appropriate Practice*. The session was very engaging and high-level, although rather heated at times. At the end, several people came up to me and heartily congratulated me, saying "You and Lilian won!" The problem was I didn't feel like we had won; I knew that Becky and Bruce were right. I needed to stop trying to defend the existing description of developmentally appropriate practice and start really listening to its critics to make it better and more useful.

Like most people, I've found that when I'm in a defensive mode, it's impossible to hear what the other person is saying. I'm too busy thinking about what I'm going to say back. We were not doing enough to help our members bridge the knowledge gap between early childhood and early childhood special education, and children with disabilities were not being served adequately as a result. I knew this. Similarly, the realities of cultural and linguistic diversity and growing doubts and anger about *Developmentally Appropriate Practice* among several groups meant that more and different voices needed to be heard. Becky's critiques were based largely on her experience in Reggio Emilia, Italy, where teachers' reflection and debate had raised practice to such a high level. Her concern

NAEYC promotes an attitude that its programs and activities are works in progress—that we operate in a dynamic, changing field and must continuously revisit, critique, and upgrade our initiatives as new information or resources are available.

— Jan McCarthy

was that the literal either/or interpretations of the 1987 *Developmentally Appropriate Practice* in our country severely limited our field's potential. She went so far as to state that she wished the book had been written with invisible ink; it is valuable to read once but shouldn't be used as a bible.

Considering all these important and very real concerns, I was faced with the charge of revising the position statement on developmentally appropriate practice, which became a more formidable task every day. In 1993 I had the good fortune to visit Reggio Emilia programs and came away with many new perspectives but one essential insight. I had been wrong in trying to rewrite alone. A complete revision could only be accomplished through a process of social construction involving disparate points of view. I returned and requested that the Governing Board appoint an ad hoc committee to undertake the task. The group represented the spectrum of critical perspectives on the document: Barbara Bowman, Victoria Fu, Lilian Katz, Rebecca New, Carol Brunson (Phillips) Day, Teresa Rosegrant, Deborah Ziegler, and myself.

The group met for three years to review all the critiques, argue and debate, conduct open hearings, collect comment, and review research and drafts. It was an exhausting but intellectually exhilarating process. One of the most significant outcomes of our work was the expansion of the definition of developmental appropriateness to include knowledge of social and cultural context. Another important change was to stress the role of the teacher as decisionmaker, simply including examples of appropriate and inappropriate practices (not as part of the position statement itself). We also enriched them so they were not so simplistic and polarized. Many elements that our colleagues in Reggio Emilia emphasize influenced the outcome as well as the process of our work. These included emphasis on creating a community of learners (children learning from each other), reciprocal relationships with families, teachers' scaffolding children's learning, and the role of representation in learning. Once the major concepts were agreed to, we faced the daunting task of putting all this into a coherent framework and "getting words in sequence," which is what I call writing. Again, I realized that this had to be a collaborative process and turned to my colleague, Carol Copple, with whom I co-wrote the 1997 edition.

The 1997 edition, *Developmentally Appropriate Practice in Early Childhood Programs,* is a much more complex document than the 1987 version (Bredekamp & Copple 1997; NAEYC 1997). The 1987 version was written relatively rapidly to meet a very

There were so many times during the early years of NANE when we would debate merging with a stronger organization rather than continue to struggle with our small membership and lack of funds. I think one reason we never gave up the struggle to build NANE was our fear of being consumed in the formalities of an established organization. We feared we might be distracted from our priority to explore the challenges, define issues and pursue solutions for the emerging field of early childhood education. We wanted to keep our focus on the questions rather than on answers derived from past history.

— Millie Almy

specific need and targeted directly to an audience of untrained personnel and the public. In 1987 we were writing a position statement in response to specific problems within a context; we were not writing a textbook, although the book was used that way. Because the 1987 *Developmentally Appropriate Practice* was highly simplified for its purpose and its audience, the unfortunate side effect was that some people drew the conclusion that NAEYC believed early childhood practice is simple. Nothing could be further from the truth. NAEYC has published hundreds of volumes and thousands of journal articles describing just how challenging early childhood education is. We hope that the 1997 edition conveys at least a little of that complexity. To help educate NAEYC leaders about the significant changes in the 1997 version and to prepare them to teach others, in 1998 NAEYC moved into the technological age by holding live, interactive videoconferences called *The Leading Edge* and disseminating videotapes for training.

LINGUISTIC AND CULTURAL DIVERSITY AND TECHNOLOGY

During the years that the articulation of developmentally appropriate practice was undergoing review and revision, key issues arose as part of that process and in their own right. One of the most significant grew out of the increasing linguistic and cultural diversity of our nation, and confusion about how best to teach young children whose home language is not English. The DAP panel discussed these issues in depth and felt that they needed to be integrated throughout the document, hence the decision to recognize social and cultural context as part of the basic core of knowledge for teacher decisionmaking. But culture and language are such critical dimensions of development and learning and are also such politically charged topics that NAEYC appointed a special panel to work on a position statement on this topic. The panel's composition was diverse as are all NAEYC panels, particularly when an issue demands lengthy discussion, debate, and review. Fortunately, the position statement was released in time to serve as a resource for members who soon began confronting political actions to eliminate bilingual education. Based on research evidence and the values that underlie NAEYC's work, the position statement supports continuing development of children's home language as they acquire English, and calls for respect for children's cultures and identities (adopted 1995, see NAEYC 1996b).

Technology was another topic on which members wanted guidance. Because of the emphasis on active learning from the begin-

> A core value of NAEYC is that 'child' comes first and the adjectives—special needs, limited hearing, Asian, African American, and so on—come second. This does not mean that there is a universal child hidden beneath these differences; it does mean that we look at the child as a unique individual and not as a representative of some group or category.
>
> — David Elkind

ning of NANE through NAEYC's present philosophy, many early childhood educators have been very skeptical about computers in settings for young children. A panel of experts on technology in the early childhood context was appointed to draft a position statement. The resulting document describes how technology can and should be used in developmentally appropriate ways with young children, and it asserts that good software creates a socially and intellectually engaging context for learning (adopted 1996, see NAEYC 1996c). The document proved very useful not only to the field but to developers, evaluators, and consumers of software. Again, to provide the strongest knowledge base for the field in this new area, NAEYC published an edited book of collected essays (Wright & Shade 1994). Here again, Patty, I'd love to know what you would think about computers with young children!

Early literacy

The 1987 *Developmentally Appropriate Practice* had enjoyed a lengthy honeymoon period. This was not the case with the 1997 edition, in part because the book had become so influential. Almost immediately, it was greeted by criticism from International Reading Association (IRA) President Jack Pikulski and a core of other IRA leaders. Although they were pleased that NAEYC had taken

major steps to strengthen the view of the teacher's role, they saw the new edition as missing an important opportunity to describe appropriate early literacy practices for young children. Several of them had in fact criticized *Developmentally Appropriate Practice* for its role in limiting educational opportunities for poor children who need more explicit attention to language and alphabetic code (see for example, McGill-Franzen 1993).

My initial reaction to this criticism was to think, "Oh, no! Here we go again!" and to get defensive after having worked so many years to revise the book very substantially. But fortunately, I had learned that defensiveness is the least effective strategy for solving problems. Having been appointed to IRA's Committee on Literacy and Young Children, I asked the group what we needed to do to fix the problem with *Developmentally Appropriate Practice*. We agreed that a joint position statement from the two organizations was the best strategy.

We used NAEYC's well-established process of position statement development, incorporating research review, solicitation of comments, open hearings at meetings, and review of drafts. For this project, we used a computer listserv process to obtain commentary on drafts, which enabled all reviewers to see and respond to all comments. This way many controversial issues were thor-

It is very important that as an Association and as individuals we avoid the inclination to respond defensively when policymakers propose different approaches for early childhood education. Over and over we have seen that when we engage in open exploration and exchange of information, we learn from each other and make new advances on behalf of young children and their families.

— Bettye Caldwell

oughly debated and resolved with little expenditure of money or time. IRA leaders were a little shocked when we held an open hearing at NAEYC's conference and allowed all our vocal critics to speak loudly and passionately about the issues! As always, I believe that those events make for better work in the end. We devised the statement using the definition of developmentally appropriate practice as our basic framework. We incorporated a thorough review of the research and framed recommended practices by age groups. In our statement we conceptualized learning to read as a developmental continuum, and we gave examples of children's progressions along that continuum.

Just as adopted and we released our statement in 1998, the National Research Council (NRC) of the National Academy of Sciences issued its comprehensive review of research, *Preventing Reading Difficulties in Young Children* (Snow, Burns, & Griffin 1998). Our statement was entirely congruent with the findings and recommendations of NRC, increasing the credibility of our work as we tried to influence practitioners in our field directly. To further explicate the position statement, NAEYC published it as part of the book, *Learning to Read and Write: Developmentally Appropriate Practices for Young Children* (Neuman, Copple, & Bredekamp 2000) and developed a related parent brochure.

The work with IRA on early literacy provides a useful framework for expanding the concept of developmentally appropriate practice and also addressing the issue of curriculum. The principles of developmentally appropriate practice can be applied to any content area, but the research in that specific area must be used to inform the curriculum content. Fortunately, in the area of literacy, a great deal of research now exists to provide guidance for curriculum about appropriate outcomes and expectations for children of various ages as well as about effective teaching strategies.

A ripe area for similar work is mathematics. The National Council of Teachers of Mathematics (NCTM) recently revised their curriculum standards to include preschool for the first time, but they describe one set of outcomes for the grades from prekindergarten through second. NAEYC and NCTM are initiating an effort, similar to the one on literacy, to develop a joint position statement and resources to inform the mathematics curriculum in early childhood programs. Other curriculum areas will no doubt follow.

So, in many ways, Patty, we've come full circle. A hundred years ago, you resisted articulating a standard curriculum for kindergarten and now we face the question for preschool and earlier. The field of early childhood is rampant with standard-setting efforts from states, agencies, organizations, and Head Start, as well as NAEYC. Articulating learning goals or outcomes is no longer a possibility but a reality. For many years, I, like you, strongly resisted the outcomes movement. Having worked through the literacy statement and learned from current research, I now believe that early childhood educators have a responsibility to take the lead rather than deferring to others who know less about young children and how they learn.

Challenges ahead

As a dynamic profession and organization, we will continue to confront new challenges and revisit old ones. For this reason alone, I think it is critical that NAEYC members understand history. Most issues are not really new, but contexts and knowledge do change. We must heed Lois Meek's words from 1929 when she said we must not "become stereotyped or static" (NANE 1929).

NAEYC and the early childhood field will continue to confront the issue of curriculum content and specifying outcomes, not only for young children but in teacher preparation programs. As knowledge continues to expand rapidly, we have to solve the challenge of recruiting and retaining a qualified workforce. We have yet to figure out how to get preservice education for all early childhood teachers, and we face the formidable challenge of reeducating practitioners on the basis of new knowledge. The field and the Association will have to look to new technology to address this challenge, while also using its traditional means of connecting with members and leaders.

We are now just beginning the universal prekindergarten debates and strategies that will occupy us for many years to come. Patty, we know that you thought putting kindergarten in public school was a tragedy and we can guess your views on putting 3- and 4-year-olds there. Yet to achieve high-quality, developmentally appropriate early education for all children, public funding is essential. How and where children receive the services will be open to debate.

Many challenges face us in the future, as described in other chapters of this book. Fundamental, I believe, is the challenge of holding on to our core values for children and practice—the vital role of play, for instance—while expanding our vision of early childhood education to reflect new knowledge about children's learning potentials and competence.

References

Bouverat, R.W., & H.L. Galen, eds. 1994. *The Child Development Associate national program: The early years and pioneers.* Washington, DC: Council for Early Childhood Professional Recognition.

Bredekamp, S., ed. 1986. *Developmentally appropriate practice.* Washington, DC: NAEYC.

Bredekamp, S., ed. 1987. *Developmentally appropriate practice in early childhood programs serving children from birth through age 8,* Exp. ed. Washington, DC: NAEYC.

Bredekamp, S. 1992. Composing a profession. *Young Children* 47 (2): 52–54.

Bredekamp, S. 1997. National Institute for Early Childhood Professional Development. NAEYC issues revised position statement on developmentally appropriate practice in early childhood programs. *Young Children* 52 (2): 34–40.

Bredekamp, S. 1999. National Institute for Early Childhood Professional Development. When new solutions create new problems: Lessons learned from NAEYC accreditation. *Young Children* 54 (1): 58–63.

Bredekamp, S. 2000. CDA at 25: Reflections on the past and projections for the future. *Young Children* 55 (5): 15–19.

Bredekamp, S., & C. Copple, eds. 1997. *Developmentally appropriate practice in early childhood programs.* Rev. ed. Washington, DC: NAEYC.

Bredekamp, S., & S. Glowacki. 1996. The first decade of NAEYC accreditation: Growth and impact on the field. In *NAEYC accreditation: A decade of learning and the years ahead,* eds. S. Bredekamp & B.A. Willer, 1–10. Washington, DC: NAEYC.

Bredekamp, S., & T. Rosegrant, eds. 1992. *Reaching potentials: Appropriate curriculum and assessment for young children, volume 1.* Washington, DC: NAEYC.

Bredekamp, S., & T. Rosegrant, eds. 1995. *Reaching potentials: Transforming early childhood curriculum and assessment, volume 2.* Washington, DC: NAEYC.

Bredekamp, S., & B. Willer. 1992. Of ladders and lattices, cores and cones: Conceptualizing an early childhood professional development system. *Young Children* 47 (3): 47–50.

Hewes, D. 1976. Patty Smith Hill: Pioneer for young children. *Young Children* 31 (4): 297–306.

Hymes, J. 1955. *The child development point of view.* Upper Saddle River, NJ: Merrill/Prentice Hall.

Goffin, S.G. 2001. Accreditation Reinvention. Thinking about the priorities of NAEYC's accreditation system in the next era. *Young Children* 56 (1): 53.

McCarthy, J., J. Cruz Jr., & N. Ratcliff. 1999. *Early childhood teacher education licensure patterns: A state by state analysis.* Washington, DC: Council for Professional Recognition.

McGill-Franzen, A. 1993. *Shaping the preschool agenda: Early literacy, public policy, and professional beliefs.* Albany: State University of New York Press.

NAEYC. 1986. Position statement on developmentally appropriate practice in early childhood programs serving children from birth through age 8. *Young Children* 41 (6): 4–19.

NAEYC. 1987. NAEYC position statement on developmentally appropriate practice in early childhood programs serving children from birth through age 8. In *Developmentally Appropriate Practice in early childhood programs serving children from birth through age 8,* Exp. ed., ed. S. Bredekamp, 1–16. Washington, DC: Author.

NAEYC. 1988. NAEYC position statement on standardized testing of young children 3 through 8 years of age. *Young Children* 43 (3): 42–47.

NAEYC. 1991. Early childhood teacher certification. A position statement of the Association of

Teacher Educators and the National Association for the Education of Young Children. *Young Children* 47 (1): 16–21.

NAEYC. 1996a. *Guidelines for preparation of early childhood professionals: Guidelines developed by the National Association for the Education of Young Children (NAEYC) and the Division for Early Childhood of the Council for Exceptional Children (DEC/CEC) and by the National Board for Professional Teaching Standards (NBPTS)* Washington, DC: Author.

NAEYC. 1996b. NAEYC position statement: Responding to linguistic and cultural diversity—Recommendations for effective early childhood education. *Young Children* 52 (2): 4–12.

NAEYC. 1996c. NAEYC position statement. Technology and young children: Ages three through eight. *Young Children* 51 (6): 11–16.

NAEYC. 1997. NAEYC position statement. Developmentally appropriate practice in early childhood programs serving children from birth through age 8. In *Developmentally appropriate practice in early childhood programs,* Rev. ed., eds. S. Bredekamp & C. Copple, 3–30. Washington, DC: Author.

NAEYC & NAECS/SDE. 1992. Guidelines for appropriate curriculum content and assessment in programs serving children ages 3 through 8. A position statement of the National Association for the Education of young children and the National Association of Early Childhood Specialists in State Departments of Education. In *Reaching potentials: Appropriate curriculum and assessment for young children,* eds. S. Bredekamp & T. Rosegrant, 9–27. Washington, DC: NAEYC.

NANE. 1929. *Minimum essentials for nursery school education.* Chicago, IL: Author.

Neuman, S.B., C. Copple, & S. Bredekamp. 2000. *Learning to read and write: Developmentally appropriate practices for young children.* Washington, DC: NAEYC.

Snow, C.E., M.S. Burns, & P. Griffin, eds. 1998. *Preventing reading difficulties in young children: Committee on the Prevention of Reading Difficulties in Young Children, Commission on Behavioral and Social Sciences and Education, National Research Council.* Washington, DC: National Academy Press.

Snyder, A., for the Early Leaders in Childhood Education Committee of Association for Childhood Education International. 1972. *Dauntless women in childhood education 1856–1931.* Washington, DC: Association for Childhood Education International.

Spodek, B. 1991. Early childhood curriculum and cultural definitions of knowledge. In *Issues in early childhood curriculum,* eds. B. Spodek & O. Saracho, 1–20. New York: Teachers College Press.

Stolz, L.H.M. 1977. An American child development pioneer: Lois Hayden Meek Stolz. Interview by R. Takanishi. Typescript. Washington, DC: National Archives. (Oral history supported by grants from the National Academy of Education, the UCLA Academic Senate Research Committee, and the William T. Grant Foundation.)

Willer, B., ed. 1994. A conceptual framework for early childhood professional development: NAEYC Position Statement. In *The early childhood career lattice: Perspectives on professional development,* eds. J. Johnson & J.B. McCracken, 4–23. Washington, DC: NAEYC.

Wright, J.L., & D. Shade, eds. 1994. *Young children: Active learners in a technological age.* Washington, DC: NAEYC.

Information exchange among early childhood professionals

Information exchange among early childhood professionals is essential to improving practice and quality in programs serving young children. This exchange involves

• posing questions and challenges to delineate key issues and priorities for further work;

• reviewing and debating the results of research as well as testing ideas for the development of standards, guidelines, and principles of best practice; and

• promulgating these ideas and promoting the integration of these concepts into actual practice.

A primary role of any professional association is to facilitate these essential processes of information exchange. Throughout NAEYC's 75-year history, two forms of communication have supported this sharing of knowledge—the exchange of ideas through print in publications and the exchange of ideas in person through conferences.

PUBLICATIONS—EARLY CHILDHOOD PROFESSIONALS CONNECTING THROUGH PRINT

The book, journal, and brochure covers on these pages portray only a sampling of the many published resources NAEYC has produced over the last 75 years.

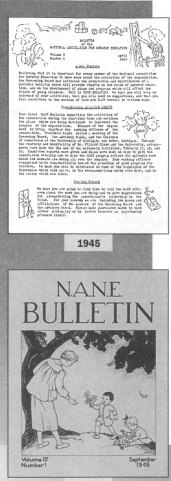

1945

1948

Since the early days of the Association, members have been linked by regular communication in print. First, a mimeographed *Bulletin of N.A.N.E.* sustained communication among members in 1945 when civilian travel was curtailed during World War II. This embryonic publication evolved into the *N.A.N.E. Bulletin* in 1948, issued four times a year. Eight years later (1956) the name changed to *The Journal of Nursery Education* and in 1964 when NANE became NAEYC, *Young Children* was introduced with an updated format and issued six times per year. After 20 years of the familiar black and white cover, *Young Children* converted to color in 1984. In 2001, color and graphic images are extensively used throughout. From the very beginning, the contents of the journal have been a mix of articles and columns addressing professional practice, research, and legislation, and Association business. The journal has consistently been comprehensive in content and purposeful in providing something of interest to all the numerous audiences working with and for young children.

For its first 20 years, the journal was created by volunteer editors and editorial committees. The editors during that time were Theo Reeve (1946–1948), Viola Theman (1948–1952), Docia Zavitkovsky (1952–1961), and Cornelia (Nell) Goldsmith (1962–1964). Elizabeth Vernon served as *Young Children* editor from 1965 to 1967, and was succeeded by Laura Dittmann. Editors over the past thirty years include: Georgianna Engstrom (1970–1976), Janet Brown McCracken (1976–1986), and Polly Greenberg (1986–2001).

2001

1956

1964

1984

NAEYC's research journal, *Early Childhood Research Quarterly,* launched in 1985, plays a vital role in stimulating improvements in professional practice and the quality of services to young children. The Quarterly encourages, recognizes, and publishes scholarly research that enables early childhood professionals to stay informed about high-quality studies and findings and their implications for practice. Four editors have guided this important contribution to early childhood education research: Lilian Katz, Doug Powell, Marilou Hyson, and Karen Diamond.

Throughout its 75-year history, NAEYC has published books and brochures to provide the field with current information on the wide variety of issues that have an impact on the quality of early childhood education. NAEYC's hundreds of titles have served to create a deeper understanding of the knowledge, skills, and dispositions required to engage in informed professional practice. For many years these publications were developed under the direction of the same individuals who served as journal editors. Then in 1993 Carol Copple was appointed to the new position of publications editor.

In recent years NAEYC has entered a new era in promoting information exchange—a Website that in 2001 was averaging four million hits a month.

Conferences—Early Childhood Professionals Connecting in Person

Conferences have been a consistent and effective means of enabling early childhood professionals to connect with one another and exchange information and viewpoints. The first conference in 1926 included 17 speakers presenting in plenary sessions, and today's conferences involve more than 1,200 presenters in close to 1,000 sessions. Yet a similar culture has characterized NAEYC conferences throughout its 75 years—a culture that fosters open exchange, debate, and dialogue among early childhood professionals. This culture is based on the develop-mental concept of the importance of active participation if growth in understanding is to occur. Also reflecting this culture and philosophy are the countless submeetings, informal gatherings, and conferring-over-coffee exchanges that take place in the course of the conferences. NAEYC staff and leaders do not organize these meetings, but they value them as a vital part of the conference's function and success. All these aspects help to make the Annual Conference the true meeting place for the entire early childhood field.

The success of these conferences as meaningful professional growth opportuni-

1951 BIENNIAL CONFERENCE
NATIONAL ASSOCIATION FOR NURSERY EDUCATION
HOTEL COMMODORE MARCH 10, 1951

ties is portrayed in the often-told stories of "my first conference" or "my most memorable conference." Another frequent response to NAEYC's conferences is the powerful affirmation experienced by conferees that comes from the energy of thousands of coprofessionals sharing the commitment to improve the lives of young children and their families. To assist each person in recalling his or her own personal memories from conferences past, every national NAEYC Annual Conference is listed by year and location on pages 122–124. Names of keynote speakers are included.

These stimulating conference experiences are not restricted to those who can travel to the national conference. NAEYC's local, state, and regional Affiliate Groups sponsor rich conference offerings, and these opportunities have become so widespread that few participants in the field would find it difficult to have a conference experience.

A new conference opportunity was launched in 1992—NAEYC's National Institute for Early Childhood Professional Development. This annual institute, offered each June, is a collaborative experience designed around the premise of mutual support and learning. The format facilitates joint work and exchange among early childhood educators who teach and support current and future early childhood professionals.

> The most memorable conference for me was the national conference that was held in Washington, D.C., in the 1990s. This was my first national conference, and it was extraordinary. I went as a parent volunteer, but after the conference I knew I wanted to spend the rest of my life working in child care; I'm now a director.
>
> — Sheila James

> [Working] in Wyoming, I never expected that my staff could afford to attend any NAEYC national conference because of the distance. But Denver was chosen as the host city in 1991, and our entire staff of teachers from Casper College slept in two rooms. The conference proved to be an event that provided the staff with a deeper appreciation for the commitment and responsibility they exhibited daily in their interactions with children.
>
> — Wilma Reever

Conference of Nursery Schools

Friday, February Twenty-Sixth
Saturday, February Twenty-Seventh
1 9 2 6

The Sun Room
Washington Hotel
Washington, D. C.

Washington, DC—1926

> In close to 30 years, I have never missed an annual NAEYC meeting and every year I experience some uncertainty about what will have changed, what will be the same, and what I think should change. But year after year I reconnect with that very special spirit that brings NAEYC members together to strive for what is best for children and am convinced once again that this organization is for me.
>
> — Ellen Galinsky

> At my first NAEYC conference in 1971 (Minneapolis), I observed that the sessions focused on what we as professionals could do for others and I noticed an uncompromising passion and commitment to making this a better world for children and families. I noted that there was a place for me to be part of a movement that would eventually pay enormous benefits to the rest of the country. The passion and commitment were contagious.
>
> — Josué Cruz Jr.

EDUCATING YOUNG CHILDREN — MORE THAN LOVE

NAEYC Annual Conference
Chicago, Illinois
November 10-13, 1977

Chicago, IL—1977

NAEYC'S ANNUAL CONFERENCES

Listed by date, location, and keynote speakers

February 1926 — Washington, DC
Arnold Gesell and Bird Baldwin

April 1927 — New York, NY
Patty Smith Hill

October 1929 — Chicago, IL
Goodwin E. Watson and John E. Anderson

November 1931 — Philadelphia, PA
John E. Anderson and William H. Kilpatrick

October 1933 — Toronto, Canada
E.A. Bott and George Stoddard

October 1935 — St. Louis, MO
Mary Dabney Davis

October 1937 — Nashville, TN
Maurice F. Seay, Lawrence K. Frank,
and O.C. Carmichael

1939 — New York, NY

October 1941 — Detroit, MI
Grace Langdon

October 1943 — Boston, MA

WORLD WAR II — TRAVEL CURTAILMENT

August 1947 — San Francisco, CA
James L. Hymes Jr., Ruth Benedict,
Erik H. Erikson, and Ernest Osborne

October 1948 — Chicago, IL
Roma Gans, W. Carson Ryan,
and Herold Hunt

March 1951 — New York, NY
Earl T. McGrath, Lawrence K. Frank,
Ira DeA Reid, and James L. Hymes Jr.

October 1953 — Minneapolis, MN
Frances Horwich

October 1955 — Boston, MA
James Marvin Baty and James L. Hymes Jr.

October 1957 — Cincinnati, OH
Ralph D. Rabinovitch and Otto Kleinberg

June 1959 — Los Angeles, CA
Abraham Kaplan and James D. Finn

October 1961 — St. Louis, MO
Donald Brieland and Glenn R. Hawkes

October 1962 — Philadelphia, PA
John Niemeyer and Lois Hayden Meek Stolz

October 1964 — Miami, FL
Paul L. Adams and Cornelia Goldsmith

November 1966 — Chicago, IL
Warner Bloomberg Jr., Ralph Ekstein,
John H. Niemeyer, and Mary Lane

November 1967 — San Francisco, CA
Arthur W. Combs and Melvin Tuman

November 1968 — New York, NY
Jerome Kagan and Barbara Biber

November 1969 — Salt Lake City, UT
Douglas H. Heath, Ogden R. Lindsley,
and Leland B. Jacobs

November 1970 — Boston, MA
Urie Bronfenbrenner and Edward F. Zigler

November 1971 — Minneapolis, MN
Herbert Kohl, Frederick C. Green,
and Walter F. Mondale

November 1972 — Atlanta, GA
Allee Mitchell and Margaret Mead

November 1973 — Seattle, WA
Marian Wright Edelman, Bettye M. Caldwell,
George Blue Spruce Jr., Donald Merle Baer,
and Robert Mondragon

November 1974 — Washington, DC
Jerome Kagan, T. Berry Brazelton,
Frederick C. Green, John H. Meier,
Constance Kamii, James P. Comer,
and Burton L. White

November 1975 — Dallas, TX
Edward F. Zigler, Florence Stroud,
George A. Gonzalez, William G. Demment Jr.,
E. James Anthony, Bettye M. Caldwell,
and Daniel C. Jordan

November 1976 — Anaheim, CA
John L. Goodlad, Lois Hayden Meek Stolz,
Ella Jenkins, Alfredo Castanedo,
Manuel Ramirez III,
and Mollie and Russell Smart

November 1977 — Chicago, IL
Barbara Biber, Blandina Cardenas,
T. Berry Brazelton,
and Marian Wright Edelman

August 1978 — New York, NY
Marian Wright Edelman, Laura Nadar,
A. Sidney Johnson III, Walter R. Allen,
Nancy J. Amidei, and Nicholas Hobbs

November 1979 — Atlanta, GA
Bettye M. Caldwell, Lilian G. Katz,
and A. Eugene Howard

November 1980 — San Francisco, CA
Wilson Riles, David Elkind, Constance
Kamii, and Glen Nimnicht

November 1981 — Detroit, MI
A. Eugene Howard, William J. Raspberry,
Sara Lightfoot, and Burton L. White

November 1982 — Washington, DC
Bettye M. Caldwell, Sheldon H. White,
Bob Keeshan, and Marian Wright Edelman

November 1983 — Atlanta, GA
Walter F. Mondale, Fred Rogers,
Asa G. Hilliard III, and Bettye M. Caldwell

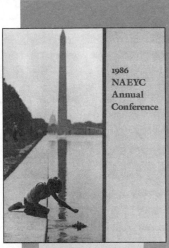

1986
NAEYC
Annual
Conference

Washington, DC—1986

*My most memorable
conference was the year
of the debate between
Bettye Caldwell and
Burton White on child
care for very young
children! The air was
charged [by] the presence
of two people who have
spent their lives caring
about children and
families modeling how
honest disagreement well
delivered strengthens both
the early childhood field
and the organization.*

— Edna Ranck

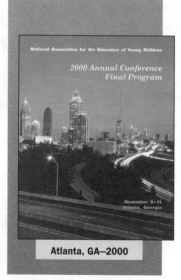

Atlanta, GA—2000

November 1984 — Los Angeles, CA
Patricia Russell McCloud, David A. Hamburg, Dwight Allen, and Docia Zavitkovsky

November 1985 — New Orleans, LA
Bettye M. Caldwell, Burton L. White, Ella Jenkins, Harold Raynolds Jr., and Eileen W. Lindner

November 1986 — Washington, DC
T. Berry Brazelton and Marilyn M. Smith

November 1987 — Chicago, IL
Patricia Russell McCloud, Constance Kamii, and David Elkind

November 1988 — Anaheim, CA
David P. Weikart and Ellen Galinsky

November 1989 — Atlanta, GA
James P. Comer, Bernice Weissbourd, and Ellen Galinsky

November 1990 — Washington, DC
Celebration with Congressional speakers at U.S. Capitol and Marian Wright Edelman

November 1991 — Denver, CO
Roy Romer and Lana Hostetler

November 1992 — New Orleans, LA
Ernest L. Boyer and Lilian G. Katz

November 1993 — Anaheim, CA
Fred Rogers and Jerry Tello

November 1994 — Atlanta, GA
Geoffrey Canada

November 1995 — Washington, DC
Shari Lewis and Jerlean Daniel

November 1996 — Dallas, TX
Richard Weissbourd, Jonah Edelman, Valerie B. Jarrett, and David Elkind

November 1997 — Anaheim, CA
Rob Reiner and Geoffrey Canada

November 1998 — Toronto, Canada
Fred Rogers and Marilyn M. Smith

November 1999 — New Orleans, LA
Patricia Montoya, James P. Comer, Edward F. Zigler, and Sharon Lynn Kagan

November 2000 — Atlanta, GA
Benjamin S. Carson Sr., M.D., Kathy R. Thornburg and panelists Roger Brown, Josué Cruz Jr., Ron Herndon, and Evelyn Moore

Chapter 5

Advocating for Young Children and the Early Childhood Profession

A Letter to Jimmy Hymes

Barbara Willer

Writing a chapter on NAEYC's policy and advocacy efforts of the last quarter century seemed a daunting task. But conceptualizing the chapter as a letter helped me a lot. I chose to write to Jimmy Hymes because his life so embodied what I believe is the central tenet of membership in NAEYC—a commitment to advocate for young children and early childhood professionals based on sound principles of child development and early childhood education.

Active in NAEYC throughout his professional life, James L. Hymes Jr. served as NANE president at a critical juncture in the Association's history (1945–1947). His leadership helped the organization resume its activities after many had been curtailed due to World War II. During the war, Jimmy had directed two Kaiser Shipyards Child Services Centers in Portland, Oregon. Perhaps it was because of this experience that Jimmy so clearly understood the relationship between public policy and programs for children. Later in his career while at the University of Maryland's Institute of Child Study, he served as a member of the National Planning Committee for Head Start.

Not only did Jimmy work diligently to advocate for stronger policies and funding to support services to children and families, he also worked tirelessly to inform others of issues and encouraged them to advocate on behalf of children. His *Notes for Parents* newsletters, sold to kindergartens and preschool programs for distribution to families, informed parents about basic principles of child development and learning. Writing for parents and the popular press was not Jimmy's original forte, but according to his wife Lucia, he consciously worked to develop a "popular" writing style because he felt that reaching parents was so crucial to informing their childrearing practices and to building support for good programs. For 20 years, he also wrote and published an annual year in review summarizing key events in early childhood education. NAEYC published the entire collection as a single volume in 1991 (Hymes 1991).

A personal anecdote may best capture Jimmy's lifelong devotion to policy and advocacy issues. Not long before his death in 1998, I received a telephone call from Jimmy asking for current information about funding levels for Head Start, the number of children served, and the status of the appropriations request in that year's budget battle. Jimmy was preparing a talk for others in his retirement community, and he wanted the current figures so that he could encourage his audience to call Congress in support of the program.

Dear Jimmy Hymes,

In 1991 you looked back over 20 years of history in early childhood education and identified three key trends that had most affected the social and political context of early childhood education: "the flooding of women into the labor market," "the breathtaking rise in enrollments in early childhood groups," and "the almost unanimous support for the *idea* of early education from the widest variety of foundations, influential public organizations, and educational associations." In the 20 years between 1970 and 1990, "the field of early childhood moved from the fringes of the educational 'establishment' to center stage" (Hymes 1991, 1, 2).

A look at current statistics underscores the importance of the trends that you identified. According to U.S. Census figures in 1970, just 30% of married mothers of children younger than age 6 were in the labor force, and roughly 10% of 3- and 4-year-olds attended a preschool program. Figures released in 2001 show that over two-thirds of mothers of young children are in the labor force, while more than half of 3- and 4-year-olds attend a group program in a preschool or child care center (U.S. Bureau of the Census 2001). Kindergarten atten-

dance has become nearly universal, and four out of five young children have attended preschool prior to attending kindergarten. Recognition of the importance of children's early years continues to grow, bolstered by well-publicized findings about the importance of early experiences to brain development. In the 2000 presidential campaign, both candidates stressed, albeit in different ways, increased attention to the early years and programs that support early learning. Similarly, at both the state and federal levels, bipartisan interest in early childhood programs has been increasingly evident.

Yet for all these trends, the United States still lacks a comprehensive *system* of services to ensure that all young children receive the high quality of programs they need and deserve. Certainly, major gains have been accomplished, with significant new investments by federal and state government as well as increased private sector support. But too many children remain in programs that fall short of the quality care and education that we know how to provide, with teachers continuing to work for low pay and inadequate benefits far below the value of their work.

The pattern of federal investments in programs for young children is illustrative. It took nearly 20 years after the 1971 presidential veto of the Comprehensive Child Development Act for Congress to enact a federal program solely focused on child care, the Child Care and Development Block Grant (CCDBG), established in 1990. CCDBG provides funds to states primarily to assist families with low incomes with their child care costs. Initially 25% of the CCDBG funds were reserved for after-school or early childhood development programs and for quality improvement efforts. Also in 1990, a parallel program was created to assist families with child care costs who were transitioning from welfare or in danger of becoming welfare dependent. This program had no funds earmarked for quality improvements. The two programs were later combined as part of the welfare reform legislation enacted in 1996, with a minimum of 4% of the total funds targeted to improve quality.

Despite the welcome infusion of new funds for child care assistance since 1990, available funds fall far short of need. It is estimated that only about 10% of eligible children are served through the CCDBG. Moreover, the majority of funds are targeted to families to assist with child care costs. Despite the high proportion of family income that child care costs represent, the amount does not reflect the costs of program provision that include equitably compensated staff. As a result, too little improvement has been made to the quality of services overall. States have developed creative approaches to use their quality improvement funds, but the meager 4% set-aside falls far short of what is needed to make systemic improvements.

Jimmy, you would be happy to learn that Head Start has enjoyed strong bipartisan support in recent years. And Early Head Start, created in 1994 to extend the lessons learned from Head Start to services for families with infants and toddlers continues to grow. Still, as you lamented many times over the years, we do not invest enough to ensure the promise of Head Start; funding is insufficient to promote program quality and to reach all eligible children.

In addition to gains at the federal level, many states have increased their investments in services for young children and their families. Forty-three states invest state dollars—a total of $2.1 billion in FY 2000—in prekindergarten programs for children ages 3 to 6, and 31 states invest state funds ($226 million in FY 2000) for child development and family support programs for infants and toddlers (Cauthen, Knitzer, & Ripple 2000). Increasingly, programs at federal and state levels are blurring the artificial distinctions between child care and preschool, recognizing that teaching and learning can—and must—occur in a variety of caring settings and that programs must attend not only to children's needs but also to families' needs.

We've made great strides over the last quarter century in providing services for children with disabilities, beginning with the enactment of P.L. 94-142 in 1974, which ensured "a free and appropriate public education in the least restrictive environment" for children in K–12. These rights were extended to children birth through age 5 with the creation of the Part B and Part H provisions of the Education for Handicapped Children in 1978 that later became IDEA (Individuals with Disabilities Education Act). Over time, the focus of the legislation has changed from identifying needs of individual children to providing supports for inclusive programs that serve children with and without disabilities, resulting in stronger ties between the general early childhood and the early childhood special education communities.

In the educational arena, concerns about children's academic achievement and national competitiveness have resulted in standards-driven assessment systems, often with high stakes for teachers, schools, and children. Of course, the move to standards-driven approaches can be good, *if* the standards reflect current knowledge about child development and learning, *if* the assessments are valid and reliable measures for individual children, and *if* the appropriate investments are made to ensure sufficient numbers of qualified teachers. Your 1991 prediction that "concern about adult-dominated, too bookish, and overly large groups for 5s and 6s will go on and on. It has for decades. And now we will have another age to try to protect 4s, doing all we can to ensure that they get a decent break in their school groups" will strike a chord with many readers (Hymes 1991, 13).

Jimmy, you always considered the childhood poverty rate in your reports, noting its shamefulness in this bountiful nation. The good news is that the poverty rate is at its lowest since the early 1970s. The bad news is that one in six American children younger than age 6 still live in poverty. This issue is especially important given the sweeping welfare reform measures enacted in the mid-1990s, because the reforms, although recognizing the need for child care assistance for family members seeking or maintaining employment, capped the length of time that individuals—including children—could receive welfare benefits.

Early childhood professionals influence agendas that are not only right for young children—they are right for the culture and society as a whole. This is what makes us 'kindred spirits' because we sit with the future of humanity on our laps and in our embrace.

— Susan Andersen

So, to sum up this quick overview of some of the key policy issues affecting young children and early childhood education over the last quarter century, although significant advances have been made, much more remains to be accomplished before all young children can enjoy the best possible start in life. The question is, what role did NAEYC play in these policy events, and how has the organization's involvement in policy and advocacy changed over the years?

Growing numbers, growing influence

Jimmy, I think that you would agree that one trend is clearly evident in NAEYC's involvement in policy and advocacy. A core cadre of leaders and members have always cared deeply about policy issues and have actively advocated on behalf of young children, families, and early childhood programs. But the Association's policy involvement and influence has directly paralleled its growth in membership size and the staff resources dedicated to policy and advocacy issues.

NAEYC's leaders have been concerned about shaping policies and attitudes to improve the quality of programs for children from day one; in fact a legislative report that included guidelines to assess state legislation

was among the initial committee reports by the group that became NANE. The *NANE Bulletin* and *The Journal of Nursery Education,* precursors to *Young Children,* regularly included public policy information and encouraged members to take action. Yet despite the active involvement and interest of Association leaders, as Dorothy Hewes noted in her article on NAEYC's first 50 years, "attempts [in the 1950s] to arouse membership involvement [in public policy] seem to have been futile" (see "NAEYC's First Half Century: 1926–1976," p. 35).

Still, Jimmy, your persistence and that of other NANE leaders in pursuing policy issues paid off. NANE was invited to send representatives from the organization to the White House Conferences on Children in 1960 and 1970. You'll likely recall that Marilyn M. Smith, who later became NAEYC's executive director for nearly 30 years, was among the six NANE representatives attending the 1960 conference.

You'll also recall that NAEYC's establish-ment of a Washington, D.C., office coincided with the birth of Head Start in the mid-1960s. No other federal program has made as great an impact on the early childhood field as Head Start has through its provision of services for young children and families and training resources. The program

Report to the President

White House Conference on Children

White House Conference on Children 1970, Washington, D.C.

has greatly increased public recognition of the importance of early childhood education. It's not coincidental that the mid-1960s was when NAEYC really began to grow, from fewer than 2,000 members in 1964 to nearly 20,000 by 1970. Many of our field's most esteemed current leaders began their professional careers working with Head Start in its earliest days, for example, by developing and providing training to launch the original summer program. Today, Head Start continues to support the development of new professionals many of whom in turn have become active and committed leaders with NAEYC at the local, state, and national levels.

Although no staff position primarily devoted to policy and advocacy existed at the time, NAEYC staff actively participated in the coalition of organizations that worked on comprehensive child development legislation in the late 1960s and early 1970s. NAEYC also provided important leadership to the consortium of child-related organizations that developed the Child Development Associate credential in 1972. With the founding of the Children's Defense Fund and National Black Child Development Institute in the early 1970s, strong collaborative relationships for policy and advocacy were forged that continue to this day.

Interest within the Association regarding policy issues increased throughout the late 1970s. This is not surprising given that public policies to adequately fund child care and preschool programs and to assure their quality had not kept pace with the rapid increase in enrollments. At the same time, NAEYC membership reached 33,000 by 1980, expanding the pool of advocates with the Association. It was about this time (late 1970s) that the NAEYC Governing Board established a Public Policy Committee to formally address policy issues. One of the committee's earliest concerns was building NAEYC's advocacy capacity. In the early 1980s, NAEYC sought and was awarded a grant from the Foundation for Child Development to fund four three-month graduate internships at the NAEYC staff headquarters. This milestone is especially important to me as I was one of these interns. I spent the summer of 1983 building the NAEYC Action Network for Children, the first of our computerized rosters to identify members and other advocates by Congressional district in order to distribute Action Alerts and generate letters or calls to members of Congress or the Administration in response to breaking policy issues.

The early 1980s also marked the beginning of NAEYC's development of formal

NAEYC is a major advocate for the importance of the early years to children's development. NAEYC helps members connect with peers in advocating for children at the national and local levels, and it partners with other organizations to influence the development of more programs that support quality of life for young children and their families.

— Rosalind Charlesworth

position statements on policy and professional practice issues, including statements on licensing and regulation of child care centers (adopted 1983; see NAEYC 1984a) and of family child care homes (adopted 1984; see NAEYC 1984b) (later combined into one statement on regulation [adopted 1987; see NAEYC 1987c]), the care of infants and toddlers, and teacher preparation guidelines. Basic teacher preparation guidelines were approved by the Governing Board in 1981 and published and approved by the National Council for the Accreditation of Teacher Education (NCATE) in 1982.

NAEYC decided to create statements on licensing for two principal reasons: the rapidly growing number of children in child care settings and the federal policy decision to drop proposed Federal Interagency Day Care Requirements (FIDCR), which left regulation of child care facilities to state discretion, often meaning very minimal standards reflecting custodial care.

These two factors also fueled the development of NAEYC's accreditation system in the early 1980s. In addition, the Association received a grant at this time from the Carnegie Corporation of New York to develop a Child Care Information Service (CCIS). This initiative was designed to complement the National Academy of Early Childhood Programs' accreditation system by creating mechanisms to generate public awareness and support for quality and was linked closely to the Association's public policy and advocacy work. Although no longer called CCIS, this initiative laid the foundation for NAEYC's communications and public outreach activities that continue to grow today.

By 1985 membership had reached 47,000. That year, the first staff position was created in which responsibility for public policy was included in the job title—Director of Affiliate Groups and Public Policy. The combined responsibilities reflected the Association's commitment to working with the network of AEYC Affiliate Groups as the primary means of building grassroots support for policy and advocacy as well as recognition of the importance of the Affiliates' role in influencing state and local policies.

The mid-1980s were characterized not only by the beginning of NAEYC's accreditation system, but also by growing concerns about inappropriate curriculum and teaching practices with young children, especially in kindergarten and prekindergarten programs. The initial position statement on developmentally appropriate practice focused solely on 4- and 5-year-olds and was followed by the statement addressing the birth to 8 age range in 1987; both were adopted in 1986 (see NAEYC 1986 and NAEYC 1987a). These statements were released using a carefully designed media strategy, generating considerable visibility for the Association's efforts. Although these statements were more closely identified with efforts to improve professional practice than public policy, they were instrumental as tools for advocates to use in local, state, and federal policy initiatives.

In the mid- to late 1980s, a coalition spearheaded by the Children's Defense Fund, with NAEYC in a critical supporting role, began organizing in support of the Act for Better Child Care. As interest in a federal bill grew, and concerns increased about the child care crisis caused by inadequate compensation, activist members and leaders urged greater visibility of policy and advocacy within the Association's budget and programs; this led to the creation of the Public Affairs Division in 1989. Designed to focus on policy and media issues, primarily at the federal level, the program had a staff of two, although responsibilities were shared across several departments, including Information Services and Membership/Affiliates, with the active involvement of other senior staff.

With its membership reaching 74,000, NAEYC celebrated passage of the Child Care and Development Block Grant and other significant legislation affecting children and early childhood programs in 1990 by holding the opening session of its Annual Conference on the steps of the U.S. Capitol. NAEYC used the occasion to launch its Reaching the Full Cost of Quality Campaign to stress the difference between the price that parents pay for child care and the costs of program provision when standards of quality, including standards for compensation and benefits, are met.

Compensation issues caused a constant struggle within the Association in the late 1980s. In fact, *Reaching the Full Cost of Quality* and the compensation guidelines it included marked a second round of position statements on the issue (Willer 1990). The initial position statement adopted in 1987 addressed quality, compensation, and affordability (NAEYC 1987b). Acknowledging the "trilemma" among quality, compensation, and affordability and urging solutions to improve all three components presented a difficult challenge in consensus building. No one disputed the inadequacy of compensation or NAEYC's focus on program quality for children. The debate was whether a focus on compensation could jeopardize program quality if parents could no longer afford programs or if *not* focusing on compensation would jeopardize program

To have good environments for children we have to have good environments for those who work with them. NAEYC has worked at that, and must continue to do so.

— Lilian Katz

quality because without good teachers there could be no quality.

NAEYC's decision to collaborate with the Administration for Children, Youth and Families in the U.S. Department of Health and Human Services to support the National Child Care Survey in the mid-1980s grew out of the perceived need for data on all aspects of program provision—including compensation—to inform public policy and advocacy efforts. Designed to complement the U.S. Department of Education's Profile of Child Care Settings, the National Child Care Survey provided the first nationally representative data from the perspective of parents for all types of early childhood settings. Together the studies provided national data regarding early childhood program costs, staff qualifications and personal characteristics, and salaries and benefits. A joint executive summary of the two reports was issued by NAEYC in 1991.

As the Association struggled with the compensation issue and ways to address it, concerns were also growing about school readiness and curriculum and assessment issues. In 1989 the nation's governors and then-President George H. Bush held an Education Summit and adopted a series of national education goals, the first of which focused on making sure that all children entered school ready to learn by the year 2000. NAEYC testified before the National Education Goals Panel, which was charged with developing plans for implementing the goals. The testimony, which formed the basis for NAEYC's original statement on school readiness (adopted 1990; see NAEYC 1990b), reflected a developmental perspective. School readiness should be a two-way street in which schools shape curriculum and teaching that correspond to children's skills and abilities. Too often, there was no such match because school's expectations were not appropriate for young children.

The push to require greater accountability for student achievement caused NAEYC to express concerns similar to those raised by the effort to promote school readiness. NAEYC adopted a position statement on standardized testing that called for a ban on standardized achievement tests prior to third grade (adopted 1987; see NAEYC 1988). NAEYC's position was upheld in the redesign, in the early 1990s, of Chapter I of the Elementary and Secondary Education Act, the largest source of federal support for education. The standardized testing statement, the position statement on appropriate curriculum and assessment strategies jointly adopted by NAEYC and the National

Association of Early Childhood Specialists in State Departments of Education (adopted 1990; see NAEYC & NAECS/SDE 1992), and the statement on developmentally appropriate practice (NAEYC 1987b) were influential in guiding policy decisions in local, state, and federal education legislation.

In the debates on both school readiness and testing, NAEYC did not object to the presumed goal—improving student success—but rather the strategy of using narrowly prescriptive approaches that fail to recognize individual differences in development and learning, that employ measures that are not valid or reliable for specific groups of children, or that base high-stakes decisions on limited and possibly inaccurate information.

By the mid 1990s, NAEYC's membership was approaching 100,000. At the same time, a major change was occurring in federal policy: federal responsibility in many areas was shifted to the states. Perhaps nowhere was this trend more visible than in the debate over welfare reform. NAEYC developed two separate positions on welfare reform—one applicable to the debate at the federal level (approved 1993; see NAEYC 1999b) and the second to guide state implementation activities (adopted in 1996; see NAEYC 1997b). As in previous legislative battles related to child care, NAEYC actively collaborated with a wide variety of organizations. As enacted, welfare reform (the Personal Responsibility and Work Opportunities Act) included major trade-offs. It allowed states to significantly increase investments for child care assistance, but also imposed lifetime limits for welfare dependency and permitted states to require mothers of infants to work in order to receive benefits.

Other issues came to the fore in the early to mid-1990s, all with policy implications. NAEYC developed position statements on media violence (adopted 1990; see NAEYC 1990a), cultural and linguistic diversity (adopted 1995; see NAEYC 1996), a conceptual framework for early childhood professional development (adopted 1993; see NAEYC 1994), and prevention of child abuse (adopted 1996; see NAEYC 1997c). It revised its statements on developmentally appropriate practice (see NAEYC 1997a), licensing and regulation (adopted 1997; see NAEYC 1998), and quality, compensation, and affordability (adopted 1995; see NAEYC 1995) to reflect new understandings of key issues and to clarify misconceptions.

A major change occurred for NAEYC in 1999 as the executive staff team of Marilyn

Smith and J.D. Andrews left after some 30 years of service, and Mark Ginsberg was named NAEYC's new executive director. Consistent with the desires of the NAEYC Governing Board, Mark was committed to increasing NAEYC's policy and advocacy capacity. A new division for public policy and communications was established, with specialized staff positions for communications, federal policy, and state policy. The creation of this division greatly expanded the Association's capacity—as a group of individual members who share common concerns and as an organization— to influence policy and public awareness of the importance of early childhood issues.

Throughout the transition in leadership, attention to key policy issues continued uninterrupted. For example, continuing concern about violence in the lives of young children led NAEYC to collaborate with the American Psychological Association and the Ad Council on ACT—Adults and Children Together— Against Violence. This national public service campaign (see Anderson 2001) stresses the message that violence is learned at an early age and that as adults we must carefully consider the lessons that our words and actions teach children. After several

NAEYC was everything I believed in. It embodied my commitment for service. Moreover it provided an opportunity for me to lead my affiliates toward those goals.

— Margaret Roth

years of development, this campaign was officially launched in spring 2001.

Another issue that spanned the transition was early literacy. Working with the International Reading Association (IRA), NAEYC adopted a position statement on learning to read and write in 1998 (see IRA and NAEYC 2000). This influential document has not only helped to change professional practice but is referred to frequently in federal and state policy discussions. Ensuring that all children successfully learn to read is a high priority of the presidential administration of George W. Bush, so attention to this issue is likely to remain high on the policy agenda for several years.

Finally, NAEYC began the new millennium by launching a restructuring initiative designed to build our capacity at the local, state, and national levels. A primary goal of the restructuring is to build states' capacities to work effectively on policy and advocacy issues as more and more decisions about child and family policy are determined at the state level. An expanded staff team with expertise in organizational development issues, policy and legislation, advocacy and communications is positioned to support the capacity building efforts, which are already showing signs of promise. NAEYC also adopted a legislative and policy agenda, based on the Association's existing position statements, but tailored for legislative action. This step marked an important evolution in our ability to proactively influence policy rather than primarily react to policy developments. Taken together, the increased capacity and formal legislative and policy agenda suggest even greater possibilities for further expansion of NAEYC's policy role in the years ahead.

Core values in NAEYC's policy and advocacy work

Jimmy, as I reflect on my years with NAEYC and your years before me, three characteristics of our policy and advocacy work stand out: the commitment to (1) take principled stands reflecting knowledge of child development and learning that respect and value every child; (2) provide tools and information that help members assess legislation and other policies and encourage them to take action on behalf of young children and early childhood programs; and (3) recognize the varied skills and resources that different individuals and groups can bring to an issue and to encourage collaborative efforts that build upon all of these strengths.

TAKING PRINCIPLED STANDS THAT REFLECT CHILD DEVELOPMENT KNOWLEDGE AND RESPECT EVERY CHILD

From its first publication as NANE in 1929, *Minimum Essentials for Nursery School Education,* through the continuing refinement of its accreditation system, NAEYC has been known and respected as a voice to improve the quality of programs for young children. At the heart of its policy and advocacy efforts are position statements or reports adopted to reflect our best professional knowledge of research and practice. Many think of NAEYC's position statements primarily in terms of their impact on professional practice, but they have had a profound impact on policy developments as well.

A good example of how NAEYC position statements can affect legislative policy is the 1989 passage of the Military Child Care Act. This bill was enacted with little fanfare, as it occurred at a time when federal child care bills were stalled. NAEYC provided guidance in the drafting of the bill so that a requirement was included for all military programs to achieve accreditation by a "nationally recognized accrediting body." This legislation became a potent force when combined with a committed military leadership,

NAEYC has been a consistent voice that has put children first in its recommendations regarding practice, regulations, and policies. It is our responsibility as NAEYC members to practice this principle of giving priority to the well-being of all children. Far too often the well-being of children gets lost as adults vie for economic, social, and political control in the complex morass of overlapping systems in which we do our work.

—Jerlean Daniel

ensuring a systemic approach to quality improvements. A comprehensive training system for program staff was linked to a compensation system that provided for salaries and benefits comparable to other positions within the military structure, and a commitment was made to ensure adequate funding for early childhood program provision. The results transformed the military's child care system—which had been viewed with derision for its near neglect of children—to a model of child development services lauded for its attention to quality.

Collaborating with several other accrediting organizations, NAEYC took the lead in developing a position statement (1999a) regarding the use of accreditation in public policies. The statement is designed to inform policymakers so that policies do not simply reward programs for achieving accreditation, but also provide support to make improvements needed to achieve—and maintain—the level of quality demanded by accreditation.

PROVIDING TOOLS AND RESOURCES TO ASSESS LEGISLATION AND ENCOURAGE GRASSROOTS ACTION

One of the first NANE committees focused on state legislation. Their report gave recommendations for assessing state legislation on programs for young children and stressed the importance of teacher qualifications, program standards, relationships with parents or families, and comprehensive approaches that link home, school, and community. These same areas are addressed today in NAEYC's legislative program.

In 1973 *Young Children* featured a year-long series of articles each titled, "Action for 'Children's Cause'" that grew out of the work of the NAEYC Commission on Legislation Education. The series included a "Do It Yourself Kit," a working tool to collect the state and local information needed to support legislative education action. The kit also provided national data for comparison purposes, addressing Head Start enrollment; the need for day care; the licensing of day care facilities; education and training requirements in day care; kindergarten enrollment, legislation, and financial aid; prekindergarten enrollment and financial aid; migrant programs for kindergarten and prekindergartens; parent and child centers; certification for early childhood personnel; and state programs for personnel development. Later articles in the series addressed how bills are passed in Congress with strategies for letter writing to influence legislation, the importance of personal encounters with policymakers, ways to expand power through link-

When we encounter setbacks in our advocacy for children and their families we should remind ourselves that we have more evidence of the importance of quality early childhood education than we do about the value of any other component of the developmental education sequence. It is up to us as early childhood educators to increase our initiatives to educate others about these facts.

—Bettye Caldwell

ages and alliances, and guidelines for evaluating proposed legislation. These guidelines were also supported by a coalition of more than 30 organizations working to achieve comprehensive child development legislation.

The Week of the Young Child marks another NAEYC activity supported by tools and resources provided to encourage member action (see section on Week of the Young Child at the end of this chapter). The national Week was preceded by local events occurring in Chicago and California. The national organization was urged to extend the event, and the first national celebration was held in 1971. Different themes and logos have characterized the event over time. What has remained constant is encouraging everyone within the community to focus on the rights and needs of young children and to take action to improve the quality of life for young children and in early childhood programs.

Today the NAEYC Website features an Action Center for Children's Champions. Various resources can be accessed from the Action Center. In addition, advocates can join an e-mail list to receive e-alerts and automatically send e-mail to their senators and members of the House of Representatives. Jimmy, you would have been one of our most frequent users if this had been around in your day! The Action Center is an example of our continuing to explore new technologies to disseminate policy and advocacy tools and information that are similar to earlier materials in their thematic approaches, if not in specific content.

ENCOURAGING COLLECTIVE ACTION THAT VALUES DIVERSE STRENGTHS AND ACTIVITIES

A third characteristic of our work has been to recognize and value individuals' differing skills and perspectives and look for ways to encourage collaborative efforts that build upon these differences. Perhaps this stems from the close ties that NAEYC strives to build between policy and practice. Perhaps it stems from our deep valuing and respect for individuals—whether children or adults. NAEYC has always encouraged its members to speak out on behalf of children and has recognized that teachers are helping to advocate for better policies when they talk to parents about the need for classroom practices that foster healthy social development as well as support literacy development. Certainly, members and others are encouraged to write their members of Congress, but these daily conversations are also important in creating public knowledge and attitudes that in turn can help to shift policy.

As early childhood educators we have intimate contact with children and families and this privilege obliges us to make their voices heard when policies are silent to the real needs of people.

— Susan Andersen

NAEYC has always made an effort to reach out to a wide range of organizations outside of education that focus on such topics as social or health services, family concerns, supervision and administration, and children with special needs. The current state of our union points to the need for an even broader outreach—finding ways to make the values of a democratic society the core of all our work.

— Mary B. Lane

NAEYC. 1987c. Public Policy Report. NAEYC position statement on licensing and other forms of regulation of early childhood programs in centers and family day care homes. *Young Children* 42 (5): 64–68.

NAEYC. 1988. NAEYC position statement on standardized testing of young children 3 through 8 years of age. *Young Children* 43 (3): 42–47.

NAEYC. 1990a. National Association for the Education of Young Children position statement on media violence in children's lives. *Young Children* 45 (5): 18–21.

NAEYC. 1990b. National Association for the Education of Young Children position statement on school readiness. *Young Children* 46 (1): 21–23.

NAEYC & NAECS/SDE. 1992. Guidelines for appropriate curriculum content and assessment in programs serving children ages 3 through 8. A position statement of the National Association for the Education of Young Children and the National Association of Early Childhood Specialists in State Departments of Education. In *Reaching potentials: Appropriate curriculum and assessment for young children,* eds. S. Bredekamp & T. Rosegrant, 9–27. Washington, DC: NAEYC.

NAEYC. 1994. NAEYC position statement: A conceptual framework for early childhood professional development. *Young Children* 49 (3): 68–77.

NAEYC. 1995. NAEYC position statement on quality, compensation, and affordability. *Young Children* 51 (1): 39–41.

NAEYC. 1996. NAEYC position statement. Responding to linguistic and cultural diversity—Recommendations for effective early childhood education. *Young Children* 52 (2): 4–12.

NAEYC. 1997a. NAEYC position statement. Developmentally appropriate practice in early childhood programs serving children from birth through age 8. In *Developmentally appropriate practice in early childhood programs,* rev. ed., eds. S. Bredekamp & C. Copple, 3–30. Washington, DC: Author.

NAEYC. 1997b. NAEYC position statement on state implementation of welfare reform. *Young Children* 52 (2): 42–45.

NAEYC. 1997c. NAEYC position statement on the prevention of child abuse in early childhood programs and the responsibilities of early childhood professionals to prevent child abuse. *Young Children* 52 (3): 42–46.

NAEYC. 1998. NAEYC position statement on licensing and public regulation of early childhood programs. *Young Children* 53 (1): 43–50.

NAEYC. 1999a. NAEYC position statement: Developing and implementing effective public policies to promote early childhood and school-age care program accreditation. Available online at www.naeyc.org/resources/position_statements/psacrpol.htm

NAEYC. 1999b. Recommendations for welfare reform initiatives. A position statement of the National Association for the Education of Young Children. In *NAEYC position statements (current as of January 1999),* 73–74. Washington, DC: Author.

U.S. Bureau of the Census. 2001. Current population survey. Table A-2. Percentage of the population 3 to 34 years old enrolled in school, by age, gender, race, and Hispanic origin: October 1947 to 1999. Online at http://www.census.gov/population/socdemo/school

Willer, B., ed. 1990. *Reaching the full cost of quality in early childhood programs.* Washington, DC: NAEYC.

Week of the Young Child and Early Years are Learning Years

Two of NAEYC's thriving, well-known public education strategies are Week of the Young Child (WOYC) and Early Years Are Learning Years (EYLY). Both initiatives are designed to support public awareness in local communities about the components and resources required to provide high-quality programs that serve the needs of young children and their families.

Several decades ago the concept of a nationwide observance of a week focused on young children and their needs was inspired by successful city and state events. Two well-known examples that began in the mid-1950s include California's Nursery Education Week (NEW) and Chicago's Week of the Young Child. Interest in taking this concept to a national level was stimulated by an article about California's Nursery Education Week published in the September 1966 issue of *Young Children*. By 1969 a high level of interest in a national week was being voiced at the annual conference. The NAEYC-sponsored national observance of the Week of the Young Child began 30 years ago in April of 1971. The first logo resulted from a nationwide competition, and a new logo and materials are introduced every few years to stimulate fresh enthusiasm and creativity in the ongoing community events.

The Early Years are Learning Years (EYLY) initiative grew out of NAEYC's ongoing efforts to improve quality, compensation, and affordability in early childhood programs and recognition that Week of the Young Child activities were not enough to focus attention on these issues. Thus, to extend public awareness efforts throughout the year, EYLY was launched in 1996. Special EYLY news releases to foster broader understanding about the importance of high-quality early childhood programs in promoting children's development and learning are posted on NAEYC's Website throughout the year. Busy early childhood teachers, parents, journalists, and advocates download these short releases for distribution.

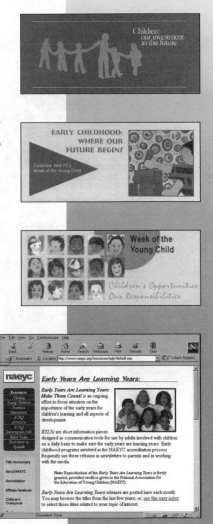

Advocacy milestones for NAEYC

1971:

NAEYC's Annual Conference meets in Minneapolis, Minnesota in November as Congress is preparing to vote on the Comprehensive Child Development Act, also known as the Mondale/Brademas Bill. Special telegram booths are set up at the conference site to allow conferees to send telegrams to Washington, D.C. Senator Mondale is a keynote speaker, and on the day he speaks, picketers protesting the bill march outside the conference hall. NAEYC President Eveline Omwake and other Board members try to engage those on the picket lines in conversation and learn they have been hired and are not well informed about the proposed legislation. The bill passes the Senate and the House, but is vetoed by the President.

1973:

The U.S. Department of Health, Education and Welfare (predecessor to today's Department of Health and Human Services) issues proposed regulations to restrict eligibility of individuals to receive child care services and to eliminate requirements for adherence to any federal child care standards. According to the Public Policy Report in the June issue of *Young Children*, "[The] NAEYC membership and other childhood workers responded as never before [as] 200,000 individuals expressed their opinion by letter and petition . . . Federal level decisionmakers are discovering within their constituencies many voices are uniting as one powerful voice to speak on behalf of young children."

1989:

Just as participants are gathering for the NAEYC Annual Conference in Atlanta, an article in *USA Today* describes child care as the "sacrificial lamb"

Children
are worth it!

Support NAEYC's Campaign
for the Full Cost of Quality
in Early Childhood
Programs

1990

in the annual federal budget reconciliation process. President Ellen Galinsky highlights this comment in her remarks at the conference's opening session and asks conferees to contact their members of Congress to support the Act for Better Child Care, the federal child care program that had passed the Senate but not the House of Representatives. Hundreds of phone calls are made, resulting in calls from Congressional offices back to the conference headquarters, begging us to "tell them to quit calling." Despite the onslaught of calls, child care is not included in the year's budget, although the Child Care and Development Block Grant is enacted the following year in 1990.

1996

1990:

The Opening session of the Annual Conference is held on the steps of the U.S. Capitol to celebrate passage of the Child Care and Development Block Grant and to launch the Full Cost of Quality Campaign. Numerous speakers from the Senate and House of Representatives speak about the grave importance of supporting the full cost of high-quality early childhood programs and give special emphasis to the importance of supporting and rewarding qualified teachers.

1996:

Thousands of NAEYC members travel to Washington, D.C., for the June 1 Stand for Children Day. They join with hundreds of thousands of other people to pledge increased effort to work on behalf of the needs of our nation's children.

2001:

More than 1500 participants register with the NAEYC Action Center within it first six months of operation to send e-mails to their members of Congress.

Looking Forward

This concluding section addresses the overarching purpose of this book—to use history to inform decisions and actions for the future. Although the book focuses on NAEYC, the concepts, principles, and questions described here are essential for anyone involved in improving early childhood care and education. The final two chapters build on the information in previous chapters and suggest two ways we can prepare ourselves to strengthen our future work on behalf of all young children.

"Organizing for the Future" (Chapter 6) by Marilyn M. Smith presents three aspects of effective organizing: Vision—focusing on mission as the guiding principle; Relationships—fostering positive energy among the participants in the organization; Change—and using strategies that constructively achieve the mission. Smith's views are gleaned from two influential experiences: being mentored by and interacting with leaders in NANE/NAEYC from 1959 to the present and teaming with J.D. Andrews to take the helm of NAEYC as the executive leadership team from 1973 to 1999. Prior to joining the staff in 1970, as a young professional she served on the NAEYC Board and committees. She currently is program associate at the Council for Professional Recognition.

"Facing the Future" (Chapter 7) by Barbara Bowman presents three areas demanding NAEYC's attention: the organizational framework and leadership, the professional knowledge base and standards for the field, and current advocacy issues. These challenges constitute an urgent agenda for dialogue and debate among those who accept leadership responsibilities for NAEYC and its Affiliate Groups. Leaders of any organization in the early care and education field could benefit from considering these challenges.

Bowman is uniquely qualified to offer this guidance to future planning. She served as NAEYC president from 1980 to 1982 and has been a contributing member of commissions, task groups, and panels that have guided the majority of our Association's position statements and initiatives the last 20 years. Her leadership extends to the broad field of early care and education as exemplified by recent responsibilities such as chairing the National Academy of Sciences Committee on Early Childhood Pedagogy, which wrote *Eager to Learn: Educating our Preschoolers,* and serving on the National Board for Professional Teaching Standards. Barbara Bowman is president of the Erikson Institute for Advanced Study in Child Development.

Organizing for the Future

Marilyn M. Smith

NAEYC has not merely survived for 75 years—it has thrived. A primary reason for this success has been effective organizational leadership. Now and in the future, the leaders who guide the organization will influence what NAEYC accomplishes or fails to achieve. Who are these leaders? Virtually every person reading this book is, or will become, an active participant in NAEYC's work.

The critical role of Association leaders permeates this book. All of the preceding chapters are replete with examples of wise decisions and actions of NAEYC leaders that resulted in building a strong organization (Hewes, Witherspoon, Daniel), improving early childhood practice (Bredekamp), and increasing public and policy support for high-quality programs (Willer). In the concluding chapter Barbara Bowman asserts, "How we handle our leadership will mark our field for years to come. It will also mark this nation's children." and she proposes three challenges that demand NAEYC's attention. As a prelude to these issues, this chapter suggests three organizing principles that can help leaders effectively meet such challenges. These are (1) Vision—focusing on mission as the guiding principle; (2) Relationships—fostering positive energy among the participants in the organization; and (3) Change—using strategies that constructively achieve the mission.

The effective organizing principles described in this chapter were derived from my personal experiences and observations from more than 40 years of intimate participation in NAEYC. During the 1960s I had the good fortune of being a young faculty member in the child development department at Iowa State University during the time that the chair of the department, Glenn Hawkes, was president of NANE, and other faculty members held positions on the Board or committees. NANE activities were a part of the conversation almost as frequently as university projects. In 1965 I was elected to the NAEYC Board, and other leaders, including the newly developed headquarters staff, became sources for my knowledge about how the organization operated.

By 1970 I was working at NAEYC and in 1973 was paired with J.D. Andrews to head the executive leadership team from that date until 1999. Throughout all of these years, I had the opportunity to work with and learn from NAEYC leaders too numerous to mention. The insights I gained from them became an integral part of my thinking, and only as I prepared to leave the NAEYC staff did I attempt to formulate these insights into

I draw great energy from concentrations of like-minded, committed people who are striving to make the world what it ought to be.

— Jerlean Daniel

explicitly stated principles for effective organizing. Reading *Leadership and the New Science* (Wheatley 1994) and *A Simpler Way* (Wheatley & Kellner-Rogers 1996) helped me frame my thoughts, but the concepts come from observations of many early childhood leaders. Working closely with J.D. Andrews, I learned much about leadership and what makes an organization flourish.

Vision—Focusing on an organization's mission as its guiding principle

Every organization calls itself into being as a belief that something more can be accomplished by joining with others.

—Margaret J. Wheatley and
Myron Kellner-Rogers

An organization is a group of people who have a mutual goal and who believe that by joining with others they can make more significant progress toward achieving that goal. Many groups fit this definition. In the world of early childhood, there are all types of private and public programs, kindergarten and primary schools, resource and referral agencies, departments in colleges and universities. Although the organizing concepts to guide the future outlined here are relevant to all types of organizations, the language and examples focus on NAEYC and its Affiliate Groups.

The first question any leader should consider is why the organization they have chosen to work for was formed—its purpose. The founding vision for NAEYC came from a handful of experts in child development and education who believed they could accomplish more as a group than as individuals. They were alarmed at the unbridled proliferation of nursery schools occurring in the United States in the 1920s and worried that the preschool movement was headed into dangerous waters, with nursery schools being started by people who knew nothing about how young children develop and learn. They shared the goal of influencing the quality of these new group programs for young children and formed a committee that quickly evolved into an official organization in order to work toward this goal as a group (Hewes [1976] 1996).

The belief that we can accomplish more together comes from our experience that creative ideas, insights, and solutions increase when we join with others to work toward a common goal. This is what attracts people to join an organization and—in the best cases—come to love it as they feel fulfilled by their contribution to the shared mission.

But that loyalty doesn't always develop, and people don't always stay. What happens?

It is important for leaders of an organization to understand that people join it for a wide variety of reasons that may or may not be related to its mission and goals. Effective leaders are able to create a shared vision among those who choose to participate and also focus attention on the principles that drive decisions that reflect the organization's core beliefs and values.

CREATING A SHARED VISION

When the participants in an organization are in agreement about its purpose and direction, they work collaboratively, beyond their individual interests, to achieve the shared goals. Of course, perceiving some personal benefit from participation is also crucial to ensuring members' continued participation. But a shared vision helps individuals to look beyond their individual needs and creates a common bond that unifies the group. Thus, it is paramount that organizational leaders give focused and persistent attention to communicating the group's mission and ensuring that sponsored activities reflect this mission. Effective leaders use every opportunity to convey

Members of NAEYC live and work in extremely diverse settings and perform a broad range of roles, yet we hold in common a deep-seated commitment to what happens to young children. This commitment to the quality of the early education and care of young children is immutable and serves to unite disparate parts of the field.

— Ellen Galinsky

NAEYC's mission to improve the quality of early care and education: they design activities based on this goal; photographs and visuals are selected to portray young children in good group programs; decisions on funding include evaluating consistency with the organization's goals.

NAEYC's mission and goals are far more likely to be conveyed through its actions and activities than its printed mission statement. Thus, leaders must work hard to avoid actions and activities that do not embody the mission and goals. Activities and behaviors that conflict with the organization's stated goals and purpose cause participants to feel they have joined an incoherent organization without focus. If many of an organization's activities don't match its stated goals, there needs to be an intense effort to determine what needs to be changed—the mission to match the actions or the actions to match the mission.

Effective leaders also listen and observe for another type of mismatch in which the interpreted meaning of the mission and goals is different from the intended meaning. It was alertness to this kind of misinterpretation that prompted our organization's name change from the National Association for Nursery Education (NANE) to National Association for the Education of Young Children (NAEYC) in 1964. Glenn Hawkes and other leaders had grown tired of explaining that the purpose of our organization was not to teach about growing plants in nurseries. Sometimes such mismatches are not difficult to detect. They just require leaders who take opportunities to observe and listen sensitively to the participants in the organization.

MAKING PRINCIPLE-DRIVEN DECISIONS

Principle-driven organizations are guided by a set of core values and beliefs that undergird their mission and goals and are shared by the group's participants. Leaders guide principle-driven organizations by effectively communicating concepts and principles rather than designing and enforcing elaborate rules to direct people into specific, predetermined behaviors. Principle-driven organizations are controlled by ideas, not by the authority of a manager, and the controlling ideas are almost never the ideas of one person but the collaborative work of many people.

From its inception, NAEYC activities have taken direction from carefully crafted and debated statements of core beliefs, values, and principles that reflect how this Association approaches its mission and goals. These beliefs about NAEYC's commitment to children are expressed most succinctly in the preamble to the *Code of Ethical Conduct and Statement of Commitment* (NAEYC 1998b).

Core Values

- Appreciating childhood as a unique and valuable stage of the human life cycle [and recognizing the value of the present in children's lives for its own sake, not just as preparation for the future]

- Basing our work with children on knowledge of child development [and learning]

- Appreciating and supporting the close ties between the child and family

- Recognizing that children are best understood and supported in the context of family, culture, community and society

- Respecting the dignity, worth, and uniqueness of each individual (child, family member, and colleague)

- Helping children and adults achieve their full potential in the context of relationships that are based on trust, respect, and positive regard

When members and others understand these core values and beliefs, those who share them find added reason to join and participate in the organization. When the organization's decisions for the future are guided by its core values and beliefs, the body of decisionmaking is consistent and adds to the shared vision of the group and what it is trying to achieve.

PRINCIPLES IN ACTION

NAEYC's core principles are at the heart of the position statements adopted throughout the Association's history, which comprise the cornerstone of all NAEYC activities and decisions. They guide behaviors and decisions of both individuals and groups. For example, teachers consult the position statement "Developmentally Appropriate Practice in Early Childhood Programs" (NAEYC 1997) for guidance in their teaching; colleges consult the position statement "Guidelines for Early Childhood Professional Preparation Programs at the Associate, Baccalaureate, and Advanced Levels" (NAEYC 1996b) regarding components of early childhood teacher preparation programs; and Association leaders consult the position statement "Guiding Principles for the Development and Analysis of Early Childhood Public Policy" (1992), to guide decisions about appropriate organizational stands and activities on local, state, or federal policy initiatives. While any of NAEYC's major projects and position state-

Core values of NAEYC affirm that each child is unique and deserves nurture, love, care, and service. NAEYC gives guidance, perspectives, directives, and management to achieve this mission of services and quality care with love for every child and family.

— Margaret Roth

ments serve as examples of an organization being driven by principles, two illustrations are presented here to amplify this concept.

NAEYC's Code of Ethical Conduct is a statement of core ideals and principles to guide decisionmaking about ethical issues. This set of guiding principles is intended to inform, but not prescribe, answers to tough decisions that teachers must make as they work with children and their families. Nor does NAEYC's Code specify behaviors members are to follow nor sanctions or rewards for specific actions. Rather, it underscores the importance of reflection, considering the unique circumstances surrounding each decision, and bringing to bear professional knowledge—along with families' knowledge and values—in determining a specific action.

The fundamental belief in decisionmaking that respects unique circumstances while bringing to bear professional knowledge is clearly visible in NAEYC's *Accreditation Criteria and Procedures of the National Association for the Education of Young Children* (NAEYC 1998a) for accrediting high-quality early childhood programs. NAEYC's accreditation system reflects the conviction that improvements in practice are more authentic and long-lasting when those who conduct the programs seeking accreditation are involved in determining the goals of their practice and their actions to meet those goals, as opposed to having to conform to externally prescribed actions or behaviors. NAEYC's accreditation system has drawn criticism for refraining from specifying upper limits on group size and adult-child ratios that, if not met, would automatically exclude programs from accreditation. Instead, NAEYC's system cites acceptable ranges for group size and ratios and relies on professional judgment about the overall quality of experience being provided to any particular group of children. Thus, the numbers are considered but within the overall context. For example, the teachers' skills and qualifications and the specific nature of teacher-child interactions are also taken into account.

The accreditation system reflects a belief that participants can and should think deeply about the relationships and educational opportunities being experienced by the particular young children served, with needs and circumstances varying greatly from program to program. This example highlights two key values intrinsic to NAEYC: the importance of professional knowledge in decisionmaking that affects early childhood program quality and the understanding that goals can be met in different ways in different contexts.

As the previous chapters in this book illustrate, NAEYC's leaders and members have been diligent and committed in creating a shared vision that reflects the Association's core principles, values, and beliefs. This is a heritage of which NAEYC should be very proud, and an important tradition to carry forward into the future.

Relationships—Fostering positive energy among the participants in the organization

Who we become together will always be different than who we were alone. Our range of creative expression increases as we join with others. New relationships create new capacities.

—Margaret J. Wheatley and
Myron Kellner-Rogers

CONSIDERING WHO IS IN THE ORGANIZATION

Organizational capacity and effectiveness is determined by who is in the group and how people work together. Articulating a shared vision and core set of principles that serve as a touchstone for all the organization's activities is essential to effective organiza-

tional leadership. But organizations need members who contribute to the vision and principles and bring them to life through action. Successful organizations actively involve all those who have a role to play in accomplishing their mission. For NAEYC to achieve its mission of high-quality early care and education for *all* young children in this nation, *all* people who work with and for young children need to be actively involved in working toward this goal.

Although NAEYC has worked hard to achieve inclusive participation, we are far from accomplishing it. The majority of NAEYC members are also members of State Affiliates and Affiliate Chapters, and a look at these organizations reveals that in many cases the membership is skewed. There is substantial participation from some segments of the early childhood education population and very little representation of others. The voids differ from group to group. Only a few Affiliates can claim significant involvement of teachers and administrators for kindergarten and primary classrooms. Imagine the potential positive result for children and families transitioning from early care and education programs to school programs if teachers at all levels had working professional relationships fostered through Affiliate activities at the community level.

The true spirit of NAEYC is the unwavering commitment to children by all of the people who make up our organization.

— Sharon Lynn Kagan

This is only one example. The lack of involvement of teachers of color, teachers working in family child care, and teachers in Even Start and Head Start programs represents lost opportunities for NAEYC and for children. This situation requires NAEYC leaders to commit to expanding the range of who is in the organization in order to effect improvements in all early childhood programs.

The greatest barrier to achieving fully inclusive participation in NAEYC, or any other organization, is a fear of differences. It is the responsibility of leaders to foster an attitude of embracing "differentness," greatly increasing the organization's capacity and effectiveness as a consequence. Such attitudes help focus participants and potential participants on the reason for being in an organization—to accomplish more together than could be achieved alone. In a vigorous organization many different people work on many different tasks. When only those who are alike participate, membership size is limited. But more important, the organization has only a limited range of ideas, approaches, and abilities to draw on. There is no value in sameness. The only sameness needed in organizations is the unifying goal that brings participants together.

Participants who choose to work toward the goal of improving early childhood educa-

tion do not need to share the same religious or political beliefs, ethnic or cultural backgrounds, academic degrees, or to work with the same age group. But these participants do need to be committed to the same goal. Based on this commitment, they need to listen carefully to the different perspectives others bring to an issue, to expand the way they think and problem solve, and to negotiate solutions no one person would have come to alone.

NAEYC leaders are not alone in facing the challenge of fostering understanding and respect for differences. Leaders of all types of organizations are paying attention to the growing diversity of our society—in 2010 no single ethnic group will constitute a majority of the U.S. population—and coming to understand that our democracy and economy require unprecedented levels of cooperation, communication, and teamwork among people who are different. For early childhood professionals this means we have a major responsibility to help prepare *all* children to *share* a society where students, neighbors, and coworkers are diverse (Washington & Andrews 1998). What better place to work toward this goal than through NAEYC?

Mentoring and other forms of outreach are extremely important strategies for attracting and involving populations who are underrepresented in an organization. There

Always assume that the people you work with have the capacities for greatness, creativity, courage, and insight. Occasionally this assumption will be wrong, perhaps. But if you always make it, you will be much more likely to uncover, encourage, strengthen, and support these qualities in them.

— Lilian Katz

are many different forms of mentoring, but to expand participation in an organization current members need to learn to coach, encourage, and give opportunities to non-members. Organizational leaders cannot assume people will just flock to participate in the group. Systematic outreach to offer opportunities to participate is essential. Ed Greene reflects on how he became involved as a participant and leader in NAEYC:

> While attending my first NAEYC conference in 1973, I met with Evangeline Ward, who had agreed to complete a survey for my master's degree project. She also talked to me about my work and interest and at the end of that conversation said, "Young man, we've got to put you to work." I am forever grateful for Evangeline [and] other people in this organization, [including] the Black Caucus, who have supported, challenged, and encouraged me. (Personal communication 2001)

Busy people make choices about where they devote their talent and time and are more likely to choose to participate when given an opportunity to do meaningful work. Some people need only the opportunity to participate; others need coaching and encouragement. Such mentoring for active involvement in NAEYC was experienced by most of our Association's current leaders, but is frequently overlooked as something we, in turn, must constantly do to involve others.

DEFINING HOW PEOPLE WORK TOGETHER

> Power in organizations is the capacity generated by relationships. What gives power its charge—positive or negative—is the quality of the relationships.
>
> —*Margaret J. Wheatley*

The second element influencing the capacity and effectiveness of an organization is *how* members are together, that is, the way participants interact and work together to achieve the organization's goals. The key question is Are the relationships in the organization generating negative energy or positive energy? In the organizations that members love, relationships generate mostly positive energy, and in the organizations members dislike or ignore, relationships generate mostly negative energy. The conclusion has to be that organizational leaders must be extremely savvy in nurturing positive relationships. Leaders can nurture positive relationships in organizations by focusing expectations and communication on the goals of the organization and the project at hand and facilitating the cooperation of different segments of the membership.

Promote goal-oriented expectations.
Leaders intent on generating constructive energy for their organization's work help

Through more than 35 years as a member and active participant in NAEYC, I have been, and continue to be,

- *inspired*
- *educated*
- *supported*
- *valued*
- *challenged*
- *determined*
- *motivated*

and the list could go on!

— Carrie Cheek

participants focus on the shared goals of the organization. They understand that participants come to an organization with multiple expectations about or purposes for their involvement, which may include social contact, professional advancement, or use of the perceived power and approval of the organization to promote the agenda of another organization. Leaders accept all of these as legitimate but give priority attention to the shared organizational goals for a particular project. An excellent example of this concept is the large cadre of volunteers who contribute their professional expertise and time to conduct NAEYC work: conducting validation visits at early childhood programs seeking accreditation; reviewing manuscripts for publication; contributing to, or critiquing, draft position statements; and planning and conducting professional development experiences promoting NAEYC position statements. Effective leaders organize the participation of these volunteers by focusing attention on what their actions will contribute to the improvement of early childhood programs and the professional development of teachers. Disagreements will naturally happen, but when volunteers' motivations are focused on their potential contribution to the field, they can more easily view such disagreements as opportunities to expand understanding. The focus

stays on the goal rather than on personal acceptance or recognition.

Organizational leaders attract higher numbers of such goal-oriented participants by adopting recruitment and retention strategies that give primary focus to mission and goals, and secondary attention to potential personal gains. Side benefits, such as insurance and discounts, may help to attract or retain members, but keeping the main focus on the mission results in more members who have a clear understanding of the major purpose of the organization. Without this understanding, participants would have no basis for constructive collaboration.

Provide goal-centered facilitation. The people who facilitate group sessions (such as study groups or the meetings of a committee, task force, or board) play a major role in achieving constructive relationships among participants. Today's organization management specialists emphasize teamwork rather than promoting rugged individualism. Facilitators promote collaboration by helping the group focus on the organization's mission and goals and establishing clear goals for the work of the specific group; they encourage the expression of different perspectives and approaches, conflicts, and disagreements. They understand that there will always be differing views about solutions, and therefore their role is to help participants listen openly and work through to a group consensus formulated around the agreed-upon goals of the group's work. Group members are helped to not take personally group decisions that don't embrace their recommendations. Participants are reminded that it is not about "liking" one person's ideas and not "liking" another's. The goal is to identify a group solution to best address the organization's needs at that time.

Effective facilitators also keep the focus on *process*—evoking problem solving, creativity, and experimentation among group members. They promote the concept that most often there is no *one* right answer, but many that could work (flexibility). What matters is picking one or two possible solutions and trying them (experimenting), collecting feedback about how well the original goal is being met (evaluation), and making adjustments as work proceeds.

Effective facilitators are also skilled at match-making—helping individuals match their experience, knowledge, interests, and abilities to responsibilities that need to be divided among the group members. Such matches move the group work forward and also help individuals feel they are making positive contributions.

Foster goal-centered communication. In healthy organizations, people support one another by being authentic in their communication and nurturing one another with trust (Wheatley & Kellner-Rogers 1996). This aspect of influencing the effectiveness of an organization requires the conscious effort of all participants, leaders and members alike. Organizations that are effective in addressing their goals practice flexibility and focus on solution-seeking activities. For group members to engage in these practices they must feel safe in exploring issues, experimenting, and probing for new understandings. Goal-centered, authentic communication among participants helps to create such a safe environment.

Members of a group support each other with authentic information when, as they speak or write, they strive for accuracy, verifying information that they give as reliable. In addition they report only information that is relevant to the task. If all early childhood educators practiced these principles, we would *not* hear the following types of statements: "First-grade teachers are destroying these children's self-confidence"; "Family child care providers don't do anything to educate children"; "College instructors don't understand or care about the inadequate compensation of child care

NAEYC continually strives to be better, but recognizes that there are many avenues to the same goal.

— Shirley Dean

workers"; "These parents aren't capable of helping their child learn to read"; "This person can't succeed at this job because he or she doesn't have a degree in early childhood education"; or "This program couldn't possibly meet NAEYC accreditation criteria—it's in a for-profit child care chain." Such blanket statements are not based on fact and ignore individual differences. But the most devastating result is that they prejudge what a person, program, or class is capable of without giving the groups or individuals the opportunity to demonstrate what they can do.

Other types of communication undermine creation of an environment of trust in which team members can feel safe to contribute, experiment, explore, and grow. Such harmful types of communication include blame statements, gossip, and statements that assign motivation to another person's action. Such communication has no value in helping a group explore issues, learn from one another, and seek solutions. Facilitators can help group members avoid such destructive comments by suggesting that all participants monitor what they are preparing to say or write, asking themselves if it is directly focused on the goal of the project, the work of the committee, or the mission of the organization. When communication centers

There is great value in open, participatory debate in furthering the mission of NAEYC. However, all participants should remember that "words, when spoken, have life," and "silence does not mean consensus."

— Alice Paul

on the shared goals of the group, that communication rarely relates to individual people.

Change—Using strategies that constructively achieve the mission

A system maintains itself only if change is occurring somewhere in it all the time.

—Margaret J. Wheatley and Myron Kellner-Rogers

Leaders must always keep in mind that organizations are open, not closed, systems. Organizations are highly dynamic, forever being influenced by the people in them and the environment in which they are operating. Successful leaders understand that members and the environment in which an organization operates are constantly changing. Recognizing this continual change, leaders are alert to signs that strategies and solutions effective in the past may need to be changed or refined to continue to accomplish the organization's goals. Change is hard, too much change is chaos, but no change is death. Four strategies and attitudes that help leaders nurture constructive change in organizations are evaluation, flexibility, experimentation, and tolerance for disequilibrium.

EMBRACE EVALUATION

Organizational leaders need to be vigilant in evaluating the effectiveness of in-place strategies and structures for accomplishing goals. They need to view their organization's strategies and structures as temporary and be sensitive to signs that old methods are losing their effectiveness. This sounds so logical, but it is difficult to do, especially for participants who played a major role in creating a particular solution or spent a lot of effort to become skilled with a strategy. It is tempting to embrace the comfort of implementing what we understand and can do well, but then we fail to make needed adjustments; we let strategies become an end goal. Bredekamp's chapter gives many examples of NAEYC positions and strategies that were helpful for a time but upon subsequent evaluation needed to be changed.

In NAEYC's past and present are many examples of embracing evaluation. Position statements are charted for intensive review every three to five years; accreditation requires that programs go through self-study and evaluation every three years; and Affiliate Groups are supported in engaging in self-study and strategic planning on a periodic basis. NAEYC's recent restructuring activities and the Board's annual identification of goals for the coming year are examples of national leaders revisiting and engaging in serious evaluation of decisions and priorities. Such processes keep the Association current with the changing needs and concerns affecting its mission to promote high-quality early childhood programs for all young children.

NAEYC maintains its traditions and core values while concurrently facing challenges and embracing change to move into new realms

— Sharon Lynn Kagan

PROTECT FLEXIBILITY

Retaining flexibility in organizations is hard, especially as they grow in size. Flexibility was the norm during the first 40 years of this Association. Membership hovered around a thousand, and activities depended on whatever resources volunteer leaders could muster or contribute. However, focus did not waver from the organization's mission, and NAEYC now stands on the firm foundation laid by early leaders. The decade from 1966 to 1976 saw the membership spiral up to 28,000, and a need for more structure and permanency became evident. These were tempestuous years, changing from NANE to NAEYC, adding paid staff to work with the volunteer leaders, and establishing a national headquarters in Washington, D.C. (Witherspoon 1976). The

When the 1968 slate for the NAEYC Governing Board was announced, all of the nominees were from the East. California AEYC members were amazed and decided to organize a write-in candidate. Lo and behold, I was elected, served my term, and then was elected to another term by the usual way.

— Esther Weir

past 25 years have seen the membership almost quadruple. Structure, policies, and systems have been essential for work to be accomplished. But within this essential framework, some flexibility has been maintained and overly bureaucratic rules avoided.

Organizational leaders should make it a point to build some flexibility into structures, systems, and policies. To be effective, every organization must respond to changing situations and resources, effectively meet the needs of a broad spectrum of participants, and enable these various participants to apply their unique and different skills, wisdom, and influence to create solutions. Structures, systems, and policies quickly lose relevance if they are treated as rigid and permanent and are incapable of being adjusted for changing circumstances and opportunities.

To grasp the necessity of protecting flexibility, consider effective early childhood teachers who are skilled in applying the principles of developmentally appropriate practice. These teachers create a learning environment that offers structure, directions, and rules based on best knowledge of the capacity and interests of the group of children. Within this framework, teachers then individualize activities, responses, and expectations for each child, taking into account children's differing developmental levels and cultural backgrounds to increase the likelihood of all in the group having successful learning experiences. The contrasting image is one of teachers who use identical methods and rigid procedures with all children, resulting in only a handful of children having successful learning experiences. These successful and unsuccessful teaching practices can easily be transferred to organizations—those that incorporate some choices and alternate strategies within a well-publicized basic structure, policies, and procedures have more success compared to organizations that offer few choices and adhere to rigid rules and regulations.

Encourage experimentation

Another essential strategy to nurture constructive change and keep organizations vibrant is to support experimentation and inquiry. Professionals well versed in developmental theory understand the importance of individuals' constructing understandings but are far more likely to apply this concept to children than with adults. Organizations, like classrooms of children, are composed of unique individuals working on problems with unique circumstances that require the collective construction of potential solutions that can be tested.

Can you imagine an organization that is constantly seeking processes to respond [to] and improve the conditions for its members and the children and families they serve nationally and internationally? That for me is the essence of NAEYC.

— Edgar Klugman

Leaders support productive experimentation by encouraging two organizational attitudes: valuing process and creativity and focusing on finding something that works as opposed to searching for one right answer. *Valuing process and creativity* translates into tolerance for ambiguity and indulgence for the messiness that inventing new solutions often entails. When process is valued, errors are expected, explored, and welcomed, because errors create more information that results in a greater capacity to solve problems. *Focusing on finding what works rather than on finding* the *right answer* involves giving more attention to "messing about" in the task of solution-creation and less attention to searching for preexisting models.

Observing the successes of other organizations can expand our thinking by suggesting new possibilities, but the experience of one organization rarely provides an exact model that would work equally well in a different organization. It is for this reason that NAEYC leaders have resisted adopting or promulgating models but rather have articulated and promoted principles to stimulate and guide experimentation to find viable solutions for particular and individual circumstances. For example, developmentally appropriate practice is a set of principles, not a curriculum model. Articles in *Young*

Children are much more likely to present concepts, ideas, examples, and guides rather than recipes or lesson plans. NAEYC's Membership Action Group grants, awarded since 1973, support innovation and exploration of ideas about a variety of issues of concern to the organization and field. Many, many examples could be added.

Use disequilibrium

Productive organizational leaders recognize that a state of disequilibrium can provide new opportunity for growth. "The things we fear most in organizations—fluctuations, disturbances, imbalances—need not be signs of an impending disorder that will destroy us. Instead, fluctuations can be a primary source of creativity" (Wheatley 1994, 20). It is not that organizational leaders seek to impose disequilibrium, but when turmoil or conflict occurs, they view it as an opportunity to tackle challenges and take the organization to a new level of productivity. Leaders attempt to redirect the energy from discord and confusion toward experimentation and solution seeking.

One example of a major disequilibrium within the early childhood field and NAEYC comes from the persistent problem of inadequate compensation in early childhood

A very important role of professional associations is to stimulate exploration of unresolved issues. During the 1950s the NANE conferences were formatted to emphasize such dialogue. I think that NAEYC should provide more opportunities in the conferences and Young Children to raise questions and debate possible solutions.

— Millie Almy

Success is a journey, not a destination.

— J.D. Andrews

education. Although the problem is far from solved, incremental progress can be attributed to individuals and groups who respond to the challenge by exploring a variety of approaches rather than crying doomsday. (See chapters by Willer and Daniel.) Another example is the so-called "reading wars" between proponents of phonics and whole language approaches to teaching reading. Two organizations—NAEYC and the International Reading Association (IRA)—responded to this discord by collaborating to develop and jointly adopt a statement of principles to guide teachers, administrators, and parents caught in this "either/or" struggle.

As successful organizational leaders nurture constructive change by promoting evaluation, flexibility, experimentation, and tolerance for disequilibrium, they never lose sight of the important role of mission and goals. They understand that with only experimentation and complete flexibility, chaos can prevail. Chaos is avoided by maintaining an unwavering focus on mission and goals in the midst of all kinds of searching for solutions and workable strategies. Effective leaders adhere to two companion principles: (1) maintaining a clear focus on mission and goals fosters order and stability; and (2) exploring, experimenting, and creating solutions fosters the identification of effective

strategies to achieve the organization's goals. Thus, the challenge to organizational leaders is to help participants see the organization's mission and goals as a reference while remembering that the role of vision and mission is to inspire, not to prescribe.

Conclusion

The source of change and growth for an organization or an individual is to develop increased awareness of who it is, now.

—*Margaret J. Wheatley and Myron Kellner-Rogers*

NAEYC's future accomplishments on behalf of children will depend on the simultaneous efforts, commitment, and activities of the individuals who comprise the Association. NAEYC is an organizational framework that enables individuals to work collaboratively. Frameworks, without purposeful individuals to make use of them, are empty buildings that can accomplish nothing.

• NAEYC as a structure or framework can't make itself into a more high-performing, inclusive organization. But NAEYC, the collective body of individuals, can foster diversity and inclusiveness in Association-sponsored activities based on the belief that these attitudes are essential to improving the quality of life for *all* children and adults.

• NAEYC as a structure can't teach a young child or improve the quality of learning opportunities available to children. But NAEYC can be the gathering place for individuals who teach and improve opportunities, plan activities that help individuals learn from each other, and support the development of positions, principles, and concepts to guide improvements in the practice of early childhood education.

• NAEYC as a structure has no authority to ratify laws and regulations or authorize public funds to support early childhood programs. But NAEYC can stimulate individuals to collaborate in seeking citizen and policymaker support for systems and funds to achieve a high-quality system of early childhood education.

These statements encompass NAEYC's three goals designed to further its mission to achieve high-quality care and education for all young children. They have effectively guided the decisions of former leaders and can guide future leaders as they direct the collective efforts of NAEYC members.

REFERENCES

Hewes, D.W. [1976] 1996. *NAEYC's first half century: 1926—1976.* 70th Anniversary reprint. Washington, DC: NAEYC.

NAEYC. 1992. *Guiding principles for the development and analysis of early childhood public policy* [Position Statement]. Washington, DC: Author.

NAEYC. 1996a. Approaching the new millennium. Lessons from NAEYC's first 70 years. *Young Children* 52 (1): 43–44.

NAEYC. 1996b. Guidelines for early childhood professional preparation programs at the associate, baccalaureate, and advanced levels. [Position Statement]. In *Guidelines for preparation of early childhood professionals,* 5–11. Washington, DC: Author.

NAEYC. 1997. NAEYC position statement: Developmentally appropriate practice in early childhood programs serving children from birth through age 8. In *Developmentally appropriate practice in early childhood programs.* rev. ed., eds. S. Bredekamp & C. Copple, 3–30. Washington, DC: Author.

NAEYC. 1998a. *Accreditation criteria and procedures of the National Association for the Education of Young Children.* 1998 ed. Washington, DC: NAEYC.

NAEYC. 1998b. *Code of ethical conduct and statement of commitment.* [Brochure]. Washington, DC: Author.

Washington, V., & J.D. Andrews, eds. 1998. *Children of 2010.* Washington, DC: NAEYC.

Wheatley, M.J. 1994. *Leadership and the new science.* San Francisco, CA: Berrett-Koehler Publishers.

Wheatley, M.J. & M. Kellner-Rogers. 1996. *A simpler way.* San Francisco, CA: Berrett-Koehler.

Witherspoon, R. 1976. From NANE to NAEYC: The tempestuous years. *Young Children* 31 (5): 333–38.

Chapter 7

Facing the Future

Barbara Bowman

W hat does the future hold for our profession and what challenges lie ahead for NAEYC? These questions are related because NAEYC is the leading voice in the field of early care and education. Of course, this does not mean that our organization is the only voice or that it dictates directions or strategies. Instead, NAEYC is one among many that have a stake in the profession, its opportunities, and its challenges. My remarks, therefore, are designed to point out to the field in general what the future may hold and how we might best respond. From time to time, I use examples from our common experience in NAEYC to highlight potential dangers. In fact, NAEYC has already responded to many of the issues I raise and I have not always noted these responses. Instead of looking at the many things we have done well, I have focused on the challenges that lie ahead for NAEYC and all concerned about the care and education of young children.

Who would have thought 75 years ago that out-of-home care and education of young children would be as prevalent as it is today and that our professional organization would speak with authority to parents, universities, governments, programs, and the public?

The early childhood field has increased in importance because research has pointed with increasing clarity to the tie between how we care for and educate young children and their subsequent development and learning. This new knowledge has become available at a time when far more children are spending at least part of the day outside the home. As a consequence, many Americans are concerned about the quality of early childhood programs and the role of parents, government, charitable organizations, and businesses in promoting the healthy development and learning of young children. As research continues to show the benefits of high-quality care and education for young children, the importance of the field will continue to increase. Looking ahead, NAEYC has an enlarging window of opportunity to influence public opinion, teacher education, government policies, and program practices. How we handle our leadership will mark our field for years to come. It will also mark this nation's children.

To get ready for tomorrow, I suggest that there are three areas that demand NAEYC's attention today. These are (1) organizational framework and leadership, (2) the professional knowledge base and standards for the field, and (3) current advocacy issues. I will present some of my ideas on these topics but I have more questions than answers. Further, new events will soon present us with new challenges. Perhaps the most important contribution this chapter can make is to encourage us to consider our past as we plan for the future.

Organizational framework and leadership

Unfortunately, the early childhood field in the United States today would have to be called chaotic. As Willer points out, "the United States still lacks a comprehensive system of services to ensure that all young children receive the high quality of programs that they need and deserve" (p. 127). Unquestionably, there are multiple reasons for this disorganized state. The major constituencies—child care, early education, and family support—arose to solve different problems and therefore, have different histories and traditions. Programs are paid for by different entities such as state and local governments, parents, or not-for-profit agencies and are located in public schools, centers, church basements, homes, park fieldhouses, factories, and settlement houses, to name a few sites. The field encompasses professionals from different disciplines: developmental psychology, education, social work, health, special education, and business, each with its own outcome expectations and professional biases. In addition, the various professions and programs have different personnel and program licensing requirements.

Despite the field's fragmentation, NAEYC has grown substantially over the past 25 years. This growth is testimony to NAEYC's ability to draw into its orbit a broad cross-section of the programs that serve young children and their families. As each of the other contributors to this volume points out, NAEYC has drawn divergent groups together by focusing on inclusiveness. It has established itself as the one organization open to all who take an interest in the field and has attracted a diverse membership. While there have certainly been tensions between various groups that comprise the field, NAEYC has included as many individuals and groups as possible under the institutional umbrella and woven their diverse perspectives into consensus on areas of practice and policy.

The Association has bound individuals and groups together by organizing its programs and policies around inclusive principles rather than dogmatic practice. For Marilyn Smith (this volume), the creation of a shared vision and a core set of principles accounts for the success. She says the original goal of NAEYC was "influencing the quality of programs" for young children and notes it has been increasingly effective in achieving this. Developing an organizational framework that focused on inclusiveness, shared vision, and core principles has not been easy and there have been many struc-tural changes in the organization through the years to facilitate cohesiveness.

Before the 1970s, membership was small and the national Governing Board and Affiliate Groups were loosely organized and connected to one another through personal relationships. Individuals and groups knew one another and were able to put together workable coalitions. As the field has grown and NAEYC's membership has mush-roomed, the informal structure and lines of communication became less viable. The Association was originally an entirely volunteer organization, but paid staff is becoming increasingly common. The national staff has grown tremendously and the number of projects initiated from the national office has also increased. Each year more local affili-ates add both staff and staff-led activities, thereby diminishing the volunteer tradition.

As any organization grows larger and its structure more formal, participants are less connected through personal relationships and more dependent upon institutional processes. The latest step for NAEYC is a role for Affiliates and how they relate to the Board that is more explicit than in the past. This change inevitably promotes different types of communication. Formalizing the structure limits flexibility and the kind of informal interactions characteristic of a smaller organization. Similarly, the number of paid staff members has increased at the national and Affiliate levels, which has expanded the number of areas in which we can be influential but may diminish the personal investment of members.

Smith points out that positive relationships are the backbone of an organization; it is through them that experience becomes meaningful. Relationships are fundamental in transmitting the common values, goals, and principles that have sustained us in the past. It is imperative to ask how changes that make processes and structures more formal will affect our relationships with one another. Can we maintain the kind of relationships that lead to belief in a common core when members have less direct contact with one another, less opportunity to directly affect decisionmaking, fewer informal opportunities to find a common agenda for action?

Another potential threat to our common core is the proliferation of groups promoting similar missions but each with its own focus and internal concerns. Head Start is certainly a case in point. Originally an active player within NAEYC at both the local and national levels, today Head Start teachers, administrators, and parents are increasingly focused on their own organization, its policy initiatives and conferences. Since Head Start and NAEYC share similar positions on major policy issues, at that level collaboration has continued. However, there is less personal contact between members of the two organizations and fewer opportunities for face-to-face relationships. Today NAEYC members and Head Start organization members are less likely to know one another or be aware of each other's interests than they were in the past. The proliferation of more narrowly focused organizations will inevitably exacerbate this trend.

There is nothing wrong or sinister about the increased number of organizations representing alternative points of view in the early childhood community. Jerlean Daniel (this volume) notes that NAEYC has itself been the spawning ground for some of these organizations. Multiple organizations offer enhanced opportunity for professional leadership and action. But as groups multiply, alternative visions will likely increase. Moreover, as allied groups focus on their own problems and needs, they may devote less time and energy to promoting the shared vision and principles. So far the diverse membership of NAEYC has held together and the forces that might splinter our organization have been kept at bay. Can

NAEYC continue to pull the various constituencies together to speak with one voice on key issues? Sue Bredekamp noted (this volume) that in the early days NAEYC's outreach was primarily for the purpose of education—convincing others of the validity of a developmental perspective; today the purpose is less to educate and more to create an arena for the negotiation of differences.

There are risks of our process for change being either too precipitous, on the one hand, or too cumbersome and difficult on the other. More specifically, as the field expands how will the NAEYC adapt its governance and define the issues to avoid these extremes? If we choose to remain broad-based as we are now—focusing on education, policy, program improvement, and so on—can we find the right mix of board members at both the local and national level to pull the various constituencies into a common agenda? Do we have mechanisms in place to debate competing proposals from self-interest groups? Will we have to become more identified with the interests of one constituency or another or will we have to ignore important issues in order to remain one organization?

NAEYC Board members have already struggled with issues of representation and communication when they considered the relationship between states and the large urban areas within them. On an ongoing basis, the boards and staffs of the Association and the Affiliates will need to be always aware of the tensions and conflict that can result as the organization grows larger and more diverse, as personal relationships become more tenuous, and as self-interest becomes a more palpable driving force. I suggest we may need to do more to develop leaders able to think clearly about the common agenda and put together coalitions, leaders ready to go beyond their own personal agendas to support programs and policies that are good for all children.

Leadership will be key to holding on to our vision and core principles. No matter what the organizational structure, NAEYC's success will depend on the quality and diversity of leadership it is able to engage. Race, ethnicity, and class continue to be overriding concerns as they compromise individuals' opportunities to lead programs and to teach and care for children and families (Moore 1997). NAEYC is not exempt from the bias that afflicts all institutions in our society. The leadership of our Affiliate Groups, for instance, must concern us. Many do not have racially, culturally, or linguistically diverse leadership. Should we

Leadership will be key to holding on to our vision and core principles. No matter what the organizational structure, NAEYC's success will depend on the quality and diversity of leadership it is able to engage.

expect our Affiliates to be as diverse as our national Board?

Similarly, some Affiliate Groups do not reach out to all types of programs. It is not unusual to find Affiliates composed mainly of preschool teachers, with few child care or proprietary programs represented. While such Affiliates are able to maintain close personal relationships within their groups, they also create a clublike atmosphere that stands in the way of the diversity we need to speak with a strong voice for the field. Should NAEYC be more proactive in proposing how to balance relationships with diversity?

Although NAEYC has policy statements addressing prejudice and discrimination, it has not actively confronted the institutions that perpetuate it. For instance, the number of minority teachers entering teacher education programs is still well below the number of minority children in schools. Further, many minority teachers who do complete teacher education programs do not pass state certification tests, presumably because their preservice education has not given them the same level of skills and knowledge that others have received. We also see this low pass rate of African Americans and Hispanics on the National Board for Professional Teaching Standards (Bond 1998). As a result, the number of minority teachers is disproportionately low compared to the number of minority children in our schools and centers. Further, of those who are in the field too many are in the lowest paid positions.

Should NAEYC become more involved in fostering leadership opportunities to groups now excluded? Practices of universities are relevant as academic credentials increase in importance in the field. Can or should we use our bully pulpit as a professional organization to demand greater emphasis on diversity in university programs? NAEYC has made its beliefs about diversity explicit when defining curricula for teachers. But should we be more active in proposing and advocating strategies to enroll students from underrepresented minorities and students from families with low incomes in higher education?

The quality of professional leadership is also an ongoing challenge. Smith wrote that our organizational leaders need to listen well and think carefully. We need leaders who are flexible, experimental, and evaluative—not ideologues. I'm not sure why the fields of education and child rearing are so vulnerable to pendulum swings in theory and practice that lock us into either/or controversies. The reading wars, developmentally appropriate versus direct instruction, progressive versus traditional, regulation versus freedom, spanking versus time out, feeding and toileting on demand versus nutritional regimens and early toilet training—these disputes seem to occur with regularity, despite the research that argues against such dichotomies. But we have too many members who do not think things through for themselves or respond thoughtfully to fads and fetishes.

How do we prepare future leaders who have the capacity to entertain different perspectives, to deal with controversy, to tolerate the discomfort of change, to embrace difference? Daniel reminds us that decisionmaking is strengthened "when the intellectual and experiential capital of each participant is considered" (p. 68). Leaders in a growing field with an expanding knowledge base must have the tools to think with. They need a substantive knowledge base designed to enable them to think about problems, not just to react.

I do not think we offer our members enough opportunities to learn the skills of professional leadership. We focus on helping members work cooperatively with others, to negotiate consensus, but leadership is not only about consensus. It is also about creating and projecting new visions for others to work towards. Leadership is about thinking ahead and guiding, inspiring, and consolidating new positions not simply rubber-stamping old measures or reflecting the opinions of others. Leaders must be willing to suggest and endorse unpopular ideas and actions when these reflect our professional knowledge base and changing social conditions.

How often do early childhood professionals have the opportunity to debate different solutions to problems? Are there enough opportunities for them to propose and persuade and to experience conflict resolution that is not capitulation? Most early childhood professionals lack experiences advocating for their positions, which often involves careful thought about how best to convey key ideas. Perhaps we need to spend less time at our conferences on methods and more on encouraging thinking, collaborating, persuading, and—in a word—leading.

Can we design programs to support the development of professional leadership skills for our members? Can NAEYC influence colleges and universities to build development of leadership skills into their programs? Can the committee structure of national and local boards promote broader discussion of the theoretical and research issues in the field?

Leadership is about creating and projecting new visions for others to work towards. Leaders must be willing to suggest and endorse unpopular ideas and actions when these reflect our professional knowledge base and changing social conditions.

Professional knowledge base and standards for practice

In 1968, Biber & Franklin wrote that it is essential for "early childhood programs to be embedded in a psychological rationale if preschool education is to be protected from the establishment of programs constructed on too narrow vision of growth needs and evaluative schema designed to test too restricted evidence of outcomes" (p. 24). They took the position that "there is available a body of theoretical concepts concerning development in early childhood and a body of practice, congruent with these concepts, which is needed to serve as a framework for early childhood education" (p. 24). In her chapter Bredekamp recommends the same lens for setting standards today. She says from the days of Patty Hill to the present *Developmentally Appropriate Practice for Early Childhood Programs* (Bredekamp & Copple 1997), NAEYC's standards have reflected new knowledge and experience.

Our field is not an easy one to define, nor do its skills and knowledge fall into neatly defined disciplines. For example, the new research on the brain has recently expanded our knowledge base by adding neurobiology to the science of child development. Our knowledge of children's growth, development, and learning keeps growing as research discovers new information in both the biological and social sciences. Teachers and caregivers need a broader sweep of knowledge and skills than are found in any single discipline. One of NAEYC's major contributions has been setting standards of practice for the field that reflect the knowledge base available. And, as the knowledge base has changed, NAEYC has reviewed and revised its standards (see Bredekamp, this volume). The latest of these documents, "Developmentally Appropriate Practice in early childhood programs serving children from birth through age 8" (NAEYC 1997) has again outlined a comprehensive approach to early care and education. It reflects the extent, depth, and complexity of caring for and educating young children.

While interdisciplinary research in child development and learning may be the underlying core for the NAEYC standards, is it enough? Research reflects particular sociocultural perspectives as a consequence of who asks what questions, what data constitute evidence, and how the evidence is interpreted (Stott & Bowman 1996). Theory and research must be supplemented by both cultural and personal experience. NAEYC

Teachers and caregivers need a broader sweep of knowledge and skills than are found in any single discipline.

has consistently recognized this intersect between research and experience and, as Bredekamp pointed out, important values underlie our standards. These core values include observing children, recognizing their individual development and interests, and listening to their families.

Balancing research with values-based practice will continue to challenge us, particularly as we try to set standards that are responsive to children living in quite different social worlds. Economic and social divisions that are reflected in child rearing place many children at risk in regard to academic achievement because they do not learn the things at home that schools expect. Others are at risk because of disabilities and developmental delays. If programs are to not perpetuate the educational trajectory of these children toward academic failure, they must find ways for all children to learn school-related skills. This means that the kind of curricula that may be appropriate for some children may be different than those for others.

This situation argues against rigid interpretations of what is and is not developmentally appropriate. Reflecting the consensus of the panel that developed the position on developmentally appropriate practice, Brede-

kamp and Copple (1997) have tried to make clear that the principles and guidelines of the position statement are not a prescription for what and how much children can learn, which many teachers have mistakenly thought.

Unfortunately, there is still considerable confusion about what developmentally appropriate means. Many teachers think that it is developmentally inappropriate for children to learn about numbers and the alphabet, to have direct instruction, or to be required to participate in an activity. They emphasize play and self-direction. In reality, it may be developmentally appropriate or inappropriate to do any or all of those things. Neither the position statement nor the book on developmentally appropriate practice tells teachers exactly what and how to teach. What is stated is a set of developmental principles from theory and research, along with guidelines and examples of strategies and activities congruent with these.

The teacher must decide what is effective for a particular child or group of children at a particular time and place. Developmental principles are not the same as recipes for practice. Principles provide a framework for thinking about practice; they don't determine the practice itself. We have not been success-

Balancing research with values-based practice will continue to challenge us, particularly as we try to set standards that are responsive to children living in quite different social worlds.

ful in conveying these distinctions to all our members. The temptation to dogmatically adhere to particular practices, even if these work for a majority of children, does a disservice to children for whom they do not work or are not sufficient.

Developmentally appropriate practices must also be determined in relation to the learning goals and achievement standards for children. As expectations for early learning have increased, the onus of accountability has created new tensions in the field. There is general agreement that standardized testing of young children is fraught with difficulties, both because of the inadequacy of our instrumentation and the volatility of young children. Nevertheless, the reality of many children failing to receive the early learning experiences that will prepare them for school success must concern us. Appropriate education and competent supervision of teachers seem the obvious answer but how do we achieve this in a field notorious for requiring little, if any, education or program direction?

The profession must bear some of the responsibility for low quality. Most professions are organized along a career ladder with clear demarcations regarding the kind and amount of training required at each level. A license to practice (based on a standard program of study) is the baseline, with graduate and postgraduate education providing pathways to program leadership. This is not the model used in preschool education and we have forged little agreement regarding the kind or the amount of training needed by direct service providers, much less by managers, trainers, allied professionals, or supervisors.

Despite 20 years of research that points to teacher education as a critical variable in program quality, the field has yet to define and build support for adequate education of early childhood practitioners. NAEYC has certainly tried to bridge the tremendous gap between what is and what should be by recommending a lattice for advancement, allowing for options in professional development. Unfortunately, these efforts have had little success in raising standards, perhaps because the lattice is an unfamiliar model and may be too complex to gain easy acceptance. What is needed are clearly defined routes to professional competence and I hope the time has come for the professional community to come together and back a single career ladder for the education of professional staff.

The field of early education requires better educated personnel, despite the cost in both money and careers. The study of human development has progressed from a series of beliefs based on observation to a richly textured knowledge base reflecting research in biology, biochemistry, neurobiology, psychology, linguistics, anthropology, and sociology as well as the pedagogy of teaching academic subjects. To fully understand and translate this complex body of research into practice requires considerable background. Teachers and caregivers who are better educated and more knowledgeable about the science of early childhood are more likely to provide the most beneficial environment for children. The National Research Council's Committee on Early Childhood Pedagogy report *Eager to Learn* (Bowman, Donovan, & Burns 2001) recommends that teachers of young children should have a bachelors degree.

There is considerable opposition to this proposal. Traditionally, the field has not had fixed educational standards and, unlike public schools, role distinctions based on teacher education were rare. The culture of preschool classroom supported equality between adults—parents and teachers—at least partially because of the widespread belief that most adults are qualified to care for and educate young children. This belief has often led to viewing early childhood programs as employment opportunities for minimally skilled adults. Pushing college degrees for teachers is still viewed by many as creating artificial distinctions between adults responsible for young children, unduly driving up the cost of programs, and professional gatekeeping.

To change these beliefs and practices will require considerable leadership from the professional community. First, we need to disseminate the research supporting higher education standards for teachers of young children (which is so robust it has led Head Start to raise its educational standards for teachers, despite the difficulty of paying the tuition for teachers enrolled in higher education.) We must get the field to agree to support a single career ladder for teachers and caregivers that not only endorses but takes steps to require increased educational credentials. Additionally, we must define roles so that differentiations between teachers take full advantage of staff with different levels of education.

The question arises, should NAEYC propose and advocate for specific programs

Despite 20 years of research that points to teacher education as a critical variable in program quality, the field has yet to define and build support for adequate education of early childhood practitioners.

and policies to implement higher levels of education for early childhood teachers and caregivers? While this issue will certainly be contentious and challenge NAEYC's consensus-building ability, the Association has a long tradition of taking leadership. NAEYC gave support to the Child Development Associate (CDA) concept when it had little public support or credibility and made a giant step toward improving the quality of care and education for young children. Now a similar issue seems to require similar leadership.

In the effort to improve program quality, NAEYC created the accreditation initiative, which outlined standards for high quality. Among the standards is the need for good supervision. Yet, management training has been and continues to be one of the weakest links in preparation of early childhood personnel. Bloom and Sheerer wrote in 1992 that directors do not have adequate "formal training in the principles of program administration, staff management, clinical supervision, or group dynamics" (p. 581). The program management problem is intensified because the personnel in early childhood programs are almost always underpaid and operating under dismal working conditions.

At various times I have proposed that our profession needs to think seriously of restructuring the career ladder at both the bottom and the top. Perhaps at the entry level we should take a lesson from business and let programs train their own staffs, delaying formal academic involvement until workers are sure of their interest and commitment. Such a change would necessitate that directors and educational coordinators be able to provide training and supervision for new workers. If we were to do this, colleges and universities would need to play an enhanced role in preparing a cadre of early childhood leaders able to carry out such responsibilities.

At the upper end of the career ladder we continue to have a vacuum. Directors, educational coordinators, and other program leaders vary even more in background and training than do teachers and caregivers. The absence of adequate training in management and supervision makes achievement of high-quality programs problematic (Bloom 1992). Should NAEYC take a position regarding the qualifications of directors? Should NAEYC become involved in verifying director competencies? Might NAEYC itself license or certify directors?

Advocacy

Willer (this volume) writes of the importance of NAEYC taking principled stands on policy and legislation that reflect knowledge of child development. In my view two issues currently stand out as areas NAEYC will need to address soon. One is how to meet the increasing need for nonfamily child care. Not only has the number of children in out-of-home care and education risen dramatically in recent years, but there is every reason to expect this trend will continue. The new worldwide economy with its downward pressure on wages, increased equality in opportunities for women, and greater freedom for alternative lifestyles will continue to fuel the demand for out-of-home programs for young children.

The most rapidly expanding type of out-of-home care is center-based group care. Between 1991 and 1993, for example, the proportion of preschoolers who were cared for in organized facilities jumped from 23 to 30 percent, a 30% increase in just two years (Casper 1996). The largest proportion increase is in center-based care for infants and toddler (Capizzano, Adams, & Sonenstein 2000; Bowman, Donovan, & Burns 2001).

A number of reasons may be contributing to the demand for center-based care. Heightened awareness of potential abuse of children by exploitive caregivers, as rare as such cases are, has made parents less trusting of care arrangements that are not transparent in their operations. Too, the research on programs for young children has shown that there are significant educational advantages to center-based programs for preschool age children, particularly for children at risk in development and school achievement (Bowman, Donovan, & Burns 2001). While many parents prefer kith and kin and neighbor care for their children, many others would prefer centers but they are unable to afford them.

Should NAEYC take a position on the desirability of center-based care? Respond to the changing demographics in the field? Should we take a position on public policies that encourage, discourage, or are neutral on the funding for different kinds of programs? Should we aggressively educate parents and the public regarding research on program outcomes, recognizing the limitations and possible bias of that research? Should we advocate universal preschool education or reserving resources for those children most in need? Should we encourage parent care through family leave policies and subsidies for parents of infants and toddlers rather than the policy of out-of-home programs with child care allowance? Should all families have the option of such subsidies? How do we measure cost and benefit? How can we create an arena to debate these issues?

A second issue is the role of NAEYC in raising the quality of early childhood programs. The switch from a manufacturing economy to a technological one is under way and business and government leaders are raising the question of how to obtain the highly educated workers needed to sustain it. Early childhood education is increasingly seen as a necessary part of the move to higher educational standards. Recent educational research has emphasized the relationship between development and learning during the preschool/primary years and later educational achievement. The success of model programs has convinced the public that early education is essential to school readiness.

Unfortunately, there is ample evidence that most programs for young children do not qualify as good quality. This means, of course, that many children are beginning life with the liability of poor care and education, and therefore, compromised opportunities for development and learning. Program quality is particularly important for children who for any of a variety of reasons are at risk of school failure. Early childhood programs can support early development and give these children a leg up on school, but only if programs are of high quality.

The reasons for the poor quality of so many programs are complex. Certainly cost is a factor. Currently families spend from 5 to 40% of their family income on the care and education of their young children, with the families with the lowest income paying the highest percentage (Capizzano, Adams, & Sonenstein 2000). Raising the education level of staffs will certainly further escalate cost, which will affect the families that need good quality most, families with low incomes. Obviously, new strategies to pay for the kind of services young children need are essential. At present, one popular suggestion is universal preschool education through the public schools. Adding a preschool year to the public schools' responsibilities offers the possibility of switching the financial burden from families to the public and aligning early childhood teacher certification requirements with those of teachers of older children.

These are some of the burning issues that NAEYC will be called upon to respond to in the next decade. The Association has

Program quality is particularly important for children who for any of a variety of reasons are at risk of school failure. Early childhood programs can support early development and give these children a leg up on school, but only if programs are of high quality.

an important role to play in making sure that its members are prepared to go out into the field and meet the challenges they find there. In 1990, the National Board for Professional Teaching Standards set as its goal to "elevate the teaching profession, educate the public about the demands and complexity of excellent practice, and increase our chances of attracting and retaining in the profession talented college graduates with many other promising career options" (NAEYC 1996, 55). The early childhood standards for the National Board call for expert teachers to not only provide exemplary education in their own classrooms but to be able to "evaluate school progress and the allocation of school resources in light of their understanding of state and local educational objectives. They are knowledgeable about specialized school and community resources that can be engaged for their students' benefit, and are skilled at employing such resources as needed" (NAEYC 1996, 57). This is a much broader definition of teacher role than is traditional and vests teachers with leadership responsibilities.

Yet many of our members do not understand the issues nor are they being educated about the options. Indeed, the least attended sessions at conferences are those related to public policy. I suggest that there are two urgent tasks. First, our members need to understand that they cannot reform the field from their own classrooms or programs. They must join others if they are to achieve their mission—the improvement of services for children and families. This should start in college and NAEYC should develop student membership programs to enroll teachers and caregivers even before they enter the field.

Second, many of the problems that professionals in the field must face are new to them and even to the service systems in which they work. Many program practices are based on family structures and work patterns that have undergone radical change. The social context within which children and families live their lives is equally unstable. Why then spend time reviewing the history of early education or NAEYC? I think knowing—understanding our past—gives us insights valuable in planning our future. Change doesn't just happen. Traditions, beliefs, principles, knowledge, and relationships give us touch points so we aren't rudderless in a sea of change. Helping our members understand how the past influences the present is the first step in considering options for the future. Can we design more opportunities for members to consider the field's past as they contemplate new challenges?

Our members need to understand that they cannot reform the field from their own classrooms or programs. They must join others if they are to achieve their mission—the improvement of services for children and families.

Change doesn't just happen. Traditions, beliefs, principles, knowledge, and relationships give us touch points so we aren't rudderless in a sea of change.

I believe we are at the brink of a sea change in our profession. We have the opportunity to help frame this change for the better or worse. It will require all of our best thinking so that what we create today we can be proud of tomorrow. The stakes for professional leadership have risen sharply. NAEYC must decide on the role it will play in addressing the problems and opportunities that lie ahead. NAEYC has a responsibility to make sure that the young children of America have the kind of care and education they need and deserve. I believe we have both the capacity and the will to take on the challenges facing us. Our history should give us hope.

References

Biber, B. & M. Franklin. 1968. The relevance of developmental and psychodynamic concepts to the education of the preschool child. In *Early Childhood Play*, ed. M. Almy. New York: Simon & Schuster.

Bloom, P.J. 1992. The child care center director: A critical component of program quality. *Educational Horizons* 70 (3): 138–45.

Bloom, P.J., & M. Sheerer. 1992. The effect of leadership training on child care program quality. *Early Childhood Research Quarterly* 7(4): 579–94.

Bond, L. 1998. Culturally responsive pedagogy and the assessment of accomplished teaching. *Journal of Negro Education* 67 (3): 242–54.

Bowman, B.T., M.S. Donovan, & M.S. Burns, eds. 2001. *Eager to learn: Educating our preschoolers*. Washington, DC: National Academy Press.

Bredekamp, S. & C. Copple, eds. 1997. *Developmentally appropriate practice in early childhood programs* Rev. ed. Washington, DC: NAEYC.

Capizzano, J., G. Adams, & F. Sonenstein. 2000. Child care arrangements for children under five: Variations across states. *New Federalism: National Survey of America's Families* Series B, no. B-7. Washington, DC: The Urban Institute.

Casper, L.M. 1996. Who's minding our preschoolers? *Current Population Reports*. Washington, DC: U.S. Bureau of the Census.

Moore, E.K. 1997. Race, class, and education. In *Leadership in early care and education*, S.L. Kagan & B.T. Bowman, eds., 69–74. Washington, DC: NAEYC.

NAEYC. 1996. NBPTS Standards For Early Childhood/Generalist Certification: Recommendations of the National Board for Professional Teaching Standards. In *Guidelines for preparation of early childhood professionals*, 53–103. Washington, DC: NAEYC.

NAEYC. 1997. NAEYC position statement: Developmentally appropriate practice in early childhood programs serving children from birth through age 8. In *Developmentally appropriate practice in early childhood programs*, Rev. ed., eds. S. Bredekamp & C. Copple, 3–30. Washington, DC: Author.

Stott, F., & B. Bowman. 1996. Child development knowledge: A slippery base for practice. *Early Childhood Research Quarterly* 11(2): 169–83.

Appendix

Leaders have always been vital to the ongoing development of NAEYC and its work to improve the quality of programs serving young children and their families. These are the people who help identify and define the issues and priorities that need to be addressed to improve practice. They are instrumental in developing and implementing strategies to address these issues. They take responsibility for creating, nurturing, and protecting the structure and support systems that enable the organization to exist and be effective.

The people listed in this chapter are all those who have been elected as presidents and Board members during NAEYC's 75-year history. For each of them there have been literally thousands of other volunteer leaders serving the Association and supporting its work through participation on appointed committees, task groups, commissions, and panels.

- **NANE/NAEYC Presidents 1926–2001**

- **NANE/NAEYC Board Members 1926–2000**

NANE/NAEYC Presidents 1926–2001

The following photographs and text are reproduced from the Gallery of NANE/NAEYC Presidents on display at the headquarters building in Washington, D.C. The photographs were selected to represent the time period when each person served as president. The text, limited by the size of the frames, presents a concise biography up to the time of their presidency and a synopsis of major events that occurred during each president's term.

Patty Smith Hill

Patty Smith Hill

Convener and Temporary Chair of Committee on Nursery Schools 1925

Patty Smith Hill (1868-1946) chaired the first Conference on Nursery Schools, which met on the last weekend of February 1926. Aware of the potential in the new nursery school movement, and concerned because it lacked unification, she worked toward that meeting for at least five years. From the careful selection of members for its sponsoring group, through preliminary planning sessions, down to her opening speech and a summary of problems confronting the venture, she was very much in control. Patty Smith Hill so dominated the early nursery school movement that it still retains a remarkable resemblance to the educational philosophy that characterized her professional and personal life.

As far back as 1921, when most of America's nursery school teachers were imported from England or sent there for training, Professor Hill summoned young Lois Meek (Stolz) from Washington to her office at Teachers College, Columbia University. They discussed the need for some sort of affiliation for professionals in preschool work, then waited and watched for the next two or three years. By the mid-1920s, alarmed at the proliferation of all types of nursery schools despite the lack of standards or curriculum plans, and with the threat of some unqualified person taking leadership, Patty Hill decided to act. After 40 years of involvement with various associations and educational theories, she believed this might be her last chance to help America's young children and their families. Her careful structuring of that first Committee on Nursery Schools led, by 1931, to formalizing the National Association for Nursery Education (NANE) which became the NAEYC of today.

Lois Hayden Meek Stolz

Chair, National Committee on Nursery Schools 1926–1929

President, National Association for Nursery Education 1929–1931

Lois Hayden Stolz

Dr. Stolz, born in Washington, D.C., in 1891, began her career as a teacher in the Washington, D.C., public schools in 1912. At Teachers College/Columbia University, while earning her M.A. (1922) and Ph.D. (1925), she became a colleague and friend of Patty Smith Hill.

As early as 1921, Patty Hill talked with Lois Meek Stolz about the rapid increase in the number of nursery schools amid a lack of consensus about the type of program the schools should offer, and by 1925 she engaged Stolz's help in calling the first meeting of early childhood educators. Hill felt she could be more influential if she remained in the background and entrusted Stolz to be the official chairperson. During Stolz's tenure as Chair of the Committee and President of NANE, debate focused on whether to build the organization as a separate entity or to disband and try to influence other organizations to give greater consideration to nursery school problems and research in child development. Dr. Stolz believed in maintaining NANE as a separate organization and spoke with pride about its accomplishments at the 50th anniversary celebration at the Anaheim, California, Conference in November 1976.

George Dinsmore Stoddard

President, NANE 1931–1933

George Dinsmore Stoddard

Dr. Stoddard, born in 1897 in Pennsylvania, received his A.B. from Pennsylvania State College (1921), a diploma from the University of Paris (1923), and his Ph.D. from the University of Iowa (1925). In 1928 he became Director of the Iowa Child Welfare Research Station.

Milton Senn, interviewing Dr. Stoddard in the early 1970s, reported Stoddard's perception that NANE was a bond that pulled the new child study centers together and provided a sense of an educational movement "to secure a better educational environment and a better educational experience." By 1935 George Stoddard would assist in organizing the Society for Research in Child Development (SRCD).

Mary Dabney Davis

Mary Dabney Davis

President, NANE 1933–1935

Dr. Davis, born in Pittsburgh, Pennsylvania, received three degrees from Teachers College/Columbia University—a B.S. in 1919, an M.A. in 1924, and a Ph.D. in 1925. From 1923 until her retirement, Dr. Davis was educational specialist in nursery-kindergarten-primary education to the United States Office of Education.

Davis's tenure as NANE president was in the midst of the Depression, and through her position in the Department of Education she had a leadership role in and involved NANE in the approximately 2,000 Works Progress Administration (WPA) nursery schools. As soon as the creation of the WPA nursery schools was announced, NANE responded with recommendations to ensure that such an extensive program would help, rather than harm, children enrolled in the schools.

Ruth Andrus

Ruth Andrus

President, NANE 1935–1937

Dr. Andrus, born in 1886, received her A.B. and A.M. from Vassar college in 1907 and 1908, respectively. During the time she served as NANE president she also served as chief of the Child Development and Parent Education Bureau, New York State Education Department.

During her presidency, the Association was concerned with federally funded nursery schools—promoting training for teachers and standards and values of nursery education. At the 1937 NANE Conference in Nashville, Tennessee, a resolution was passed that no future conference would be headquartered at a location where racial discrimination was known to exist. Twenty-seven years passed before another NANE conference was held in the south—Miami, Florida, in 1964. At the 1939 Conference, a representative of the New York Board of Education said the Board would not be interested in nursery education until there was proof of its value. Ruth Andrus replied that the Board of Education should first show proof that first grade was important.

Ruth Updegraff

President, NANE 1937-1939

Ruth Updegraff

Dr. Updegraff, born in Iowa in 1902, studied and taught at Vassar College (1923 to 1925), then went to the University of Iowa where she completed her Ph.D. in 1928 and became a professor of child development and guidance. During the time she was president of NANE, she published two books for the field: *Practice in Preschool Education* and *Iowa Studies Preschool Education*.

During Dr. Updegraff's presidency the nation was recovering from the Depression and confronting increasing concerns about national defense. Both of these events increased the number of children being cared for by someone other than a parent. During these times NANE tried to address a number of troubling issues: fast preparation programs to "qualify" preschool teachers; the establishment of programs under many different auspices with no standards; and the need for parent education. A Distribution Center was established at the University of Iowa under Updegraff's supervision to institute a central location for NANE correspondence.

Grace Langdon

President, NANE 1939-1941

Grace Langdon

Dr. Langdon was born in Nebraska in 1889, began her career as a teacher in rural elementary schools, and became a supervisor of kindergarten-primary grades before going to Teachers College/Columbia University for three degrees—a B.S. in 1926, an A.M. in 1927, and a Ph.D. in 1933. During the time she served as president of NANE, she was the specialist in Family Life Education in the Work Projects Administration located in Washington, D.C. A few of Grace Langdon's books include *Home Guidance for Young Children; The Discipline of Well-Adjusted Children; Teacher-Parent Interviews;* and *Helping Parents Understand Their Children's School.* During these pre-war and war years, NANE almost faded away with fewer than 100 members.

Amy Hostler

Amy Hostler

President, NANE 1941–1943

Dr. Amy Hostler, born in Iowa in 1898, attended St. Cloud Normal School and taught kindergarten and first grade prior to starting a nursery school at Teachers College. She earned advanced degrees from the University of Chicago and Western Reserve University. When Amy Hostler became president of NANE she was the student personnel director and administration officer at Bank Street College of Education. During her presidency she became dean of Mills College of Education.

During this period, the increased activity within nursery education caused strife within NANE. Although the Lanham Act of World War II increased the number of nursery schools, it lacked the support of many Americans who felt that women should be at home taking care of their children and of many early childhood professionals who felt that the national conscience was focused on providing child "watchers" rather than quality experiences for young children. Conflicts within NANE stemmed from disagreement about who was answerable for the sponsorship, funding, and monitoring of nursery schools.

N. Searle Light

N. Searle Light

President, NANE 1943–1945

Mr. Light was born in New York in 1886 and received his B.A. in education from Yale University. During the major part of his professional career he served as chief of the Bureau of School and Community Services in the Connecticut State Department of Education. Mr. Light served as NANE president during the end of World War II, and, in an audience with President Truman, he presented proposals on behalf of a number of educational organizations recommending that the Office of Education and the Children's Bureau continue to fund child care services originated under the Lanham Act. However, after a six-month extension, federal funds were withdrawn. NANE conferences were not held during the war years because of travel curtailment, but the first *NANE Bulletin* was published in April 1945.

James L. Hymes Jr.

President, NANE 1945–1947

James L. Hymes Jr.

Dr. Hymes earned his A.B. in 1934 from Harvard College and received both his M.A. (1936) and his Ed.D. (1946) in child development and parent education at Teachers College/Columbia University. At the time of his election as NANE president, Jimmy Hymes was the director of two wartime child care centers of the Kaiser Company, Inc., in Portland, Oregon. Following the war he was professor of education and coordinator of Early Childhood Education at the State University of New York–New Paltz. He is known for many books including *Teaching the Child Under Six; Discipline; Effective Home-School Relations;* and *Listen Teacher: The Children Speak.*

With the end of World War II came reductions in services for children: the Lanham nursery schools were closed and the federal government returned to its traditional role of non-involvement in child care; and full-day kindergartens were changed to half-day programs to accommodate the increasing number of 5-year-old children. Jimmy Hymes noted the frightening honor of becoming NANE president during this period of retrenchment and the "horrible lag between what most parents of young children want (and what professional workers want) and what most communities actually offer in facilities and arrangements for young children." The *NANE Bulletin* continued to be the main source of communication for members. In August 1947 conferences resumed.

Frances Horwich

Frances Horwich

President, NANE 1947–1951

Dr. Horwich spent her childhood in Ohio then studied early childhood education at the University of Chicago (Ph.B. 1929), Teachers College/Columbia University (M.A. 1933), and Northwestern University (Ph.D. 1942). After teaching first grade and supervising WPA nursery schools, she taught at Teachers College and Mills College and was at Roosevelt University during her tenure as NANE president. Immediately following her presidency she began writing, producing, and appearing in the televised "Ding Dong School" where she was known as "Miss Frances."

During Horwich's presidency, increasing numbers of mothers were working outside the home and the demand for child care was greater than during the war. NANE focused on the lack of concern about the quality of child care among the nation's officials, parents, and public, which translated to a lack of attention to qualifications for personnel and regulations for facilities. This visible indifference to young children fed into a declining interest in NANE, thus Association activities focused on rebuilding and revitalizing membership through national conferences and the *NANE Bulletin*. The Distribution Center moved to Roosevelt College in Chicago.

Millie Almy

Millie Almy

President, NANE 1952-1953

Dr. Almy, born in New York, majored in child study at Vassar College (A.B. 1936) and received her A.M. (1945) and Ph.D. (1948) from Teachers College/Columbia University. Her early career was devoted to teaching/supervising in nursery schools and child care centers and was followed by teaching/research/writing at universities (including Columbia University during her presidency). In addition to publishing numerous articles, Dr. Almy is well known for the following two books: *Child Development* and *The Early Childhood Educator at Work*.

The years of her presidency were quiet times—the activity surrounding the WPA nurseries and the Lanham emergency centers was gone. However, hope for federal support lingered as reflected by the phrase printed on NANE's stationery: "Nursery Schools—The Next Step in Public Education." A NANE merger with ACE (now known as ACEI, Association for Childhood Education International) was considered, as it had been in almost every previous president's tenure. Time after time the conclusion was the same—NANE was not willing to lose its identity by merging with another group. The Distribution Center moved to the University of Rhode Island.

Harriet Nash

President, NANE 1954-1955

Harriet Nash

Dr. Nash, born and educated in Connecticut, received her B.A. (1933) in child study at Vassar College and her M.A. (1936) and her Ed.D. (1953) in early childhood from Teachers College/Columbia University. Her early career experiences included camp counseling and teaching/directing nursery schools, followed by a lengthy tenure (including the time of her presidency) as consultant of early childhood and parent education of the Connecticut State Department of Education.

Dr. Nash's view of America's attitude toward young children during her presidency was one of widespread compassion for human rights worldwide, but little concern for early childhood education in this country. This attitude was reflected in the lack of concern over poor quality programs as child care expanded to meet the needs of mothers employed outside the home. It was a time of struggle for NANE as the Association tried to determine what breadth of membership the organization should serve. A merger with ACEI or the Child Welfare League was considered and rejected. An official designation for affiliated groups was also considered.

Theodora Buckland Reeve

President, NANE 1956–1958

Theodora Buckland Reeve

Ms. Reeve received her B.A. (1929) from Mt. Holyoke College, her M.Ed. from Teachers College of Winnetka (1937), and her M.A. (1947) from Columbia University. Following early teaching experiences in the Institute for the Blind, in Beirut, Lebanon, and in public schools, Ms. Reeve served the rest of her career as a consultant in the New York Education Department's Bureau of Child Development and Parent Education.

Ms. Reeve recalls the tone of the country during her presidency as uninterested in funding public kindergartens in spite of the demand for nursery education. During her tenure as NANE president, she and two previous presidents (Nash and Almy) worked out the details for implementing an official NANE Affiliate structure, the *NANE Bulletin* became *The Journal of Nursery Education,* and a desk space in Chicago became the first national headquarters.

Edna Mohr

Edna Mohr

President, NANE 1959–1960

At the time of her presidency, Edna Mohr was consultant on day care in the Bureau of Family and Child Welfare, Department of Public Welfare, Pennsylvania. Ms. Mohr's term as president was a time when the Association looked inward at its structure and capacity to become a more forceful voice for children. The need for clarifications in the new Affiliate structure was addressed jointly with the Midwest Association for Nursery Education. The NANE Board held serious discussions about the need to employ an executive secretary for the Association.

Glenn Rogers Hawkes

Glenn Rogers Hawkes

President, NANE 1961–1962

Dr. Hawkes, born in Idaho, served in the Army (from 1941 to 1945) then earned his B.S. (1947) and M.S. (1948) in psychology from Utah State University and his Ph.D. (1950) in psychology from Cornell University. He served as professor and head of the Department of Child Development at Iowa State University during his tenure as president of NANE. Dr. Hawkes co-authored *Behavior and Development from Five to Twelve,* and *The Disadvantaged Child: Issues and Innovations.*

During Dr. Hawkes's term as president, NANE focused on the systematic identification of goals and strategies to strengthen the Association so that it could speak more effectively as a national organization and provide much-needed services. Goals included increasing membership, providing yearly conferences, establishing a permanent headquarters staff and base, and converting the journal to a more scholarly, professional publication. Priority was given to raising funds for these activities, and incremental steps began to be achieved.

Ralph Leo Witherspoon

President, NANE–NAEYC 1963–1966

Ralph Leo Witherspoon

Dr. Witherspoon was born and earned three degrees in Michigan—his B.A. at Central Michigan College (1932) and his M.A. (1940) and Ph.D. (1949) at the University of Michigan. Following teaching and principalship experiences, he spent the greatest portion of his career as professor of psychology at Florida State University. As an author he is best known for his collaboration on *Good Schools for Young Children.*

As Dr. Witherspoon assumed the presidency, NANE still had limited financial resources. However, the vision of what needed to happen grew stronger, inspired by such significant events in the field of early childhood education as the launching of Head Start. A cadre of NANE leaders invested untold amounts of time, travel, and expertise to assist Witherspoon in making the following things happen: the Association's name was changed to the National Association for the Education of Young Children (NAEYC) in order to project and invite a broader base of participation; the format of the journal was updated and the title was changed to *Young Children;* a major contribution was received from The Grant Foundation to improve the publications program; Cornelia Goldsmith was installed as the first executive secretary in 1964 and worked in New York City until the move to Washington, D.C., in 1966; and Milton E. Akers became the first executive director. Membership grew from less than 2,000 to more than 9,000 during this period.

Eveline Beaver Omwake

Eveline Beaver Omwake

President, NAEYC 1967–1970

Eveline Omwake, born in 1911, received her A.B. from Ursinus College in 1933 and her M.A. from Teachers College/Columbia University in 1937. She taught at the Dalton School and Vassar College prior to becoming assistant professor of the Child Study Center and director of the nursery school at Yale University from 1952 until her retirement. She also directed the Nursery School and Children's School at the Vassar Summer Institute from 1948 to 1957 and consulted for the White House nursery school during the Kennedy Administration.

The flurry of NAEYC growth continued during Ms. Omwake's presidency—the membership grew from 13,000 to close to 18,000. With this growth came concerns about meeting the needs of a more diverse membership—diverse in race, ethnic group, cultural perspective, and type/degree of preparation to work with young children. This prompted renewed discussion about licensing and training needs and new discussion regarding full recognition for all NAEYC members. A special task force was formed at the 1969 Salt Lake City conference. Recommendations from the task force were presented at the 1970 Boston conference and led to viable goals that strengthened the ability of NAEYC to respond to membership needs. Milestones during Eveline Omwake's presidency included a contract awarded to NAEYC by the Bureau of Indian Affairs to train teachers of Indian reservation schools and the Association's purchase of its first national Headquarters building at 1834 Connecticut Avenue, N.W., in Washington, D.C.

Evangeline H. Ward

President, NAEYC 1970–1974

Evangeline H. Ward

Dr. Ward, a native of Virginia, received her B.S. from Hampton Institute, her M.A. from Atlanta University, and her Ed.D. from Teachers College/Columbia University. After teaching at the early childhood, elementary, and secondary levels, she returned to Hampton Institute to develop an early childhood major. She served as the director of the St. Louis Comprehensive Day Care Service Agency prior to her longstanding professorship in early childhood education at Temple University.

During Dr. Ward's tenure as NAEYC president, the nation demonstrated conflicting commitments to young children—the Comprehensive Child Development Act passed Congress only to be vetoed, and Head Start funding became less and less certain. One positive development, however, was the establishment of the Office of Child Development (OCD). Dr. Ward focused the NAEYC Board's attention on institution building so that the Association could have "vitality and strength regardless of the tornadic-style whims and fancies of society and legislative feats of a temporary nature." Conferences became highly visible events during this period, and when Senator Walter Mondale spoke at the 1971 Minneapolis conference, paid picketers demonstrated in front of the Conference hotel. By the 1972 Atlanta conference, J.D. Andrews, who had provided voluntary conference consultation, was appointed to the staff. Milton E. Akers resigned as executive director because of failing health, and Marilyn M. Smith accepted the Board's appointment to that position with the understanding that she and Dr. Andrews would administer the Association as a team. Membership Action Group (MAG) grants were initiated as an avenue for encouraging individual responsibility toward achieving the Association's goals. The MAG concept was dedicated to Milton Akers. The first national observance of the Week of the Young Child (WOYC) occurred in 1971.

David Bruce Gardner

President, NAEYC 1974–1976

David Bruce Gardner

Dr. Gardner, born in Salt Lake City, received two degrees from the University of Utah (a B.S. in 1948 and an M.S. in 1949) and a Ph.D. from Cornell University in 1952. Following professorship and administrative responsibilities in the child development departments at Utah State University and Iowa State University, he was professor and chairperson of the Child Development Department at Colorado State University during his term as president of NAEYC. Child development instructors are familiar with his book, *Development in Early Childhood: The Preschool Years.*

The Association continued to look inward—studying, reaffirming, and modifying governance, communications, and services. An outside consultant conducted a governance study, President Gardner conducted the first membership survey, a Meet the Candidate opportunity was introduced, and the number of full Board meetings was increased from two to three per year. For the first time in its history the Association began to accumulate savings. A restricted reserve for emergencies was established, and funds were accumulated to amortize the mortgage by the Association's 50th anniversary in 1976.

Bernard Spodek

President, NAEYC 1976–1978

Bernard Spodek

Dr. Spodek, born in Brooklyn in 1931, received his B.A. from Brooklyn College and two degrees from Teachers College/Columbia University—an M.A. in 1955 and an Ed.D. in 1962. Following teaching experiences at the nursery, kindergarten, and primary levels he moved to higher education—first at the University of Wisconsin and then in 1965 to early childhood education at the University of Illinois. Two of his books well-known at the time of his presidency were *Teaching in the Early Years* and *Early Childhood Education.*

The Association's 50th anniversary was celebrated throughout 1976 and culminated with special activities at the 1976 Anaheim Conference. All living past presidents were guests including the first president, Lois Meek Stolz, who addressed the conference. Fire marshals would not permit a symbolic copy of the mortgage for the Headquarters building to be burned (as originally planned), so the copy was torn up instead. NAEYC continued to grow stronger and focused intensely on effective communication with the Association's growing membership—31,000 by the end of Dr. Spodek's term.

Jan McCarthy

President, NAEYC 1978–1980

Ruth Updegraff

Dr. McCarthy attended one-room schools in rural Indiana, earned two degrees at Ball State University, and obtained her Ed.D. from Indiana University. All of her professional studies have focused on early childhood and elementary education, and she has taught children ranging in age from the age of infancy through 8 years. In 1962, the dean of education at Indiana State University enticed her to join that faculty and develop a program in nursery school education. She was head of ISU's early childhood education department during her tenure as NAEYC president.

Two concurrent agendas prevailed during Dr. McCarthy's presidency: (1) maintenance and improvement of the Association and (2) leadership responding to political issues and the state of the field of early childhood education. New internal procedures included establishing more specificity in the criteria and review of NAEYC officer and Board candidates; replacing formal business meeting resolutions with a process for the entire membership to prioritize problems (later to evolve into the Membership Expression of Opinion); and, arranging for the NAEYC archives to be housed at the Cunningham Memorial Library at Indiana State University. NAEYC initiatives related to external events included requesting the Department of Labor to change its rating of child care workers to collect more accurate data on their salary status; identifying NAEYC's ethical beliefs and practices, and issuing the "Commitment to Children" in response to the nation's concerns about political scandals; issuing guidelines for NAEYC members to review and respond to the Federal Interagency Day Care Regulations (FIDCR); and joining the National Council for Accreditation of Teacher Education (NCATE) to influence early childhood teacher preparation programs.

Barbara T. Bowman

Barbara T. Bowman

President, NAEYC 1980–1982

Ms. Bowman, born in 1928, earned her B.A. from Sarah Lawrence College in 1950 and her M.A. in 1952 in the Department of Education at the University of Chicago. Following a variety of experiences teaching children and adults in this country and in Iran, she joined the faculty of the Erikson Institute for Early Education/Loyola University in 1966 and was the director of graduate studies during her term as NAEYC president.

Following a decade of institution building, NAEYC moved boldly into the arena of standard setting and promotion during the 1980s. Teacher education guidelines for four- and five-year programs were adopted and submitted for NCATE approval, and work began on guidelines for associate degree programs. It was during Barbara Bowman's presidency that the milestone decision was made to develop NAEYC's accreditation system for early childhood programs. Throughout the Association's history concern about the quality of programs and teachers had manifested itself in published statements, but the accreditation initiative went further by stating its intention to stimulate programs to improve and to provide a form of recognition for programs that demonstrate high quality.

Bettye McDonald Caldwell

Bettye McDonald Caldwell

President, NAEYC 1982–1984

Dr. Caldwell grew up in Texas and completed her A.B. at Baylor University in 1945, her A.M. at the University of Iowa in 1946, and her Ph.D. in 1951 at Washington University. Following a variety of positions at universities in Missouri, Illinois, and New York, she joined the faculty at the University of Arkansas at Little Rock. At the time of her presidency she was the Donaghey Distinguished Professor of Education. Her prolific research publications focus on all aspects of early care and education, and she is known for her promotion of the term educarer.

During Dr. Caldwell's term as president, attention focused on the accreditation program—developing and approving the organizational structure system and accreditation criteria and conducting the field test. Amazingly, standard setting was not limited to the accreditation project—position statements were adopted on child care licensing; family day care regulation; and nomenclature, benefits, and wages. A grant from Carnegie Corporation of New York supported the establishment of a new Information Service Department, and the First Annual Spring Conference for NAEYC leaders was held in 1983. By the end of Dr. Caldwell's term membership had increased to 43,000 and staff had outgrown the headquarters building.

Docia Zavitkovsky

President, NAEYC 1984–1986

Docia Zavitkovsky

Docia Zavitkovsky grew up in Panama and earned two degrees from the University of Southern California—a B.S. in education and an M.S. in administration. She became director of a Lanham Act day care center in Santa Monica during World War II, and, when the California Department of Education continued funding these centers after the war, became the director of the Santa Monica Children's Centers until her retirement in 1983. From 1956 to 1966 she edited and distributed the *Journal of Nursery Education* out of her home's garage.

Rapid growth in size and projects continued during Docia Zavitkovsky's presidency. With developmental work on accreditation completed (the National Academy of Early Childhood Programs began accepting applicants in September 1985) work began to more explicitly define developmentally appropriate practice—a term referenced frequently in the accreditation criteria. In 1986 the first position statement on developmentally appropriate practice was adopted, and work began on developing a position on compensation, quality, and affordability. Two other initiatives were launched during Ms. Zavitkovsky's term: the development of a code of ethics, and publication of the *Early Childhood Research Quarterly*. With no remaining space at NAEYC headquarters, two departments moved to rented space and an expansion fund campaign began.

David Elkind

David Elkind

President, NAEYC 1986–1988

Dr. Elkind received his doctorate at the University of Southern California, Los Angeles, and from 1964 to 1965 he was a National Science Foundation Senior Postdoctoral Fellow at Piaget's Institut d' Epistemologie Genetique in Geneva. During his tenure as NAEYC President, he was professor of child study at Tufts University, Medford, Massachusetts. Dr. Elkind is a prolific writer of research, theoretical, and popular articles/books but at the time of his presidency was best known for *Miseducation of Young Children* and *The Hurried Child*.

The Association continued to assert leadership in the field by adopting and promoting position statements on issues of concern. Statements adopted during Dr. Elkind's term included "Quality, Compensation, and Affordability in Early Childhood Programs"; "Guide for Developing Legislation Creating or Expanding Programs for Young Children"; "Standardized Testing of Young Children"; "Guidelines for Advanced Degree Programs; and an anti-discrimination statement. Public policy efforts were primarily focused on the Act for Better Child Care and the Economics of Child Care Study that was launched as a joint initiative with the Administration for Children, Youth and Families (ACYF). In 1987 the Association purchased the 1832 Connecticut Avenue, N.W., property adjacent to the existing headquarters, and, following renovations to join the two buildings, reunited all departments into one location in the spring of 1988. Membership reached 62,000 in 1988.

Ellen Galinsky

President, NAEYC 1988–1990

Ellen Galinsky

Ellen Galinsky grew up in West Virginia and received her B.A. at Vassar College in 1964 and her M.S. from Bank Street College of Education in 1970. At the time of her election to the NAEYC Board she had been on the faculty of Bank Street College for 24 years, and by the end of her term she was co-president and founder of the Families and Work Institute. Two of her best known books are *The New Extended Family: Day Care That Works;* and *Between Generations: The Six Stages of Parenthood.*

During Ellen Galinsky's presidency attention again turned inward, and, with the help of an organizational consultant, three aspects of NAEYC were examined: identity and mission; Board/staff roles and relationships; and the role of Affiliate Groups and membership. A separate Public Affairs Department was established, the Full Cost of Quality Campaign was launched, and the Membership Action Group project was expanded to include a separate fund for grants related to compensation issues. Two milestones in 1989 were the release of *Anti-Bias Curriculum: Tools for Empowering Young Children* and adoption of the "Code of Ethical Conduct: Guidelines for Responsible Behavior in Early Childhood Education." Work began on two new position statements: a model for professional development and guidelines for curriculum and assessment that would extend the work that began with the positions on developmentally appropriate practice. Membership continued to grow and reached over 73,000 in 1990.

Lana L. Hostetler

Lana L. Hostetler

President, NAEYC 1990–1992

Lana Hostetler grew up in Illinois and received her baccalaureate degree at Illinois Wesleyan University in 1963 and her masters degree at Illinois State University in 1967. Following experiences teaching children and adults she joined the faculty of Lincoln Land Community College in the Child Care Services Department in 1970. Starting in 1981 she was also a legislative consultant for not-for-profit organizations in the state of Illinois.

Lana Hostetler began her term as NAEYC President by presiding over the Opening Session of the 1990 Conference on the steps of the U.S. Capitol—launching The Full Cost of Quality Campaign and celebrating the enactment of the Act for Better Child Care. Work was completed on a number of position statements during her term including those on early childhood teacher certification; school readiness (in response to Goal 1 of the National Education Goals); guidelines for appropriate curriculum content and assessment; and the first revisions to the accreditation criteria. The results of a monumental economics of child care study were released at the November 1991 Denver conference in the book *Demand and Supply of Child Care in 1990*. Two new, major initiatives were launched with the aid of grants: the Goal One Project funded by the Kellogg Foundation; and the establishment of the National Institute for Early Childhood Professional Development with funding assistance from Carnegie Corporation of New York. Continued attention to institutional matters was reflected in the adoption of "Guiding Principles to Enhance Governing Board Leadership" and the initiation of a structure study. The need for an expanded headquarters was a concern throughout Ms. Hostetler's presidency, and during the last weeks of her term, J.D. Andrews successfully negotiated the purchase of a much larger building at 1509 16th Street, N.W., in Washington, D.C.

Lilian G. Katz

President, NAEYC 1992–1994

Lilian G. Katz

Born in London, Dr. Katz spent her childhood in Great Britain and emigrated to the San Francisco area at age 15. She received her B.A. from San Francisco State College and her Ph.D. from Stanford. In 1970 Lilian Katz became director of ERIC/Elementary and Early Childhood Education in conjunction with her faculty position at the University of Illinois, Urbana-Champaign. A prolific writer and speaker, two of her best known books are *Engaging Children's Minds: The Project Approach* and *Talks with Teachers of Young Children: A Collection*.

NAEYC's move to expanded headquarters space at 1509 16th Street, N.W., in Washington, D.C., occurred during the first months of Dr. Katz's presidency. With the additional space, it was possible to add much needed staff—a 38% increase during her two year tenure. A study of NAEYC's structure resulted in initiatives to strengthen communications and strategic planning among NAEYC and its Affiliate Groups and to streamline and improve membership processing at all levels. Other milestones include the adoption of three major position statements ("Violence in the Lives of Children"; "Conceptual Framework for Early Childhood Professional Development"; and "Guidelines for Preparation of Early Childhood Professionals"), the launching of a revision process for the positions on developmentally appropriate practice, and directing the Full Cost of Quality Campaign towards strategies for promoting high-quality early childhood programs. As NAEYC's membership grew to 90,000 in 1994, President Katz reminded members and leaders to value and protect the Association's practice of soliciting and respecting diverse opinions in all of NAEYC's planning and work on behalf of young children.

Jerlean Daniel

Jerlean Daniel
President, NAEYC 1994-1996

Dr. Daniel grew up in Sacramento, California, then moved to Pennsylvania and earned three degrees from the University of Pittsburgh—a B.A. in political science, an M.S. in child development, and a Ph.D. in higher education. Having devoted 18 years to directing child care and development centers, she currently applies her experience and knowledge to teaching courses relating to child development and child care at the University of Pittsburgh.

Dr. Daniel's presidency occurred during a period of increased public attention to early childhood development and education, and she provided leadership for NAEYC to both respond to and influence such changes. She was NAEYC's public voice for such varied events as the devastating Oklahoma City bombing April 19, 1995; the joyous Stand For Children rally at the Lincoln Memorial, June 1, 1996; and press conferences releasing results of national studies relating to the cost and quality of child care. Her leadership skills facilitated adoption of a number of new or revised position statements including: "Responding to Linguistic and Cultural Diversity" ; "A Call to Action on Behalf of Children and Families" ; "Technology and Young Children" ; revision of "Developmentally Appropriate Practice" ; and "Prevention of Child Abuse in Early Childhood Programs." NAEYC created the Young Children International program to create strategies identifying and disseminating international information on early childhood practices. Among the major initiatives to enhance organizational capacity that took place during Dr. Daniel's presidency were the Association Development Process and a revised system for affiliation of new groups; revised roles and functions of NAEYC committees and panels; and a foundation-sponsored think tank to consider lessons learned from a decade of NAEYC accreditation and formulate goals for the next decade. In these activities and throughout her tenure, Dr. Daniel emphasized that early childhood professionals are developmentalists.

Richard M. Clifford

President, NAEYC 1996-1998

Richard M. Clifford

Dr. Clifford was born in North Carolina, where he completed all of his formal education. His degrees include a B.S. in physics from Wake Forest University, and a M.Ed. and a Ph.D., both in educational administration, from the University of North Carolina at Chapel Hill (UNC-CH). From 1965 to 1973 Dr. Clifford held teaching and administrative positions in elementary, junior high, and high schools prior to beginning his long and distinguished tenure on the research faculty at the Frank Porter Graham Child Development Center, UNC-CH.

During Dr. Clifford's presidency, NAEYC membership surpassed 100,000 and unprecedented public attention was focused on the importance of quality in early childhood programs—partially due to two White House Conferences on early childhood development and child care. Although the 105th Congress responded by addressing quality in various ways, federal funding was not significantly expanded. More successful was NAEYC's work to improve practice. Major revisions in *NAEYC's Accreditation Criteria and Procedures*, and minor revisions in the licensing position statement and the "Code of Ethical Conduct," as well as collaboration with the International Reading Association to develop and adopt the joint position "Learning to Read and Write: Developmentally Appropriate Practices for Young Children" all occurred during Dr. Clifford's tenure. Quality, Compensation, and Affordability (QCA) initiatives continued with the QCA Program Recognition Project. NAEYC's first videoconference seminar, The Leading Edge, was launched to enhance the ability of early childhood leaders to communicate the principles of developmentally appropriate practice. While the above achievements are significant, Dr. Clifford may be most remembered for his leadership in addressing two major organizational challenges—an in-depth examination of organizational structure to better prepare NAEYC for the next millennium (summits held in 1997 and 1998), and the first change in the Association's executive staff since 1972. President Clifford's integrity and deep commitment to NAEYC's core values were applied as the Board developed and implemented a systematic transition plan throughout 1998.

Sharon Lynn Kagan

Sharon Lynn Kagan

President, NAEYC 1998-2000

Dr. Kagan grew up in Detroit, Michigan. She graduated from the University of Michigan with a B.A. and teaching certificate in English and later received her masters from Johns Hopkins University and Ph.D. from Teachers College, Columbia University. Dr. Kagan is respected for her scholarly contributions to policy and practice issues impacting children, families, communities, and early childhood professionals. At the time of her presidency, she was a senior research scientist at Yale University's Child Study Center.

Dr. Kagan's tenure as NAEYC's president occurred at a pivotal point in the organization's history. During the transition in executive staff—the first in 30 years—she helped to create a smooth transition and fostered the development of a strong working relationship between the members of the Governing Board and the newly appointed executive team. Also during her presidency, the Board adopted a far-reaching restructuring initiative and public policy efforts were greatly expanded. She established important precedents in the nature of Board proceedings, providing for greater dialogue of emerging issues and their implications for the early childhood field and NAEYC. The National Commission to Reinvent NAEYC Accreditation was appointed to guide a project funded with support from the Carnegie Corporation of New York and the McCormick Tribune Foundation. The reinvention project was designed to provide for the next era of accreditation recommendations that both maintain the system's integrity and purpose and respond to the changing context of early childhood program delivery.

Kathy R. Thornburg

Kathy R. Thornburg

President, NAEYC 2000-2002

Dr. Thornburg grew up in Topeka, Kansas and became a third-grade teacher after graduating from Pittsburgh State University with a degree in elementary education. After receiving both a M.A. and Ph.D. degree in child and family development from the University of Missouri, she became a professor at the University of Kentucky. In 1981, she became a professor in human development and family studies and director of the Child Development Laboratory at the University of Missouri—Columbia.

Dr. Thornburg began her term as president in 2000, ushering in a new millennium and the implementation of a revised organization structure for the Association. Celebration of NAEYC's 75th anniversary, and preparation of this book, occurred during her presidency. Thus a complete description of accomplishments during her term was not possible.

NANE/NAEYC Board Members 1926–2000

The following compilation of all people who have served on the NANE/NAEYC Governing Board during its first 75 years is clustered in four time periods: 1926–1950; 1950–1970; 1970–1990; and 1990–2000. Accompanying each person's name is the date they were elected to the Board and their state of residence at the time of their election. Persons who served more than one term and in more than one position are noted each time they were elected. Asterisks designate deceased former Governing Board members for whom the Association has received notification.

Compiling this information for the earliest years of the Association was a challenge. When there was doubt, inclusion seemed the best course—as was the case in a memorable October 1937 Board meeting. According to the Minutes, "the president suggested and the members agreed that since we all have trouble remembering who is on the executive board and who on the advisory board, we for this meeting grant advisory board full voting privileges."

NANE Governing Board members

1926–1950

*Patty Smith Hill, 1927, New York	*Harold H. Anderson, 1936
*Lois Hayden Meek Stolz, 1927, 1929, New York	*Ruth Andrus, 1935, New York
*Grace Abbott	*Edna D. Baker, 1931
*Charles A. Aldrich	*William E. Blatz, 1931, Canada
*Winifred Allen, 1945, New York	*Marguerite P. Burnham, 1945, Connecticut
*Rose H. Alschuler, 1927, Illinois	*Helen Christianson, 1948, California
*John Anderson	*Marjorie Craig, 1943, New York
	*Mary Dabney Davis, 1927, Washington, D.C.

*Abigail A. Eliot, 1927, Massachusetts

*Josephine C. Foster, 1936

*Marie Fowler, 1929

*Elizabeth M. Fuller, 1943, Minnesota

*Hazel Gabbard, 1945, Washington, D.C.

*Arnold Gesell

*Christine Glass, 1936

*Barbara Greenwood, 1932

*Ethel Gordon, 1946, Ohio

*Christine Heinig, 1931

*May Hill

*Frances R. Horwich, 1943, North Carolina; 1947, Illinois

*Amy Hostler, 1941, 1943, New York

*James L. Hymes Jr., 1945, Oregon; 1948, New York

*Arthur T. Jersild

*Emma Johnson, 1936

*Harriet M. Johnson, 1927

*Mary Cover Jones, 1927, New York

*Alice Keliher, 1936

*Lulu Lancaster, 1931

*Howard Lane, 1943, Michigan, 1948, New York

*Grace Langdon, 1939, Washington, D.C.

*N. Searle Light, 1943, 1945, Connecticut

*Virginia Messenger

*Lynette Messer, 1943, California

*Elizabeth Moore, 1929

*Harriet E. O'Shea, 1945, Indiana

*Willard C. Olson, 1931

*Ernest Osborne

*Lulu Palmer, 1943, Alabama

*Anna L. Payne, 1936

*Anna E. Richardson, 1927

*Katherine Roberts

*W. Carson Ryan, 1945, North Carolina

*George D. Stoddard, 1929, Indiana

*Edith Sunderlin, 1948, Indiana

*Ruth Updegraff, 1937, Indiana

*Majorie C. Upton, 1931

*Lee Vincent, 1936

*Charles W. Waddle, 1927

*Lovisa C. Wagoner, California

*Edna Noble White, 1927, Michigan

*Helen T. Woolley, 1929

*Myra Woodruff, 1945, New York

NANE/NAEYC Governing Board members

1950-1970

June E. Aimen, 1959, Illinois

*Millie Almy, 1952, New York

*Katherine H. Read (Baker), 1956, Oregon

Evelyn Beyer, 1952, Massachusetts

Alma Bingham, 1967, Oregon

Donald Brieland, 1961, Illinois

Beryl Campbell, 1954, California

*Judith Cauman, 1954, New York; 1959, Pennsylvania

*Gertrude E. Chittenden, 1954, Michigan

Oneida Cockrell, 1952, Illinois

*Helen Dawe, 1950, Wisconsin

*Edith M. Dowley, 1958, California

*Isabelle Diehl, 1954, Indiana

*Mary Ellen Durret, 1964, California

*Hope Eagle, 1958, Maryland

*Lola Emerson, 1959, Washington, D.C.

Barbara Fischer, 1956 , Missouri

*Ira Gibbons, 1968, Washington, D.C.

*Sadie D. Ginsberg, 1969, Maryland

Adele Goldstein, 1962, Ohio

Marjorie M. Green, 1954, California

Helena Guernsey, 1966, Florida

NAEYC Governing Board—1969

Standing: Ann K. Doss, Mary Ellen Durrett, Bernard Spodek, Marjorie Maynard, Phyllis Richards, Elizabeth Ann Liddle, Ira Gibbons, Alma Bingham, Evangeline H. Ward, Mary B. Lane, Ethel Macintyre, Esther Weir, Mildred A. Reed

Seated: Milton E. Akers, Blanche Persky, Eveline B. Omwake, Marilyn M. Smith, Ralph L. Witherspoon, Ethel W. Kunkle

Not present: Sadie Ginsberg

W. Willard Hartup, 1960, Iowa

Glenn R. Hawkes, 1956, 1961, Iowa

Ruth Highberger, 1957, Tennessee

Rebecca Pena Hines, 1970, California

*Frances R. Horwich, 1952, Illinois

Ruth E. Jefferson, 1965, Florida

*Flo Gould (Kerckhoff), 1958, Michigan

*Dorothy Jean Lane, 1958, Iowa

Mary B. Lane, 1968, California

*Catherine Landreth, 1956, California

Sylvia Lapin, 1964, Rhode Island

Norma Law, 1963, Oregon

Elizabeth Ann Liddle, 1967, Massachusetts

Leone List, 1956, Tennessee

*Margaret McFarland, 1952, Pennsylvania

Ethel L. Macintyre, 1967, Illinois

*Polly McVickar, 1956, California

Theresa Mahler, 1950, California

Mary Alice Mallum, 1950, California

Esther Mason, 1950, Pennsylvania

Marjorie Maynard, 1968, Massachusetts

Mary V. Minnie, 1961, California

*Edna Mohr, 1958, 1959, Pennsylvania

Shirley Moore, 1964, Minnesota

Harriet C. Nash, 1954, Connecticut

Josephine Newbury, 1963, Virginia

Paul H. Nolte, 1956, Wisconsin

Eveline B. Omwake, 1958, 1967, Connecticut

June Patterson, 1958, California

*Blanche Persky, 1962, New York

Mildred A. Reed, 1966, Washington

Theodora B. Reeve, 1952, 1956, New York

Katherine M. Reeves, 1961, New York

Eleanor Reich (Brussel), 1950, New York

Phyllis Richards, 1961, Texas

Julius Richmond, 1952, Illinois

*Judith A. Schoellkopf, 1956, Massachusetts

Harold Shane, 1950, Illinois

Aladine Shomaker, 1956, Missouri

*Rebekah Shuey, 1957, New York

Russell C. Smart, 1950, New York; 1960, Rhode Island

Marilyn M. Smith, 1965, Iowa; 1969, Tennessee

Bernard Spodek, 1965, Illinois

*Edith Sunderland, 1952, Iowa

Viola Theman, 1952, Illinois

*Evangeline H. Ward, 1964, Missouri

Esther Weir, 1969, California

Miriam Wiggenhorn, 1956, Oregon

*Ralph L. Witherspoon, 1960, 1963, Florida

Elizabeth Woods, 1950, 1954, California

Julia Zimmerman, 1966, Missouri

NAEYC Governing Board members

1970–1990

Phyllis A. Antone, 1983, Arizona

Nathaniel Archuleta, 1975, New Mexico

Rebeca Barrera, 1989, Texas

Barbara T. Bowman, 1980, Illinois

Samuel J. Braun, 1971, Massachusetts

Nancy H. Brown, 1985, Washington, D.C.

Owen C. Cahoon, 1975, Utah

Bettye Caldwell, 1982, Arkansas

Carrie Cheek, 1972, 1982, New York

Frances E. Cherino, 1978, New Mexico

Mae A. Christian, 1979, Georgia

Vernon L. Clark, 1974, North Carolina

Meg Barden Cline, 1984, Massachusetts

Margaret H. Cone, 1970, Texas

Josué Cruz Jr., 1978, California

Brenda Dabney, 1989, New Mexico

Jerlean Daniel, 1986, Pennsylvania

Therry N. Deal, 1973, Georgia

Shirley M. Dean, 1976, Illinois

*Robert J. Dematteis, 1980, Oregon

Lucille Echohawk, 1974, New Mexico

Patricia Eggleston, 1971, Illinois

David Elkind, 1986, Massachusetts

Linda Espinosa, 1989, California

Governing Board—1972

First row: Eveline Omwake, Frank Self, Elvie Watts, Pat Eggleston, Evangeline Ward, Alma Bingham

Second row: Ethel Macintyre, Esther Weir, Vincent Randall, Milton Akers, Lilian Derow

Third row: Mildred Reed, Ann Doss (Nanninger), Ethel Kunkle, Dorothy Sanchez, Sam Braun, Rebecca Pena Hines, Margaret Cone, Georgianna Engstrom, J.D. Andrews (hidden behind Ira Gibbons), Ira Gibbons, Marilyn M. Smith

Fourth row: Bernard Spodek

Not present: Bruce Williams

Stephanie Feeney, 1980, Hawaii

Marjorie V. Fields, 1983, Alaska

*Marcia L. Fochler, 1987, California

Mary Elizabeth Fraiser, 1976, North Carolina

Victoria R. Fu, 1985, Virginia

Ellen Galinsky, 1988, New York

Bruce D. Gardner, 1974, Colorado

Elsie W. Gee, 1975, California

Robert C. Granger, 1984, New Jersey

Janice E. Hale, 1988, Michigan

Dorothy W. Hewes, 1977, California

Richard Hinze, 1975, Hawaii

*Richard Hirabayashi, 1978, Canada

Betsy Hiteshew, 1983, California

Randy Hitz, 1985, Oregon

*Lana Hostetler, 1990, Illinois

Betty L. Hutchison, 1987, Illinois

Sharon Lynn Kagan, 1988, Connecticut

Barbara Kamara, 1980, North Carolina

Lilian G. Katz, 1981, 1983, Illinois

Earline D. Kendall, 1979, Tennessee

Sally J. Kilmer, 1981, 1983, Ohio

Edgar Klugman, 1977, Massachusetts

*Ethel W. Kunkle, 1970, Wisconsin

John E. Kyle, 1974, Pennsylvania

Jane E. Lannak, 1986, Germany

Joan Lombardi, 1987, Virginia

Mary London, 1977, California

*Ivalee Long, 1973, Kansas

Jan McCarthy, 1978, Indiana

*Grace Mitchell, 1974, Massachusetts

Gwen G. Morgan, 1982, Massachusetts

Jim Morin, 1986, Wisconsin

*Ann K. Doss (Nanninger), 1970, Colorado

Roger Neugebauer, 1989, Washington

Alice S. Paul, 1988, Arizona

*Ann DeHuff Peters, 1979, California

Lucy C. Peterson, 1979, California

Jeanne W. Quill, 1980, Washington

Vincent E. Randall, 1971, Arizona

Consuelo Rocha, 1976, Texas

Margaret B. Roth, 1977, Minnesota

Patricia Jo Salisbury, 1982, New Mexico

Dorothy Sanchez, 1972, Colorado

Margaret H. Sanstad, 1975, Washington

Frank Self, 1970, Connecticut

Jan Silverman, 1981, Missouri

Bernard Spodek, 1976, Illinois

Cheri Sterman Miller, 1985, Ohio

Carolyn Thomson, 1973, Kansas

*Evangeline H. Ward, 1970, Pennsylvania

Billie Warford, 1986, Montana

Jeannette Watson, 1981, Texas

Elvie C. Watts, 1970, California

Bernice Weissbourd, 1982, Illinois

Bruce M. Williams, 1970, Mississippi

*C. Ray Williams, 1981, Ohio

David Wright, 1984, Oregon

Jackie Yamahiro, 1973, Colorado

James C. Young, 1982, Georgia

Docia Zavitkovsky, 1984, California

NAEYC Governing Board members
1990-2000

Shizuko Akasaki, 1993, California

Susan Andersen, 1994, Iowa

Gina Barclay-McLaughlin, 2000, Tennessee

Roger H. Brown, 1995, Massachusetts

Richard Clifford, 1996, North Carolina

Moncrieff Cochran, 1997, New York

Ken Counselman, 1991, Massachusetts

Josué Cruz Jr., 1996, 1999, Florida

Jerlean Daniel, 1993, Pennsylvania

Governing Board—1990

First row: Sharon Lynn Kagan, Jerlean Daniel, Lana Hostetler. Rebeca Barrera, Roger Neugebauer

Second row: Lilian Katz, Ellen Galinsky, Michelle Seligson, Betty Hutchison, Alice Paul, Linda Espinosa, Billie Lynn Warford, Jane Lannak, Jim Morin, Joan Lombardi, Brenda Dabney

Not present: Janice Hale-Benson

Louise Derman-Sparks, 1997, California

Diane Trister Dodge, 1990, Washington, D.C.

*Walter Draude, 1992, California

Amy Driscoll, 1996, Oregon

Stephanie Fanjul, 1993, North Carolina

Cheryl L. Foster, 1998, Arizona

Martha Norris Gilbert, 1997, Virginia

Ed Greene, 1994, New York

Amos Hatch, 1998, Tennessee

Julienne Johnson, 2000, Washington, D.C.

Jamilah Jor' dan. 1999, Illinois

Ellen Junn, 1997, California

Sharon Lynn Kagan, 1997, Connecticut

Lilian G. Katz, 1991, Illinois

Margaret King, 1994, Ohio

Mary Lou Kinney, 1995, Idaho

Marjorie Kostelnik, 1994, Michigan

Ann K. Levy, 1999, Florida

Elena Lopez, 1998, Massachusetts

M.-A. Lucas, 1992, Virginia

Muriel Wong Lundgren, 1994, 1996, Florida

Anne Mitchell, 1999, New York

Christina Lopez Morgan, 2000, California

Patricia A. Phipps, 1992, Texas; 1998, Virginia

Karen Ponder, 1998, North Carolina

Nila Rinehart, 1994, New Mexico

Bea Romer, 1991, Colorado

Larry Schweinhart, 1993, Michigan

Hanne Sonquist, 1990, California

Maurice Sykes, 1999, Washington, D.C.

Marjorie Warlick Tate, 1992, North Carolina

*Helen Taylor, 1991, Washington, D.C.

Diane Turner, 1995, Colorado

Kathy Thornburg, 1990, 1999, Missouri

Marce Verzaro-O'Brien, 1993, Florida

Valora Washington, 1990, Michigan

Jane Wiechel, 1996, Ohio

Kathleen Wright, 1990, Michigan